THE SPATIALITY OF THE NOVEL

The
SPATIALITY
of the
NOVEL

by JOSEPH A. KESTNER

The University of Tulsa

WAYNE STATE UNIVERSITY PRESS
Detroit, 1978

Kestner, Joseph A
    The spatiality of the novel.

    Bibliography: p.
    Includes index.
    1. Fiction-Technique.   2. Space and time in
literature.   I. Title.
PN3365.K4   809.3'3   78-14377
ISBN 0-8143-1612-3

For my parents

Contents

Preface

The development of a spatial poetics for the novel involves two considerations: first, the use of space as a formal construct in the text; and second, the nature of spatiality as a critical method of reading the text. Spatiality in the novel is founded on the concept of *secondary illusion.* According to an extensive tradition including Horace and Lessing, the arts are divided between the temporal arts, based on inherent succession and irreversibility (the novel, music), and the spatial arts, inherently reversible and simultaneous (painting, sculpture, architecture). The concept of spatial secondary illusion evolves from the idea that the temporal arts use spatial qualities like simultaneity for their realization, extension, and development. Likewise, in the spatial arts, a temporal element like succession constitutes a temporal secondary illusion. Spatiality in the temporal art of the novel, therefore, involves methods of spatial properties, like volume, point, or simultaneity. In a temporal art like the novel, spatial secondary illusion thus means the exercise of spatial elements to extend the essential temporal nature of the novel.

The spatial method, the study of spatiality in the novel, is therefore inherently a critical approach which must integrate several disciplines, including literary theory, scientific thought, spatial artistic practices, and philosophic query. One must study the spatiality of the novel in the context of space as well as in the context of literature: since space is a property not only of literature but of science and art, a study of space in the novel is therefore integrative.

This book is designed to examine spatiality in the novel in as complete a context as possible. Studies of time in the novel, including A. A. Mendilow's *Time and the Novel* and Hans Meyerhoff's *Time in Literature*, have examined one facet of the nature of the novel—its temporal essence, characterized by succession and irreversibility. However, it is important to recognize, as Mendilow has observed, that the novel relies on spatiality for its operative secondary illusion to elaborate this temporal essence. Therefore, a study of the novel must account for several relations, including the relation of the novel as a temporal art to other temporal arts like music, and the relation of the novel, through its spatial secondary illusion, to space in science and in the arts. The idea of spatial secondary illusion in the temporal art of the novel becomes the foundation of a spatial methodology.

For this reason, I first locate the development of spatial methodology in the context of artistic, philosophic, and literary theory, beginning with the most prominent concepts of space, extending from Plato to Kant to Einstein. This investigation details the properties of space which contribute to the elements of its secondary illusion in temporal art. After this survey of spatial ideas in science and in philosophy, the first chapter reviews concepts of space in literary and artistic theory. The decisive documents of the theory of the novel, including Percy Lubbock's *Craft of Fiction*, Henry James's *Art of the Novel*, E. M. Forster's *Aspects of the Novel*, and Wayne Booth's *Rhetoric of Fiction*, contain implications important for spatial methodology. For literature, Joseph Frank's "Spatial Form in Modern Literature," which examines the achievement of reversibility and simultaneity in the novel, is an important statement, although Frank does not use explicitly the concept of secondary illusion and draws only marginally on science and the plastic arts in his essay. Studies of literature in connection with the arts, originating with Lessing, are particularly crucial in evaluating spatial illusion; in the twentieth century, these include Rensselaer Lee's *Ut Pictura Poesis*, Heinrich Wölfflin's *Principles of Art History*, Helmut Hatzfeld's *Literature through Art*, Wylie Sypher's *Four Stages of Renaissance Style* and *Rococo to Cubism*, and Jean Hagstrum's *The Sister Arts*. These studies are significant not only in themselves but also because they indicate how cautious such investigations must be in their conclusions.

In addition to these integrative studies of the arts and to English language theories of the novel, an important body of European theory influential on spatial studies has become prominent during the last decade, particularly the work of Russian Formalists and French theoreticians. One must note Tzvetan Todorov's *Theory of Literature*, which includes Boris Eichenbaum's "Theory of the 'Formal Method'" and "How Gogol's 'Overcoat' Is Made"; Jurij Tynianov's "On Literary Evolution"; and Victor

Shklovsky's "Construction of the Short Story and of the Novel," as well as Shklovsky's complete *On the Theory of Prose*. Important recent French theory includes Todorov's *Poetics of Prose* as well as his "Poétique," contributed to *What is Structuralism?*; Gérard Genette's crucial essays on space in *Figures I* and *Figures II;* Michel Butor's theories of structure included in his *Essays on the Novel;* and Jean Ricardou's studies of narrative and narration in *Problems of the New Novel*.

From this foundation for a spatial poetics of the novel come several key concepts, particularly the three kinds of spatiality identified as the *geometric,* the *virtual,* and the *genidentic*. Geometric spatiality concerns Euclidean spatial elements like point, plane, and line in the novel. This form of spatiality is the most basic of spatial methods. A second and more intricate type of spatial method concerns virtual spatiality, which defines the relation of the novel to the spatial arts of painting, sculpture, and architecture. The relation of scene to painting, particularly the concept of framing or *encadrement,* the connection of characterization to sculptural volume, and the clear nexus of novelistic structure to architectural functional form all reveal an extensive range of alternatives within virtual spatiality. The final form of spatiality, the genidentic, involves both a theory of text generation and a method of reading any text. Genidentic spatiality rests on the concept of genidentity developed in physics by Hans Reichenbach in *Space and Time,* as well as on Michel Butor's theory of the book as an object capable of creating its own dynamic field producing an interpenetration of text and interpreter. E. D. Hirsch's notion of genre in *Validity in Interpretation,* Victor Zuckerkandl's study of the dynamism of music in *Sound and Symbol,* and Walter Ong's and Wolfgang Iser's theories of the audience provide important insights into the concept of the text as a spatial dynamic entity. Interpretation of the novel must involve not only its temporal essence but also its spatiality, for, as Gérard Genette has observed in *Figures I,* "Language spaces itself so that space, in itself, becomes language, speaks it and writes it."

Each of these three forms of spatiality is examined in a separate chapter. Within each chapter, representative texts are selected to illustrate the function of spatiality in the novel. These individual texts, however, imply the applicability of such spatiality to other texts. For instance, a form of geometric spatiality like parallelism is as apparent in *The Wild Palms* as in *War and Peace;* superimposed planes of texts exist in *The Waves* as well as in *Don Quixote*. Similarly, a form of virtual spatiality such as sculptural volume is as applicable to *The Red and the Black* as to *The Marble Faun* or *Women in Love*. One may examine the idea of space-time in Andrey Biely's *Petersburg* as well as in Proust's *Time Regained,* or the concept of dynamic language in *Finnegans Wake* as well as in *Absalom, Absalom!*. The idea of the act of reading as dynamic and genidentic is relevant to the interpretation of any single text. This evolution of a spatialist poetics from the geometric to the virtual to the genidentic follows the insights and practices of novelists themselves. The successive observations of Longus, of George Eliot, of Proust, of Joyce, and of Butor constitute a continuum of thought about space in the context of novelistic creation. A spatialist poetics recognizes what Thomas Mann states in *The Magic Mountain:* "Space . . . possessed and wielded the powers we generally ascribe to time."

Conversations with Joseph Frank at Princeton University were significant in the initial development of the ideas that led to this book, while correspondence with Gérard Genette of the Centre d'Études transdisciplinaires of the Sorbonne has been a source of great encouragement. For their long-standing professional support I would like to thank Carl Woodring, Columbia University, and A. Walton Litz, Princeton University. Maurice Wohlgelernter of The City University of New York has been an abiding inspiration.

I am grateful for the many courtesies extended to me by the following institutions: the libraries of Columbia University, Princeton University, and Rensselaer Polytechnic Institute; the Vatican Museum; the Galleria Borghese; the Museum of Modern Art, New York; the Metropolitan Museum; and the Musée national d'Art moderne, Paris, where Madame Magalie Lamasse-Savoie was especially helpful. I also wish to express my gratitude to the Research Foundation of The City University of New York for a grant during 1974–75 which enabled me to pursue this work.

Portions of this book have been published in a different form in *Poétique, Modern Fiction Studies, bye-cadmos, The Classical World,* and *Modern British Literature.*

CHAPTER ONE

Spatial Secondary Illusion

> All these things made of the church for me something
> entirely different from the rest of the town; a building
> which occupied, so to speak, four dimensions of space—
> the name of the fourth being Time.
>
> Proust, *Swann's Way*

> "You have to be like Rodin, Michael Angelo."
>
> Lawrence, *Women in Love*

Analyses of spatial form and spatiality in the novel develop from Greco-Roman philosophic discussions of the nature of space and time. Since most literary forms, including the novel, have their origins in Greco-Roman literature, it is necessary as well as desirable to establish premises for the investigation of space in the context of the development of Western prose. Discussions of spatiality in the novel cannot be meaningful without such a context, and the extent of spatiality in the novel becomes apparent only when one realizes that spatial form in literature is inextricably involved at its origin with the prevailing philosophic, artistic, and scientific attitudes toward physical space. Space was never completely the concern of any one intellectual discipline. From the beginning it influenced philosophy, science, and artistic form simultaneously. This pervasive importance of space comes to influence not only the content but especially the form of the novel. Marcel Proust's statement in *Swann's Way*, D. H. Lawrence's insight in *Women in Love*, and James Joyce's acknowledgment in *Finnegans Wake* reveal the importance of spatial theory in art, science, and philosophy to the novelistic text. Such theory originated with the Greek Milesian philosophers.

In the ancient world the debate about the existence of space began with Thales of Miletus, the sixth-century thinker who concluded that the basic substance of the universe was water. But while Thales believed that a

13

concrete, tangible substance was the basic matter of the universe, the opposite position was taken by Anaximander (ca. 610) in the succeeding generation. He called the primary substance "the Infinite" or "the nonlimited." The irreconcilability of these two modes of thought, the tangibility of Thales and the intangibility of Anaximander, is the central dilemma of any writer concerned with spatiality. The younger associate of Anaximander, Anaximenes, followed his teacher to the extent of believing in an "underlying substance"; he did not, however, accept its intangibility, declaring that it was air. These three thinkers of the Milesian school contributed to thought about space, therefore, in two ways: in their attempt to confront the problem of "one versus many" by seeking a unity, and in their ideas regarding the tangibility or intangibility of the substance.

According to Aristotle in the *Metaphysics*, the Pythagoreans (ca. 531) conceived a kind of spatiality in their theories of numbers, for them the primary elements of the universe. Their central contribution is the concept of "spatial vacancies," for they found some opposition between space as *pneuma apeiron* ("endless air") and as *kenon* ("void"). One of the Pythagoreans, Archytas (ca. 428–347), contributed two further propositions: there is a distinction between *topos* ("place") and space, and space "differs from matter and is independent of it."[1]

Heraclitus (ca. 500) pursued the ideas of the Milesians. Declaring that fire was the "basic substance," he nevertheless posited the theory of flux and strife, that the universe existed by "an attunement" of opposite tensions: the fire, like the same river into which we cannot step twice, is a visible manifestation of this central idea of change. Parmenides (ca. 450), the founder of the Eleatic school, rejects these theories, regarding the universe as absolute, single, and permanent, a monistic theory of "being" as opposed to the Heraclitean theory of "becoming." To Parmenides, change and motion are illusions. Empedocles, compromising between Heraclitus and Parmenides, accepted the idea of permanency, but also declared the permanency of process.[2]

A pupil of Empedocles, the nihilist Gorgias (ca. 483–375), placed space and matter in separate categories. It was against this distinction that Plato himself rebelled in the *Timaeus* (ca. 348), the major source of his thinking about space. While admitting the difficulty of believing in space, Plato declared that space was "eternal and indestructible," providing "a position for everything that comes to be." Furthermore Plato, as Max Jammer observes, "conceived the elements as endowed with definite spatial structures." Earth was a cube, air was an octahedron, fire was a pyramid, and water was an icosahedron; the universe itself was a dodecahedron. These shapes, except for the dodecahedron, are various permutations of the

most simple elementary plane figure, the triangle. Plato's identification
of space and matter remained central to European philosophy through the
Middle Ages. The importance of geometric configuration in the novel,
mirrored in its theories of point of view, finds its source in this Platonic
text.[3]

For Aristotle, the distinction of place and space is a crucial one in
theory, but in practice it is equivocal. "Place" is the adjacent boundary of
a containing object, while space is the inner boundary of the containing
receptacle; a thing's place can be quitted, but its space cannot. A character, according to Aristotle in the *Physics*, would occupy space, but not
always the same place. Likewise in the *Physics*, Aristotle formulated the
concept of "long" and "short" time, that the only determination of time is
the magnitude of movement. His ultimate conclusion is that the space of
the universe is finite, and its center is, predictably, the earth. For as Plato's
transcendentalism is proved by his theory of space, Aristotle's materialism
and pragmatism are based on his.[4] Plato's ideal geometrizations involve
space with separation; Aristotle's theory supports containment. In these
thinkers the novelist was to find two alternatives to his problem. Form and
matter for Plato are separate; for Aristotle, they are one.

Although the problem of space continued to disturb men after the
classical period, as is apparent, for example, in the constant questioning of
Augustine in the *Confessions*, it is really with the seventeenth century
that the problem surfaces in the context one calls "modern," that is, in the
debate concerning whether space is relative or absolute. The relational
theory of space was propounded by René Descartes and Gottfried Leibniz,
and the absolutist theory by Isaac Newton and John Locke. Descartes, in
the *Principles of Philosophy* (1644), stated that there was no difference
between body and space, that a vacuum could not exist, that the Aristotelian distinction between place and space is actually a difference of thought
only, and that extension in "length, breadth, and depth" is the only spatial
determinant. These concepts influenced the thinking of Leibniz, who
declared boldly: "I hold space to be something merely relative, as time
is." For him, "space... results from places taken together." Ideas of
space and place "consist only in the truth of relations, and not at all in any
absolute reality." Time rests completely on the order of situations: "Time,
without things, is nothing else but a mere ideal possibility."[5]

Isaac Newton opposed these ideas in his *Mathematical Principles of
Natural Philosophy* (1687). He declared that relative time and space were
merely concrete measurable dimensions of absolute time and space; relative time and space are explained as duration or distance. Time is determined by an order of succession, space by the order of situation. Relative
space and time, i.e., that which is measurable by the succession of places

or by motion, is merely the measured quantity of absolute space or time. John Locke, in *An Essay Concerning Human Understanding* (1690), declared that space is the distance between two points, while place is "the relation of distance between anything and any two or more points." Locke distinguished between a solid body and space, which is characterized by infinite extension and continuity; time, measured duration, itself defined as "fleeting extension," rests ultimately on space. Immanuel Kant added support, in the *Critique of Pure Reason* (1781), to the absolute theory of space, emphasizing that "space . . . is a pure intuition," "the subjective condition of sensibility," an idea that became crucial for the novelist in the theory of characterization; this transcendental space makes it "possible that things should be outer objects to us." In other words, one's relation to the universe depends entirely on space. Time likewise is absolute, and neither time nor space depends on any object for its existence; both are a priori. Kant established clearly what became a central artistic element of twentieth-century thought, the important distinction that space is characterized by simultaneity, but time by succession: "While the parts of the line are simultaneous the parts of time are always successive."

It was in the late nineteenth and early twentieth centuries that these absolutist theories of space and time were assailed and refuted. In *The Science of Mechanics* (1883), Ernst Mach declared that space and motion provided only relative knowledge of themselves. Any absolutist theories, he contended, were "arbitrary fictions of our imaginations." Henri Bergson, in his *Introduction to Metaphysics* (1907), began to focus on the relative nature of space and time, but via this imagination. Concentrating on perceived rather than scientific time, he explored the nature of duration and memory, thereby isolating a problem central to the spatiality of the novel. That is, novelists have not been scientists, or even pure philosophers, in dealing with space, but have nevertheless, in delving the individual consciousness, aligned themselves with relativist theories.[6]

Modern scientific theories of space rest on several ideas, among them those of non-Euclidean space, of the relativity of space, proved by Albert Michelson in 1881, and of the relativity of time, demonstrated by Albert Einstein in 1905. Hermann Minkowski boldly declared: "Henceforth space by itself, and time by itself, are doomed to fade away." Emphasizing that "nobody has ever noticed a place except at a time, or a time except at a place," Minkowski eloquently formulated the theory of space-time, a hypothesis that denies both the absolute existence of space and the absolute existence of time, but does not refute the idea of absolute space-time. Space-time is four-dimensional space, the fourth dimension of which is time. Since such a world is tenseless, it has provoked investigation of the spatial nature of language in the novel.[7]

It was in the 1930s that the influence of space-time began to permeate theories of language and its use to express temporal relations. C. D. Broad emphasized that an event and its utterance, expressed by *is*, could mean only that the event was simultaneous with the utterance; the copula *is* immediately becomes nontemporal. J. N. Findlay, returning to some of the dilemmas presented by Augustine in the *Confessions*, is inclined to blame language for its inadequacy in presenting temporal ideas. Nelson Goodman argues that past, present, future, and "passing time" are so ambiguous as to be false categories, determined least of all by linguistic utterances. He concludes: "Strangely enough it turns out not that time is more fluid than (say) space but rather that time is more static."[8] Émile Borel has enunciated in *Space and Time* the idea that causality, which we presume to be based on time, is in reality much more spatial, dependent on distance and our identity with a particular group of observers. Thus, the position one chooses to take vis-à-vis a novel is critical to whether he perceives causality in the work at all; the concept of "temporal" causality is hardly certain. Once the idea of space-time is accepted, one may see, as Hans Reichenbach points out in *Space and Time*, the feasibility and even transparency of it. Reichenbach, however, contends that space-time may well be absolute, free from "subjective grounds."[9]

The work of Richard Taylor is likewise relevant to literary theory, for Taylor argues that basic concepts such as place, distance, length, extension, and direction are equally applicable to space or time. Time, he asserts, can have a "backward" movement, an idea influential on someone like Roland Barthes, who contends that language is reaching "degree zero" by a negative, and therefore reversible, momentum. Adolf Grünbaum has declared that happenings in themselves are tenseless, following the ideas of Moritz Schlick, who declared that "the structure of the past is inferred . . . from the spatial arrangement of objects."[10] The significance of this structure not only for the novelist but also for his reader, who regards the novel as "past" merely because it is recorded, is that it suggests that one's confrontation with a text is much more spatial than temporal. Seen in this light, the novel can be regarded as evidence for our modern theory that language, and the events it records, are to be ascribed to space more than to time, as Thomas Mann realizes in *The Magic Mountain*.

These theories of space, of course, are given perspective by notions of time. Time, no less than space, has provoked uncertainty among its philosophers. Augustine asked in the *Confessions*, Book 11: "What, then, is time? If no one asks of me, I know; if I wish to explain to him who asks, I know not." Thinkers after Bergson and Russell have debated whether there are such categories as past, present, or future; whether only "now" (following the paradox of Zeno) exists; whether timeless memory and expectation are more significant than the problem of time. It was Augustine, however, in his long exploration in the *Confessions,* who enunciated what remains the central conclusion about time: "I say that I measure time in my mind." Such a statement, clearly developing the concept of subjective, psychological time, was maintained by Hobbes and Locke, and even provides a basis for Bergson's theories in *Time and Free Will* (1889). There are, as Hans Meyerhoff has expressed it, "two dimensions of time," which account for "the divergent philosophical interpretations of time." One of them is chronological and objective; the other, psychological and subjective, depends on memory, expectations, and a fully developed emotional awareness of concepts of future and past. [11]

For the novelist the time problem remains a decisive challenge. Meyerhoff has listed six forms in which time is significant in literature, and within *Time in Literature* he explores them all. His six aspects include subjective reality; continuous flow, or duration; "dynamic fusion, or interpenetration, of the causal order in experience and memory," or the relation between external events and the formation of the self; "duration and the temporal structure of memory in relation to self-identity," an idea emphasizing the recollection of events during the formation of a self-identity; eternity, which means "timelessness," not infinite time; and "transitoriness, or the temporal direction toward death." Investigations by such critics as Leon Edel, in *The Modern Psychological Novel,* and Robert Humphrey, in *Stream of Consciousness in the Modern Novel,* have expanded our awareness of the novelist's problem of time. [12] Fielding's use of an almanac for *Tom Jones,* the rigid time scheme of *Wuthering Heights,* the opposition of psychological and chronological time in *Tristram Shandy,* the year-and-a-day quest time of *The Return of the Native,* as well as the experiments of Joyce and Proust, testify to the intricacy of this dilemma for the novelist, concerned as he is with four times—of his characters, his era, himself, and his reader. In his preface to *Roderick Hudson,* James expressed the problem of summary and foreshortening as one of great "delicacy" but also, somehow, "exquisite." Forster could state, in *Aspects of the Novel,* that "in the novel, the allegiance to time is imperative." [13]

But time is not all. One must confront the proposition that while time is the essence of the novel, it is not enough for its existence; the temporality of its medium, language, cannot suffice. The qualities of the temporal and of the spatial arts received elucidation in Gotthold Lessing's consideration of the Laocoon group. In *Laocoon* (1766), explicitly in chapter four, he examined the contrast between the bodily pain expressed by the sculptor and the cry represented by Vergil in the *Aeneid,* concluding: "A review of the reasons here alleged for the moderation observed by the sculptor of the Laocoon in the expression of bodily pain, shows them to lie wholly in the peculiar object of his art and its necessary limitations. Scarcely one of them would be applicable to poetry." In the words of A. A. Mendilow in *Time and the Novel,* Lessing distinguished "between two categories of art: those based on co-existence in space, and those based on consecutiveness in time." The essential attribute of spatial art is simultaneity, of temporal art, successiveness. There is a further distinction in that the temporal arts are irreversible in essence, while the spatial arts are not inherently irreversible. Thus literature, cinema, dance, and especially music, are temporal, that is, in essence consecutive and irreversible; painting, sculpture, and architecture are spatial, in their essence simultaneous and reversible. At any one moment, Keats's entire Grecian urn is *there;* the nightingale's song or Beethoven's Fifth Symphony is the very image of ourselves, that is, of temporal men.[14]

However, Lessing's failure as an aesthetician, as Mendilow observes, rests in his acceptance of the logical limitations of the two forms of art, his belief that the arts achieve their best results by remaining within the confines of their respective essences. Lessing does not consider the extramedial effects by which the spatial arts may convey the effects of succession and the temporal arts the effects of simultaneity. The "simultaneity" of the spatial arts implies a temporal relation; the "succession" of the temporal arts implies a spatial relation. In the spatial arts, time constitutes the *secondary illusion;* in the temporal arts, space is the secondary aesthetic illusion. The secondary illusion of the novel is thus a spatial agent inherent in the temporal art of the novel by which the complete realization of the form is effected. The catalytic agent or secondary illusion of one form of art is an element of the other art.[15] For example, the spatial juxtaposition of the auction and the seduction during the agricultural fair of *Madame Bovary* produces an atemporal effect in the temporal text. In the temporal art of music, the echo of *Tristan and Isolde* in *Die Meistersinger* associates the works in a spatial relation beyond their temporal essence. The fact that *Lohengrin* was composed beginning with act three, or *Caleb Williams* beginning with volume three, demonstrates how spatial reversibility operates in the seemingly irreversible temporal art. While the initial experience of each work is successive, the complete form of an interreferential opera or of a detective text is preeminently spatial. In the spatial arts, however, time becomes the secondary illusion. Auguste Rodin's *Burghers of Calais* contains, by the simultaneous grouping of the six men, in reality the succession of each in his progress to self-sacrifice for the city. Gustave Courbet's *Interior of My Studio* presents in a simultaneous form the temporal sequence of his life. Umberto Boccioni's bronze *Unique Forms of Continuity in Space* by its title as well as its execution explores its temporal illusion.

Joseph Frank, in "Spatial Form in Modern Literature," has argued that images and word groups, for example, do not rely for meaning on "temporal relationships," but rather on reflexiveness and spatial simultaneity "not . . . in unison with the laws of language." "Modern literature is moving in the direction of spatial form. . . . These writers intend the reader to apprehend their work spatially, in a moment of time, rather than as a sequence." Quoting Flaubert's famous statement that "everything should sound simultaneously," Frank analyzes the *comice agricole* of *Madame Bovary*, arguing that the "time-flow of the narrative" halts in favor of a juxtaposition "independent of the progress of the narrative." Similarly, for Frank, Proust's "pure time" is perception in a moment of time, that is to say "space." Murray Krieger has declared that the language of the spatial arts is really the only satisfactory vocabulary for exploring temporal art forms: "I am being pressed to metaphors of space to account for miracles performed in time"; one "gives the temporal game away to space."[16] Therefore, if as critics like Mendilow and Susanne Langer contend, space is the secondary illusion of all temporal art (as time is of spatial art), it is the indispensable secondary illusion.[17] "Secondary" is a nominal, not evaluative, word in such a context. Likewise "illusion," although indelibly of the vocabulary of aesthetics, connotes a genuine agent in the arts. Space is a function; spatial functions in the novel are properties, not analogies.

From this concept of space as a secondary illusion or agent, a second proposition emerges: that spatial elements have controlling functions in the novel. Its theoretical components include point of view, line, and plane. Included in the concept of place is the important point of view, a spatial artistic concept brought into temporal art. As Barthes remarks, language itself is more "vertical" or spatialized than horizontal or successive. Distance, on which, as Wayne Booth observed, irony rests, depends on relational planes of places. The process of perception itself compels a delimiting separation from the object, and thus the origin of reflective thought is the origin of spatial awareness.[18]

A third concept evolves from the presence of these general spatial properties in the novel, which is that each of the spatial arts has lent its peculiar properties to the novel. Scene, characterization, and functional form derive from the pictorial, sculptural, and architectural spatial arts respectively. From the pictorial art the novel derives setting and scene, two-dimensional elements of one-point perspective. Examples include Andrey Biely's Petersburg, Honoré de Balzac's houses, Jane Austen's Sotherton, and Alain Robbe-Grillet's actual map in *Jealousy*. The creation of character employs sculptural elements against the background of this location. The implication of E. M. Forster's use of the terms "flat" and "round" to describe characters is the perception of relief and of statue. A

character of "high relief," like Isabel Archer in *The Portrait of a Lady*
(James emphasizes the "portrait"), lacks the ability of statues to incorporate the area which surrounds them. Quentin Compson of *The Sound and
the Fury* and Natasha Rostov of *War and Peace* are statuesque in their
power to infold their surroundings into themselves. Thus Rupert Birkin
declares in *Women in Love:* "You have to be like Rodin." Such spatialization, simultaneity, is at the heart of the concluding scene of *The Sentimental Education* or of the protagonist's stasis in *Oblomov.* Lastly, the fundamental property of architecture, that it be the form of its function, has
importance for the novel when we recall, with Bertrand Russell for example, that all order is spatial. The rhetorical figures and the elements of
word, sentence, paragraph, and chapter in a novel are architectural in
their tendency toward spatial enclosure. As time can be circular and
motionless (thus spatial and nonlinear), and as causality is spatial rather
than temporal (as Émile Borel has shown), so language itself is more
spatial than temporal. [19]

A fourth and compelling concept of spatiality in the novel applies to the
critic himself. Paul de Man in *Blindness and Insight* has remarked that
the critical process necessitates "the notion of circularity or totality" for
"true understanding." The interpretive act, itself therefore spatial, cannot
ignore the spatial elements of the work it contemplates. Novelists have
always considered spatial illusion. Longus described his objective in
Daphnis and Chloe as *antigrapsai te graphe,* to write in answer to the
picture which generates the novel; *grapho,* the root in both "write" and
"picture," indicates the necessity of spatial illusion in temporal writing.
Geometric dances become the protagonists of *The Princess of
Monpensier;* James, critic of the "house" of fiction, writes a *Portrait;*
Andrey Bolkonsky of *War and Peace* is bounded by windows until the
epiphany of space at Austerlitz; Virginia Woolf records in her *Writer's
Diary* her attempt to write "so that one had the sense of reading the two
things at the same time"; Conrad's intention was, "before all, to make you
see." Faulkner has declared that "the aim of every artist is to arrest
motion," which is a spatial, nontemporal objective. Spatial, as de Man has
proved, means not frozen but total. The interpretation of literature derived from space-time aesthetics provides a spatial explanation of the
critical act, an explanation which recognizes the spatial secondary illusion
of the novel. Such an idea explains the presence of what Wolfgang Iser has
called *The Implied Reader.* [20]

There are, therefore, four possible functions of space in the novel.
First, space functions as the operative secondary illusion in the text, the
agency by which spatial properties are realized in the temporal art. Its
second function is revealed through geometric qualities like point, line,

plane, and distance. The relation of the novel to the spatial arts of painting, sculpture, and architecture constitutes its third spatial function.
Proust's belief that a character is "virtual" in the sculpture of a cathedral
provides a useful term to describe this third form of spatiality. Finally,
spatiality influences the interpretive act, for the text creates a "genidentic" field, incorporating the reader in a dynamic relation with it.

These four functions must be examined, however, against the background of previous integrative studies of the arts. Writing in Newton P.
Stallknecht and Horst Frenz's *Comparative Literature,* Mary Gaither
called such investigations "a touchy field of exploration." Murray Krieger
has provided cautionary words about Joseph Frank's theories; for example, is Frank examining effects or causes? Are the properties he isolates
inherent in the works of art, or merely in the perception of them? Heinrich Wölfflin's *Principles of Art History* (1915), with its terms "linear" and
"painterly," generated a desire to pursue such properties in other works
of art; such an approach has led to Helmut Hatzfeld's *Literature through
Art,* Jean Hagstrum's *Sister Arts,* and Wylie Sypher's *Four Stages of
Renaissance Style* and *Rococo to Cubism.* [21]

The practice of comparative aesthetics has been difficult almost from
the beginning, as Rensselaer Lee summarizes in his *Ut Pictura Poesis.*
Simonides of Ceos is stated by Plutarch in *De Gloria Atheniensium* to
have declared: "Painting is mute poetry, poetry a speaking picture." So
far as we may judge, he was the first to juxtapose the two art forms,
temporal and spatial, in a single critical aphorism. In the second chapter
of the *Poetics,* Aristotle is quick to point out that both painters and poets
deal with imitation and representation, some showing us as we are, some
as better than we are. Within the *Poetics,* Aristotle frequently uses
analogies between the two art forms, as when discussing plot: "The plot,
then, is the first essential of tragedy . . . and character takes the second
place. It is much the same in painting; for if an artist were to daub his
canvas with the most beautiful colors laid on at random, he would not give
the same pleasure as he would by drawing a recognizable portrait in black
and white." In the *Ars Poetica,* Horace declared: "A poem is like a painting [*ut pictura poesis*]: the closer you stand to this one the more it will
impress you, whereas you have to stand a good distance from that one;
this one demands a rather dark corner, but that one needs to be seen in
full light, and will stand up to the keen-eyed scrutiny of the art-critic." It
is clear from this quotation that in context, as Lee indicates, such a
passage calls primarily for critical flexibility. In the hands of the Renaissance critics, however, as was also the fate of the "Aristotelian" unities,
the phrase *ut pictura poesis* became the rallying aphorism for questionable critical theories as much as for serious aesthetic philosophy. It must be

noted that Lessing's *Laocoon*, along with Horace's treatise a central point in comparative theory, nevertheless directly opposes the Renaissance abuse of the Horatian dictum, as Lessing argues for demarcation of the arts and against the "transgressions" encouraged by Renaissance critics' misunderstanding of Horace.[22]

During the sixteenth and seventeenth centuries, critics concerned themselves with representation and imitation, attempting further interpretations of the Aristotelian *mimesis*. Leonardo perceived that in describing a battle scene the poet had to resort to successive, piecemeal segments of narrative, whereas a painter could present "the action of a battle in a single instant." The same distinction prevailed when the poet and the painter attempted to depict a portrait; here, as Lee observes, Leonardo anticipated many of Lessing's theories. In *Dialogo della pittura* (1557), Ludovico Dolce regarded the province of the painter as representation, but felt his concern should be life "as it ought to be." Dolce supports the method of Zeuxis, whereby one selects the finest features from a number of models or individuals to depict the beauteous Helen.[23]

In the late seventeenth and eighteenth centuries, these ideas about succession and simultaneity were extended and debated further. Lessing's beliefs were current before the publication of *Laocoon*. In his preface to Du Fresnoy's *De Arte Graphica* (1695), Dryden wrote his famed "Parallel of Poetry and Painting." He begins by citing the theories of Bellori, particularly his advocacy of the Platonic posture of imitating the idea rather than nature; Dryden cited the example of Zeuxis and his Helen. Aware of the ideas of Leonardo, critical of the Dutch painters for their adherence to nature rather than the ideal, Dryden declared that "the art of painting has a wonderful affinity with that of poetry" in their "common imagination." Dryden listed the elements common to both painting and poetry, the "sister arts": (1) pleasure; (2) the use of deceit; and (3) "great and noble" subject matter. He was also aware of their central difference: "I must say this to the advantage of Painting, even above Tragedy, that what this last represents in the space of many hours, the former shows us in one moment." Poetry and painting also have their principal parts in common: (1) invention; (2) imitation of "the best Nature"; (3) order; (4) controlling idea; (5) economy of detail; (6) consistency; (7) "centrality" of focus; and (8) avoidance of "absurdities and incongruities." Dryden even drew analogies between words and color: "Expression, and all that belongs to words, is that in a poem which colouring is in a picture." Lights and shadows correspond to tropes and figures: "Strong parts of a poem require to be amply written, and with all the force and elegance of words; others must be cast into shadows, that is, passed over in silence, or but faintly touched."[24]

During June 1712, Joseph Addison, praising the pleasures of the eye, could declare: "Description runs yet further from the things it represents than painting; for a picture bears a real resemblance to its original which letters and syllables are wholly void of." Later he emphasized: "Colors speak all languages, but words are understood only by such a people or nation." After Dryden, the eighteenth century begins to erode the theory; beginning with Addison, and succeeding to Abbé DuBos and Lessing, the proper philosophy of the time seems *non ut pictura poesis.* DuBos formulated yet another difference in *Critical Reflections on Poetry and Painting* (1739), where he subtly advocated intuitive perception, but especially the concept, expressed earlier by Benedetto Varchi, of the province of poetry as *di dentro,* the inner life, and of painting as *di fuori,* the features of the outer world. The temporal arts can represent, as painting cannot, subtleties of the soul and "intricacies of moral character" because of the successive events they portray. Sir Joshua Reynolds in the *Discourses* could conclude that the great alignment of poetry and painting lay, ultimately, in "nobleness of conception." But as Lee notes, with the ascendency of Rousseau, the resurrection of Longinus, and the growth of neo-Gothic sensibility, the debate rests.[25]

The nature of space in the temporal arts became a difficult issue in the twentieth century. This controversy originated in 1915, with the publication of Heinrich Wölfflin's *Principles of Art History.* It was with Wölfflin's book, or rather with the adaptation of his theories, that this debate was renewed. Using the oppositions of "linear" and "pictorial," "closed" and "open," "flat" and "deep," the categories Wölfflin adopted to distinguish Renaissance from baroque art, critics attempted to apply these criteria to literary works, beginning with Oskar Walzel's analysis of Shakespeare in 1917. This study was soon followed by Oswald Spengler's *Decline of the West* (1918), in which analogizing led to the rise of *Geistesgeschichte,* history based on the theory of "the spirit of the time" and its pervasive existence in all art forms of any one epoch. An entire series of these studies, mostly from Germany, flourished.[26]

Less extravagant claims were made for the method in England. In 1918 Lawrence Binyon, using the central concept of "rhythm" and somewhat influenced by Walter Pater, studied relationships such as those between Wordsworth's poems and Constable's paintings, between the Elgin marbles and Keats's *Hyperion,* and between Shelley's and Turner's works, resting much of his case on imagery. The correspondences he found are more interesting than convincing, ignoring as they do the problem of inherent essences of the art forms and concentrating on purely affective responses to the art works. Edmund Blunden, pursuing the same material in 1942, also analyzed the presence of images in different media, such as architecture in Keats and extravagant color in Byron. In his essay "Parallels in Painting and Poetry" (1936), Herbert Read observed affiliations between Dryden and Wren and cited the significant "rebirth of English painting" which occurred "precisely with the birth of the English novel." Read is cautious enough to question the "analogical method," declaring that the "manifestations of the separate arts" must be "distinct in separate individuals," particularly as the art forms in any one era do not keep pace with each other.[27]

In 1941, however, René Wellek published an extensive criticism of the methods of *Geistesgeschichte* in "The Parallelism between Literature and the Arts." He first discounts the idea of "mood" as purely affective response. The second idea, of artistic intention, is discounted because of the quite observable gap between intention and execution. Third, the argument from "common social and cultural background" is specious, especially as the arts do not progress at the same speed in any single era. The only sound investigations, he claims, must rest on "structural relationships." The other three criteria, especially the popular "time-spirit" argument, do not provide convincing arguments for comparative aesthetics.[28] The concept of secondary illusion which underlies the geometric, the virtual, and the genidentic forms of spatiality in the novel rests on the type of sound norm advocated by Wellek, "structural relationships."

Wellek's criticisms did not go unheeded. Following World War II, the field of comparative aesthetics was approached with more defined norms and yet with more aspiring hopes than before. Helmut Hatzfeld, in "Literary Criticism through Art and Art Criticism through Literature" (1947) and in *Literature through Art* (1952) cited examples from medieval times to the twentieth century to support six relations: (1) the interpretation of literary texts through pictures (Rimbaud/Gauguin); (2) the interpretation of pictures by literature (Millet/Hugo); (3) "literary concepts and motives made evident by art" (Rousseau/Greuze); (4) "artistic concepts and motives made clear by literature" (Poussin/Racine); (5) "literary-linguistic forms interpreted by art forms" (metonymy in Lamartine/Ingres); (6) "art forms explained by literary-stylistic expressions" (*esprit de finesse* in Pascal/Molière). In "Method in the Study of Literature in Its Relation to the Other Fine Arts" (1950), Giovanni Giovannini, after considering the problems of representation, harmony, and design, questions the logic of Joseph Frank's theory of "spatial form," declaring that Frank is discussing elements of perception, not elements of the artistic product per se, and that the novels of Flaubert and Joyce do not in essence change their temporality. The problem of comparative aesthetics, Giovannini argues, rests in what is given and what is suggested. He focuses, for the first time in any such criticism, on the novel and its relation to painting by probing the influence of impressionism on *The Ambassadors*. While granting the existence of such an influence, he reaffirms that this occurs in the tradition of the novel, not in the tradition of painting. In 1951, Wallace Stevens, in *The Necessary Angel*, discussed "The Relations between Poetry and Painting," declaring the arts to have in common elements of composition, labor, and above all, imagination.[29]

Three recent texts illustrate the state of comparative aesthetics: Wylie Sypher's *Four Stages of Renaissance Style* (1955) and *Rococo to Cubism* (1960) and Jean Hagstrum's investigations of the English eighteenth century in *The Sister Arts* (1958). While Sypher's theory of "continual discontinuity" applied to both cubism and Gide is suggestive, for example, the problem of inherent essence is raised disturbingly.[30] Hagstrum surveys the history of comparative aesthetics in the same manner as Wellek, and is critical of Sypher's tendency to use artistic terminology separate from analyses of visual imagery. Such language becomes, for Hagstrum, under such rubrics as "icons," "ekphrasis," and "the picturesque," the cornerstone of his study of Dryden, Pope, Collins, Thomson, and Gray. Hagstrum's book has the virtue of a well-clarified and bounded focus which the works of Sypher and Hatzfeld lack; by concentrating on the visual, he produces what is probably the most satisfactory study of comparative aesthetics yet achieved.

In addition to the scholarship of comparative aesthetics, other texts involve spatial problems in the theory of the novel. Hans Meyerhoff's *Time in Literature*, A. A. Mendilow's *Time and the Novel*, and John Henry Raleigh's "English Novel and the Three Kinds of Time" have provided numerous insights into the literary use of time. Raleigh's classifications of "cosmic time," "historical time," and "existential time" are particularly striking because he uses spatial configurations as their symbols (the circle, horizontal line, and vertical line respectively). Such critical works gloss James's assertion in the preface to *Roderick Hudson:* "This eternal time-question is accordingly, for the novelist, always there and always formidable; always insisting on the *effect* of the great lapse and passage . . . and on the effect of compression, of composition and form, by the terms of literary arrangements." The novelist is concerned not only with the opposition of chronological and psychological time (enunciated by Bergson in *Time and Free Will*), but also with the technical problems of dealing with time in the art of the novel itself. The investigations by Georges Poulet, *Studies in Human Time* and *The Interior Distance*, examine the relation of existence versus essence, of subject and object, in writers from the seventeenth to the nineteenth centuries. Robert Humphrey's *Stream of Consciousness in the Modern Novel* studies this technique in relation to time and timelessness in the work of Joyce, Woolf, and Faulkner; his analyses provide concrete evidence of the techniques these authors use to seize spatial effects and to study spatiality. Poulet's third and most important work, *Proustian Space*, is a crucial document in spatial studies, examining atemporality, self-reflexiveness, and spatial art in the seven novels of *Remembrance of Things Past*. Along with Gérard Genette's "Discourse of the Récit" about Proust from *Figures III*, it constitutes the most significant application of spatial theories to a single author yet published. [31]

There is concern with spatial functions not only in the studies of critics like Humphrey or Poulet, but also in an important body of criticism about the techniques of the novel. This criticism originates in the twentieth century with the work of Henry James, particularly the prefaces he wrote for the New York edition of his works, later edited by R. P. Blackmur as *The Art of the Novel*. These prefaces and James's essays are most important in their recognition of spatial aspects of the novel. In "The Art of Fiction," James declares that "as the picture is reality, so the novel is history," to the extent that the novelist has "so much in common with the philosopher and the painter; this double analogy is a magnificent heritage." His statement that "a novel is in its broadest definition a personal, a direct impression of life" is undoubtedly the remark that generated interest in the Impressionists' influence on *The Ambassadors*. His insight about the relation between point and picture appears in his assertion: "I see dramas within dramas in that, and innumerable points of view. A psychological reason is, to my imagination, an object adorably pictorial; to catch the tint of its complexion—I feel as if that idea might inspire one to Titian-esque efforts." He pursues the insight in his final advice: "Try and catch the color of life itself." In his notice of *Our Mutual Friend*, he acknowledges the relation between character and sculpture in his preoccupation with "figure": "But the prime requisite was that they should *be* characters: Mr. Dickens, according to his usual plan, has made them simply figures." James's remarks foreshadow Forster's conceptions of "flat" and "round."[32]

Furthermore, in his brief review of *Middlemarch*, James provides the clue to yet another artistic concept, the architectural, which he will use throughout the prefaces: "*Middlemarch* is a treasure-house of detail, but it is an indifferent whole." Reverting to the sculptural relationship to character, he declares Bulstrode of "a slightly artificial cast"; he develops the sculptural concept in later criticism. It occurs, for example, in the essay on Balzac, where he refers to Balzac as "*penetrating* into a subject; his corridors always went further and further." The remark sounds as if the subject of discussion were the proper placement of a statue in a house. Again: "Let me add . . . that [Balzac's faults] are faults, on the whole, of execution, flaws in the casting." Foreshortening, mentioned here and throughout the prefaces, constitutes yet another spatial technique. Emma Bovary, James observes in the essay on Flaubert, is a figure living "without evaporation under the painter's hand," a statement which does not so much relate character to painting as character to flat and high relief. *Madame Bovary* itself has a "firm roundness," "that sign of all rare works that there is something in it for every one," which again results from the architectural element. [33]

James refers to spatial elements throughout his prefaces, calling them variously the "germ," "spot," "*donnée*," "seed," or "point." He also refers to the "centre," the organic theory, foreshortening, the importance of scene and dramatization, the concept of the "fictive picture" from Turgenev, and the "flatness" of *Daisy Miller*. His discussion of character, which as Susanne Langer has shown involves "volume," is especially concerned with the sculptural. In addition, he frequently refers to the novel itself as an architectural product. For example, he observes in the preface to *The Portrait of a Lady:*

The house of fiction has in short not one window, but a million—a number of possible windows not to be reckoned, rather; every one of which has been pierced, or is still pierceable, in its vast front, by the need of the individual vision and by the pressure of the individual will.

Later, in the preface to *The Awkward Age,* he again recognizes the architectural:

The dramatist has verily to *build,* is committed to architecture, to construction at any cost; to driving in deep his vertical supports and laying across and firmly fixing his horizontal... I rejoiced, by the same token, to feel my scheme hold.

His critique of *The Wings of the Dove* similarly involves architecture:

It is in Kate's consciousness that at the stage in question the drama is brought to a head, and the occasion on which, in the splendid saloon of poor Milly's hired palace, she takes the measure of her friend's festal evening, squares itself to the same synthetic firmness as the compact constructional block inserted by the scene at Lancaster Gate.

The briefest survey of the prefaces gathered by Blackmur into *The Art of the Novel* attests to James's conscious use of actual spatial technique in his novels and in his critical theory. [34]

The Jamesian use of pictorial, sculptural, and architectural metaphors and techniques provoked, of course, the great twentieth-century interest in the theory of fiction, beginning in 1921 with Percy Lubbock's *Craft of Fiction*. Although Lubbock does not specifically discuss spatial techniques, he analyzes the relation of characters to their environments

(Emma Woodhouse); the relation of these characters to our environment (Pierre and Natasha); pictorial elements (in Flaubert, and Balzac); the problem of freestanding characters (in Thackeray); the "scenic" method; the problem of life from within (in *Anna Karenina*); *War and Peace* as the "form of time"; and of course point of view, which Lubbock declares is "fixed in space," and "free in *time*," clear indications of the spatial origin of this conception in secondary illusion. Forster's *Aspects of the Novel* (1927) from the beginning assumes James's attitude toward works of fiction as "mansions" or "edifices," develops the idea of detachment (essential to Wayne Booth as "distance"), declares in contrast to Lubbock that "space is the lord of *War and Peace*, not time," calls Austen a "miniaturist," espouses the idea of infinity in relation to Dostoyevsky's characters, finds the hourglass patterns in *Thaïs* and *The Ambassadors*, and develops the idea of rhythm as "repetition plus variation," a welding of the ideas of space and time.[35]

Later in the twentieth century, the theory of fiction properly came into its own. Edwin Muir, in *The Structure of the Novel* (1929), developed a theory of the dramatic novel and character novel, according to which the province of the former is time, and that of the latter space. This argument, inconclusive because of its adherence to a single concept of time, remained more suggestive than convincing. Wayne Booth's *The Rhetoric of Fiction* (1961) relied for its central thesis on the concept of distance and its relation to point of view. This influential study, with its distinction between author and narrator, and its notion of the implied author, evolved into the theory of rhetorical persuasion of the reader. Booth, however, uses the term "distance" without adequately pursuing its clearly pictorial implication. Recent critical studies of the novel have been concerned with architecture: Alan Friedman's *Turn of the Novel* (1966), with its distinction between the "closed" and the "open" novel; Philip Stevick's "Fictional Chapters and Open Ends," with its concepts of "enclosure" and "openness"; E. K. Brown's *Rhythm in the Novel* (1950), in which he finds that design is closely aligned to language; Frank Kermode's *Sense of an Ending* (1967), which incorporates the insights of Robbe-Grillet to show the changing attitude toward fictional "end"; and R. S. Crane's "The Plot of *Tom Jones*," with its conception of "plot" as a verb. Gaston Bachelard's *Poetics of Space* has shown, by phenomenological reduction, that the sense of space undoubtedly is dominant over the sense of time in an individual's perceptive process.[36]

Recent criticism in France of the novel and of language has demonstrated again the importance of spatiality in the novel. In "The Space of the Novel," from his *Essays on the Novel*, Michel Butor observes: "In that which concerns space, [the novel's] interest is no less great, especially in its tight bond with the arts which explore it, painting in particular." More recently, Gérard Genette in "Space and Language," from *Figures I*, has observed: "Language, thought, contemporary art are *spatialized* [*spatialisés*]." For Genette, the relations of connotation to denotation, the appearance of devices abolishing linearity of discourse, the discontinuity and atemporality of the novel, reveal that "language *spaces itself* [*s'es-pace*] so that space, in itself, becomes language, speaks it and writes it." Tzvetan Todorov, in his "Poétique" from *What is Structuralism?*, has isolated four types of spatiality of language, including written, verbal interreferential, architectural, and literal. [37]

In addition to the spatiality of simultaneity, of secondary illusion, of language, and of atemporality, there is the further spatiality of the written text, as Genette observed in "Literature and Space" from *Figures II*: "The clear spatiality of writing can be taken as a symbol of the profound spatiality of language." This idea has been further pursued by Michel Butor in "The Book as Object," where he emphasizes that the book, itself a diptych, exploits its typographical and spatial layout for part of its existence. What Proust said in *Against Sainte-Beuve* is true: "Time has here taken the form of space." In his further work on individual authors, such as "Proustian Palimpsest," "Fixed Vertigo" (on Robbe-Grillet), and "Silences of Flaubert," Genette has drawn on spatiality to explain dimensions of these authors. In "Frontiers of the Récit," Genette argues that description in narrative is spatial, a representation "of objects in their single spatial existence," serving a role "purely aesthetic, like that of the sculpture in a classic building," its essence "spatial simultaneity." His study of Proust, "Discourse of the Récit" from *Figures III*, reflects Einsteinian thought in such a definition as that of *diegesis*, "the spatial-temporal universe indicated by the récit." [38]

Michel Butor has pointed out striking elements of space in the novel in several essays. In "Research on the Technique of the Novel," he declared that linear arrangement (succession) has little to do with events or even with word and sentence order; time is rarely experienced as continuous, and therefore does not greatly concern the novelist. Rather, time in the novel is three superimposed sequences, those of the narrative, of the writing, and of the reading. Balzac was properly an architect, using his novels to build the edifice of *The Human Comedy*: his recurring characters demonstrate simultaneity and spatial reversal. Butor observes in "The Space of the Novel" that framing and perspective occupy the novelist as much as the painter. [39]

The work of the Russian Formalists, collected in *Theory of Literature* by Tzvetan Todorov, demonstrates the importance of spatial study in early twentieth-century studies of language and narration. For example, in the second and third parts of "The Construction of the Short Story and of the Novel," Victor Shklovsky probed the importance of parallelism, of *ralentissement* (retarding the speed of narration), of *encadrement* ("framing") and of *enfilage* ("linking") in the construction of narratives. Jurij Tynianov and Roman Jakobson declared that Ferdinand de Saussure's ideas of *la langue* (the norms of a language) and *la parole* (the individual utterance within that language) must be studied in conjunction: that is, any use of the language in an individual novel is always a palimpsest, because underlying the individual utterance is a simultaneous utterance of linguistic norms. In an essay from *On the Theory of Prose*, Shklovsky argued that the architecture of chapters in *Little Dorrit* was itself a mystery greater than the events of the story. [40]

The influence of the Formalists' theories is pervasive in the work of Tzvetan Todorov himself. In "The Categories of the Literary Récit," distinguishing between *histoire* ("story") and *discours* ("narration"), Todorov demonstrated how devices of antithesis, gradation, and parallelism achieved the *histoire*. For the expression of the *discours*, the novelist resorted to various devices, all concerned with spatial placement, to handle the problem of time: *l'enchainement* ("coordination"), *l'alternance* ("alternation") and *l'enchâssement* ("subordination"). In *The Poetics of Prose*, Todorov shows how the theories of the Russian Formalists, particularly of Vladimir Propp, revealed that the word or sign, in the connection of its *signifiant* to its *signifié*, was always involved in an atemporal state of relationships. In "How to Read?" Todorov argued that the interpretation of a work was involved with layers of significations. The procedures of reading, particularly "superposition" and "figuration," represent spatialized methods of approaching the text, concerned as they are with connections, whether within one text or between texts, as, for example, among all the works of one author. The reader experiences a dynamic field in space-time. Concurrent investigations by Roland Barthes and Jean Ricardou explored spatial or atemporal concepts about narrative. Ricardou, for example, in two essays in *Problems of the New Novel*, demonstrated that the relationship of the two times of a novel is spatial, inasmuch as one is "behind" the other in all situations exclusive of dialogue. Likewise, the relationship between a part of a narrative and its whole, the narrative within a narrative, and the novel the reader creates are critical nontemporal elements of a novel. [41]

As Paul de Man observes in *Blindness and Insight:* "literature first moves away from itself and then returns."

In describing literature, from the standpoint of the concept of modernity, as the steady fluctuation of an entity away from and toward its own mode of being, we have constantly stressed that this movement does not take place as an actual

Clinker, the epistolary form shows separate reactions by persons of diverse intelligence and social rank to Matt Bramble or to each other. On the thematic level, the letters in a sense end at the novel's conclusion not merely because the events are finished, with marriage and discovered sons, but because Bramble has been rescued from the misanthropy that dominated his life. The isolation of the form no longer applies. In *The New Héloïse,* Rousseau employs the device to emphasize the loneliness of Julie and Saint-Preux in the midst of their adulterous love. In Richardson's *Pamela,* the introspection inherent in the privacy of letters, the presentation of reaction rather than action, leads to the statement by the heroine: "I have been delivered from a worse enemy, myself."[1] With *Dangerous Liaisons* the epistolary form, the "novel of point," reaches a formal climax: here are indeed two principal, but six essential, correspondents, or points. It is a novel of tortured solitary mental harassment, as in the frequent instances when Valmont could have seduced Madame de Tourvel physically but could not be sure of her mental despair. Only when the distraught woman begs mentally for her seduction does he grant what she formerly would have "yielded." Laclos's creation of this form of mental rape achieved the greatest exploitation of the epistolary novel, although Goethe in *Young Werther* could hint at its possibilities. It is Laclos who recognized the supremely cerebral function of the epistolary novel and its isolation, nearly existential, which it exacerbates rather than alleviates. Geometric point here clearly supports thematic isolation.

Throughout *Wilhelm Meister's Apprenticeship* and *Henry von Ofterdingen,* Goethe and Novalis propound what is styled the "organic" theory of the novel's formation. Deciding whether or not to present the uncut *Hamlet,* Wilhelm tells Serlo: "It is a trunk with boughs, twigs, leaves, buds, blossoms, and fruit. Is not the one there with the others, and by means of them?" He adds: "From youth, I have been accustomed to direct the eyes of my spirit inwards rather than outwards; and hence it is very natural that to a certain extent I should be acquainted with man, while of men I have not the smallest knowledge." The intention of this novel, as a prototypical *Bildungsroman,* is to move from within to without, like the tree of any artistic work. Wilhelm is in this sense his own author, or would be, to paraphrase Beckett, but for the pronoun, the use of the third rather than the first person. In Hölderlin's *Hyperion,* the protagonist writes to his friend Ballarmin:

Men began and grew from the happiness of the plant, grew until they ripened; from that time on they have been in ceaseless ferment, inwardly and outwardly, until now mankind lies there like a Chaos, utterly disintegrated, so that all who can still feel and see are dizzied; but Beauty forsakes the life of men, flees upward into Spirit; the Ideal becomes what Nature was, and even though the tree is dried out and weatherworn below, a fresh crown has still sprung from it and flourishes green in the sunlight, as the trunk did once in its days of youth; the Ideal is what Nature was. By this, by this Ideal, this rejuvenated divinity, the few recognize one another and are one, for one thing is in them.

In the startling preface to his novel, Hölderlin states: "He who merely inhales the scent of my plant does not know it, and he who plucks it merely in order to learn from it does not know it either." For Novalis, the protagonist is literally the word made flesh: "The ladies liked to dwell on his attractive figure, for it was like the simple saying of a stranger, which one hardly notices until long after his departure, when its deep and unpretentious bud opens up more and more and finally reveals a gorgeous flower in all the glory of closely entwined leaves so that one never forgets it, never tires of repeating it." He reinforces the idea instantly: "From time to time the flower of his heart flashed upon his inward eye like heat lightning." Henry and the novel both are the famed organic blue flower.[2]

This connection between the novel as point and the individual as point is explicit in Sartre's *Nausea:* "Nausea... is made of wide, soft instants, spreading at the edge, like an oil stain." "The Nausea... is I." Roquentin's introspection formally is close to Valmont's letter, for it realizes the epistolary isolation in the more explicit form of the diary, a chronicle that does not use even the specious excuse of communication; the conflict between the ostensibly public letter and the writer's closet has, simply, been dispensed with. Robbe-Grillet provides the clue to the word as stain, as point, by the centipede crushed on the wall in *Jealousy* with its "sections of legs and the partial form of a body convulsed into a question mark." One notes that the stain of the centipede is presented long before the actual event of its appearance and crushing. The climax of the novel is the application of the typewriter eraser to the question mark stain; "erasing a stain or a badly chosen word" are the same.

Besides, it is not practical to wash the wall. This dull-finish paint is much more fragile than the ordinary gloss paint with linseed oil in it which was previously used on the walls of this room. The best solution would be to use an eraser, a hard, fine-grained eraser which would gradually wear down the soiled surface—the typewriter eraser, for instance, which is in the top left desk drawer.

The slender traces of bits of legs or antennae come off right away, with the first strokes of the eraser. The larger part of the body, already quite pale, is curved into a question mark that becomes increasingly vague toward the tip of the curve, and soon disappears completely. But the head and the first joints require a more extensive rubbing: after losing its color, the remaining shape stays the same for quite a long time. The outlines have become only a little less sharp. The hard eraser passing back and forth over the same point does not have much effect now.

A complementary operation seems in order: to scratch the surface very lightly, with the corner of the razor blade. Some white dust rises from the wall. The precision of the tool permits the area exposed to its effect to be carefully determined. A new rubbing with the eraser now finishes off the work quite easily.

The stain has disappeared altogether. There now remains only a vaguely outlined paler area, without any apparent depression of the surface, which might pass for an insignificant defect in the finish, at worst.

The question mark, however, remains: "The stain formed by the remains of the centipede is scarcely visible because of the oblique light."[3]

In the preface to *Roderick Hudson,* James declared: "The work... remains in equilibrium by having found its centre, the point of command of all the rest. From this centre the subject has been treated, from this centre the interest has spread, and so... the thing had acknowledged a principle of composition and contrives at least to hang together." In the preface to *The American,* he praised "the effort of the artist to preserve for his subject that unity and... that effect of a *centre* which most economise its value. Its value is most discussable when that economy has most operated; the content and the 'importance' of a work of art are in fine wholly dependent on its being one." Quoting Turgenev on the "fictive picture," James declared that Isabel Archer constituted "the germ of my idea." And finally, in the preface to *The Tragic Muse,* James announced: "I delight in a deep-breathing economy and an organic form." Throughout his New York edition prefaces, James reiterates the theory of the "grain," the "germ," the "seed," the "grease-spot"—what in "The Art of Fiction" he called the *donnée.* The Jamesian novel, therefore, elevates point in two ways, as the central force for its tale (the *donnée*) and as the foundation of its technique (the centre). So spatial and geometric is this conception that James can connect these two points, provoke the exposure of the *donnée* to the centre, by a line, the *ficelle.*[4]

A particularly fine instance of how the point influences both character and the formation of plot material is found in the work of George Eliot. Many of James's observations about point are implicit in the opening sentence of *Adam Bede:* "With a single drop of ink for a mirror, the Egyptian sorcerer undertakes to reveal to any chance-comer far-reaching visions of the past. This is what I undertake to do for you, reader." This theory of "concentric circles," all radiating from a single event, the consequences of the seduction of Hetty Sorrel, finds reinforcement in chapter titles such as "The bitter waters spread." The only two incontestable descriptions of novelistic art in *Adam Bede* are the drop of ink in chapter one (that is, a point) and the Dutch paintings in chapter seventeen, "In which the story pauses a little."[5] Pictorial art is seen in its essential two-dimensional, one-point perspective.

The point was all in all to George Eliot, both as an ethical idea and as an aesthetic practice. Morally, it is the ego, the individual as point; it is the small cancer from which evil grows, like the radiating lines on the silver in *Middlemarch* or the web in the same novel. The point, likewise, is the convergence of all the radiating lines, like Hetty's arrest in *Adam Bede*, like the boat trips in *The Mill on the Floss* or *Daniel Deronda*, like the revelation of paternity in *Felix Holt*. To recall André Gide, no point is more a beginning than an ending, more centrifugal than centripetal. The "drop of ink" which opens the novel, as Darrell Mansell has shown, is indeed the organic method applied to an organic meaning: there is no public life not determined by a private life. The well-known problem of egoism in the novel, clarified for George Eliot so well in the positivist writings of Comte and Feuerbach, finds its expression in this drop, which is both as contracted and expanded as the human being, who like Adam Bede (whose first name suggests he is the paradigm of postlapsarian man) must accommodate himself to the larger structure of society. [6] Frequently in the novel the reader is asked to "peer into windows," or to recognize the originating point of all activity, as at Hall Farm where "the life . . . has changed its *focus*, and no longer *radiates* from the parlour, but from the kitchen and the farmyard" (italics added).

What is more striking in *Adam Bede* is the explicit evocation of point in many places in the novel, and particularly in book one, in such a way as to prepare for the discussion of Dutch genre painting when "the story pauses a little." In the second chapter, Eliot adopts such an attitude in describing Mr. Casson, the Donnithorne's landlord: "On a front view [he] appeared to consist principally of two spheres, bearing the same relation to each other as the earth and the moon: that is to say, the lower sphere might be said, at a rough guess, to be thirteen times larger than the upper." Clearly this is apprehension by geometry, the first sketches a charcoal artist would employ in establishing a geometric outline. A traveler views the surrounding country in a similar painterly fashion: "High up against the horizon were the huge conical *masses* of hill. . . . And directly below them the eye rested on *a more advanced line* of hanging woods. . . . *Then came* the valley. . . . Doubtless there was a large sweep of park and a broad glassy pool in front of that mansion, but the swelling slope of meadow *would not let our traveller see them* from the village green. He saw instead a *foreground*" (italics added). At Broxton, for one's first sight of the Reverend Irwine, "we will enter very softly, and stand still in the open doorway. . . . At present we *can only see* that he has a broad flat back and an abundance of powdered hair. . . . He will perhaps turn round by-and-by" (italics added). When George Eliot evokes the Dutch paintings in chapter seventeen, she is doing far more than analogizing: she is defining what inductively she has practiced during the entire first book of *Adam Bede*. The "pause" of the story has been justified by the fact that the form of the novel has been pictorial in a technical sense—by construction, with a one-point, organic perspective.

An examination of both chronology and presentation of character in *Adam Bede* substantiates its truly spatial intention. This spatiality is easily demonstrated, for example, by pointing to the completion of the hymn in chapter one with which the novel began, or to the sudden introduction of the present tense after the historical present: "Hetty walked hastily across the short space," but then "She is at another gate now," or "She doesn't know that there is another turning to the Hermitage, that she is close against it." Or, to serve the same spatial intention, Eliot introduces the progressive present, frequently with a present participle: "Adam Bede is passing with his undoubting step"; "an elderly woman is looking out." The tenses take us back to the conclusion of chapter one with Adam finishing the hymn. The effect of this technique is one of reversion to the point. *Adam Bede* as a novel works consistently against itself. It is for this reason that the clocks at the Hall Farm and the Chase, in a famous passage, do not correspond. After the fight between master and man, George Eliot tells us that the psychological clock alone mattered: "It was only a few minutes measured by the clock—though Adam always thought it had been a long while—before he perceived a gleam of consciousness in Arthur's face." The use of "always" establishes the atemporal quality this momentous event had for Adam; he retells it as abiding not in the momentary present but in *now* for the rest of his life.

The most notable example of geometric point is in "The Two Bed-Chambers," in which a unit of spatial effects is established through Eliot's description of the contrasting simultaneous activities of Dinah and Hetty upon retiring. It is not only the contrast between Hetty toying with her garnet earrings and Dinah meditating on divine love that arrests; the technique of such juxtaposition itself is startling. The chapter has become the spatial point, which literally welds the separate actions into a composite whole. The next chapter, "Links," emphasizes this point as a genuine welding of Adam and Arthur; both these chapters prepare for the succeeding chapter in which the story "pauses."

The chronology of *Adam Bede* has been carefully analyzed by W. J. Harvey. It is instructive to realize that the first two books of the novel comprise only a single week, from Tuesday, 18 June 1799, to the following Monday. On Tuesday, Adam returns from the carpenter shop and Seth returns from the preaching; by 7 a.m. on Wednesday, Thais Bede's body has been found, and that evening Dinah Morris visits the Bedes' home. Thursday is particularly crowded with events, as Arthur goes to

Norburne in the morning and meets Hetty around 4:30 that afternoon; at about 9:30 p.m., the events of chapter fifteen, "The Two Bed-Chambers," occur. On Friday Adam has an evasive meeting with Mr. Irwine, and the first book concludes. At this point "the story pauses a little" while George Eliot reflects on her art. Book two is concerned with only two days— Sunday, including Thais Bede's funeral, and Monday, 24 June, when Adam visits the Hall Farm, walks with Hetty in the garden, and then goes to Bartle Massey's school. Book three occurs on a single day, that of the coming of age of Arthur Donnithorne. With each of the first three books thus containing progressively less chronological time, there is a clear narrowing to a point in the structure of *Adam Bede*. Book four, however, continues from August until the following February; book five embraces the events of approximately three weeks; book six, after summarizing the period from March 1800 to September 1801, moves to the marriage of Adam and Dinah in November, with the epilogue taking the reader to June 1807. Despite the care devoted to the calendar chronology, how- ever, the central element of Eliot's style is its reversal.

Two statements indicate her genuine intention. If one keeps in mind the elements of reversion (for example, the hymn, the chambers, the "links," the discrepant clocks, the reduction of time to a single day in book three, or the progressive present tense), then two observations in the novel verify that this spatiality of point is moral as well as formal. Adam sees Hetty and Arthur in the woods: "Adam was still motionless, looking at him as he came up. He understood it all now—the locket, and every- thing else that had been doubtful to him: a terrible scorching light showed him the hidden letters that changed the meaning of the past." Adam sees Irwine after his futile search for Hetty: "He saw the whole history now by that terrible illumination which the present sheds back upon the past." The most striking word in each passage is "now," and it is particularly striking in that it is not the past which forms the present, which would make spatiality considerably less important, but the present which forms the past. This fact is startling, involving a genuine apprehension of the now, of the point as both morality and as technique, of the tenseless. Cause and effect are important in the novel, but Eliot clearly did not consider temporal structures alone. The formal, spatial techniques em- ployed in *Adam Bede* are moral and ethical. Indeed, as Harvey has shown, the spatiality provides the most disturbing ironies of missed con- nections. Hetty parts from Arthur at the same time as Dinah leaves the Bedes' cottage; when the two women meet, there is only Dinah's intuition to guide her into Hetty's chamber.

Adam is greatly disturbed by his father's death, not because the loss of his father leaves a void, but rather because for the first time Adam realizes he himself has been a void. During the funeral he ruminates "to himself": "It seems to me now, if I was to find father at home to-night, I should behave different; but there's no knowing—perhaps nothing 'ud be a lesson to us if it didn't come too late." This question never leaves him. After all the intervening events, when Adam and Arthur again meet in the woods, Adam confesses: "I've known what it is in my life to repent and feel it's too late: I felt I'd been too harsh to my father when he was gone from me—I feel it now, when I think of him." The deliberate echo of the previous internal meditation during the funeral, again with the word "now," is the spatial technique concentrating on this point of no time, this point of self. In her brief "Notes on Form in Art" (1868), Eliot discussed the definition of "form" in both the temporal and the plastic arts, particularly emphasizing its quality of "limit" by which an "intrinsic" whole was realized and distinguished. [7] Thus the moments of self-revelation are distinct and reversible points in the development of the organism, timeless in perception and in influence. At the end of the essay she declared: "Speech is to a great extent like sculpture." *Adam Bede* explores geometric point, as Eliot intended when she applied her "drop of ink."

The most formal point in the novel, however, is the word. For if indeed the characters are points experiencing "collisions," as George Eliot thinks, characterization is effected by the collision of words. The young Marcel observes about Swann: "As he spoke I noticed... whenever he used an expression which seemed to imply a definite opinion upon some important subject, he would take care to isolate, to sterilise it by using a special intonation, mechanical and ironic, as though he had put the phrase or word between inverted commas." Later Swann's own name provokes this reaction in Marcel: "And then I would be obliged to pause for breath; so stifling was the pressure, upon that part of me where it was for ever inscribed, of that name which, at the moment when I heard it, seemed to me fuller, more portentous than any other name, because it was burdened with the weight of all the occasions on which I had secretly uttered it in my mind." This connection between the character as point and the word as point, by which the flesh becomes the word, is best demonstrated in *The Scarlet Letter*. Pearl, the point at which Hester and Dimmesdale unite, is herself the scarlet letter containing a radiating point: "The child's whole appearance... irresistibly and inevitably reminded the beholder of the token which Hester Prynne was doomed to wear upon her bosom. It was the scarlet letter in another form; the scarlet letter endowed with life." In the twentieth century this independence of the word, symbolized by Pearl, is a standard result of the symbolic novel, especially one which exploits poetic suggestion. The great moments in which a word, such as "suck," "hot," "cold," or "Dedalus," takes on independent power, therefore, reveal a spatial point of Joyce's *Portrait of the Artist.* For Virginia Woolf, this independence is a cause for despair: "Little words that broke up the thought and dismembered it said nothing. . . . The urgency of the moment always missed its mark." Susan tells Bernard in *The Waves:* "I am tied down with single words. But you wander off; you slip away; you rise up higher, with words and words in phrases." By the novel's end, Bernard abandons this proclivity in order to embrace solitude and silence: "I have done with phrases."[8] Even more important, he recognizes that "time tapers to a point," which is to recognize spatial point as the origin of his novel.

The challenge of spatial point for the novelist was well expressed in Edouard's journal in *The Counterfeiters:* "Life never presents us with anything which may not be looked upon as a fresh starting point, no less than as a termination. 'Might be continued'—these are the words with which I should like to finish my *Counterfeiters.*" The problem and a potential solution are as follows: "No doubt it would have been simpler to go straight to the point; but going straight to the point is a thing particularly foreign to my nature, whose irresistible bent is toward moving obliquely." As did a condemned man in *The Weir of Hermiston,* so does the novelist, his character, and his word: "The creature stood in a vanishing point," facing the challenge that Jinny recognizes in *The Waves:* "The distance closes forever in a point; and we forever open the distance wide again." Forster's behest in *Howards End* to "Only connect!" demonstrates that for the novelist the point as character must be joined to the point as word. For Heyst in *Victory,* the points of the universe are experienced as "laying him under an obligation, but giving him no line of action."[9] The novelist must find the line.

The study of line in the novel is complicated for a reason best stated by Eugène Delacroix in his *Journal:* the straight line, the curved line, and the parallel "never occur in nature; they exist only in the brain of man." As Rudolf Arnheim emphasizes, the straight line does not appear on the human body. Yet ideas about line have been frequent and pervasive in the theory of the novel. For example, Henry James used the linear image *ficelle* ("string") to describe one of the most important structures of the novel. In the preface to *The Ambassadors,* he reveals that Maria Gostrey was above all a function:

> She is the reader's friend . . . and she acts in that capacity, and *really* in that capacity alone, with exemplary devotion, from beginning to end of the book. She is an enrolled, a direct, aid to lucidity; she is in fine, to tear off her mask, the most unmitigated and abandoned of *ficelles.*

> Her function speaks at once for itself, and by the time she has dined with Strether in London and gone to a play with him her intervention as a *ficelle* is, I

hold, expertly justified. Thanks to it we have treated scenically, and scenically alone, the whole lumpish question of Strether's "past."

In his recognition of the *ficelle* as an aid to the reader James emphasizes that the theory of line, between *ficelle* and centre and between novelist and reader, is a central geometric element of the novel.[10]

A second kind of line, *enfilage* ("threading"), defines methods of constructing the *histoire*, as Shklovsky observes. There are two kinds of threading: "In the first, the hero has a neutral role, his exploits pursue him and he himself does not seek them. . . . Other compositions link the action and the agent to motivate the adventures." Thus there is one method used when the agent and action are not linked (as when pirates kidnap helpless adolescents), and another when the action and the agent are linked, as in *The Golden Ass, Lazarillo de Tormes,* or *Don Quixote.* Finally, in "The Secret of the Récit," Todorov recognizes in a Jamesian tale "two lines of force"—a horizontal, concerned with the revelation of events, and a vertical, the quest of knowledge of these events. Systems of parallelism, such as Todorov examines in "The Categories," depend for their achievement on the necessity of convergence.[11]

Spatial line in the novel appears particularly, as Todorov has observed in "The Categories," in the *histoire*. The author, constructing the internal relations of the narrative, uses line in the forms of antithesis, gradation, or parallelism to design the *histoire*. The parallel, as it appears in *Vanity Fair* and *The Old Wives' Tale* in the stories of Becky and Amelia and of Sophia and Constance, provides an easy method of construction. The only difficult technical problem is that of creating the illusion of the meeting of the parallel lines. The revelation by Becky to Amelia before Waterloo in *Vanity Fair* demonstrates a successful solution to this challenge. On the other hand, the lives of Sophia and Constance Baines in *The Old Wives' Tale*, separated geographically, are told as two separate accounts; one does not feel the influence of one life on the other. Masterpieces of this form, like Tolstoy's *Anna Karenina* and Joyce's *Ulysses*, show how parallels may be used convincingly if their points of intersection are motivated and inevitable. The system of antithesis, as Shklovsky notes in "The Construction of the Short Story and of the Novel," is really the device of parallelism used in literal opposition. For example, in *War and Peace* the opposition of Kutuzov and Napoleon is clear, but the opposition of Pierre Bezukhov and Andrey Bolkonsky, where Nicholas Rostov "serves as an axis of reference to the one and the other," is more complex.[12] Shklovsky's reference to the axes of *War and Peace* isolates the preeminence of geometric line in its text.

The foundations of *War and Peace* were laid by 1860 in Tolstoy's fragmentary novel *The Decembrists*, about events occurring when Nicholas I ascended the throne. By 1864 the earliest sections of *War and Peace*, then called *The Year 1805*, were scheduled to appear, and Tolstoy wrote about its genesis. One of the drafts of his foreword to *The Year 1805* is important for the study of the spatiality of the novel, since it indicates that *War and Peace* did not grow by consecutive elements, but rather by evolution against them, as the narrative moved reversibly from 1856 to 1812 to 1807 to 1805.

In publishing the beginning of my projected work, I do not promise a continuation or a conclusion. We Russians generally speaking do not know how to write novels in the sense in which this genre is understood in Europe, nor is the projected work a long short story; no single idea runs through it, no contention is made, no single event is described; still less can it be called a novel with a plot, with a constantly deepening interest, and with a happy or unhappy denouement destroying the interest of the narrative. In order to explain to the reader what the projected work is I find it most convenient to describe how I began to write it.

In 1856, I began to write a story with a definite tendency, the hero of which was to have been a Decembrist returning with his family to Russia. From the present I involuntarily moved to 1825, the period of the delusions and misfortunes of my hero, and I abandoned what I had begun. But even in 1825, my hero was already a grown-up man with a family. In order to understand him, I had to carry myself back to his youth, and his youth coincided with Russia's glorious period of 1812. Once again I discarded what I had begun, and took as my starting point the year 1812, the smell and sound of which can be apprehended by us and are dear to us, but which is now so far removed from us that we can think about it calmly. But for a third time I abandoned what I had begun, not now because I needed to describe my hero's early youth: on the contrary, in the midst of the semi-historical, semi-public, semi-imaginary great typical faces of a great period, the personality of my hero receded into the background, and the young and the old, the men and the women of that time interested me equally and came to the fore. I turned back a third time. . . .

And so having gone back from 1856 to 1805, I now intend to lead not one, but many heroes and heroines of mine through the historical events of 1805, 1807, 1812, 1825, and 1856. I do not foresee in any one of these periods a denouement in the relationships between these people. However much I tried at first to think up a novel-like plot and denouement, I was convinced that it was not within my means, and I decided in describing these people to bow to my own practices and my own powers.

This document, and the remaining three drafts for the foreword, define the specific nature of geometric spatiality in *War and Peace*. In the first draft Tolstoy had declared: "Traditions both of form and content oppressed me. I was afraid to write in a language different from that in which everybody writes. I was afraid that my writing would fall into no existing genre, neither novel, nor tale, nor long poem, nor history." It is evident that by the second draft he had distinguished what is unique and non-

European about his novel. It is not compelled to have either continuation or conclusion; it has no single idea; it is concerned with no single event; it has no central plot; and above all, it has no denouement. By the end of this second draft, the structural elements of "open form" and "decentralization" analyzed by Käte Hamburger have appeared. Tolstoy emphasizes these two qualities in the third draft:

This work is more similar to a novel or tale than to anything else, but it is not a novel because I cannot and do not know how to confine the characters I have created within given limits—a marriage or a death after which the interest in the narration would cease.

He further develops the notion of decentralization in a declaration about the independence of the parts of the novel:

I am convinced that interest in my story will not cease when a given section is completed, and I am striving toward this end. It seems to me that if my work is of any interest, then the reader's interest will not only be gratified at the end of each part of the work but will also continue. As a result of this special quality, this work cannot be called a novel.

Because of this special quality, I think that this work can be printed in separate parts without in any way losing the reader's interest and without inciting the reader to read the subsequent parts.

It will not be possible to read the second part without having read the first, but having read the first, it will be very possible not to read the second.

This particular draft is profoundly significant for *War and Peace*. By his rejection of climax, denouement, plot, and limits to the characters, Tolstoy denies much of the temporal quality of the novel. However, he indicates the alternative, a theory of parts, any one of which will comprise in essence the entire novel. Tolstoy himself was clear in later pronouncements about geometric point:

The most important thing in a work of art is that it should have a kind of focus—i.e., some place where all the rays meet or from which they issue. And this focus should not be capable of being completely explained in words. This, indeed, is the important thing about a good work of art, that its basic content can in its entirety be expressed only by itself.

The aim of an artist is not to solve a problem irrefutably but to make people love life in all its countless inexhaustible manifestations. If I were to be told that I could write a novel whereby I might irrefutably establish what seemed to me the correct point of view on all social problems, I would not even devote two hours' work to such a novel.[13]

The results of Tolstoy's radical theories of the novel are directly evident in his treatment of time in *War and Peace*. The time sequences in the novel either accelerate the speed or intensify *ralentissement*. Volume one involves three parts, all of which occur in 1805: part one, the soirée and

Natasha's name day; part two, Schon-Grabern; and part three, Austerlitz, where Andrey is wounded. In the second volume, Tolstoy accelerates the novel, going from 1806 to 1812: part four, in 1806, includes Pierre's duel and Nicholas's return home; parts five, six, and seven concern events from 1807 to 1811, including the meeting of Pierre and Andrey on the raft, Natasha's debut, and the fox hunt; part eight ends the volume with the aborted elopement of Natasha and Anatole, and Pierre seeing the comet. Volume three, including parts nine, ten, and eleven, concerns only 1812, particularly the battle of Borodino and the burning of Moscow. Parts twelve, thirteen, and fourteen, in volume four, likewise involve 1812, especially Andrey's death and the retreat of the French army; part fifteen concerns the growth of love between Pierre and Natasha from 1812 to 1813. In the first epilogue, Tolstoy concentrates on the time from 1813 to 1820 by focusing on Nicholas and Mary's love and the growing consciousness of young Nicholas Bolkonsky. The four volumes are thus characterized by both similarity and *alternance,* as one and three concentrate on the events of single years, 1805 and 1812, while two and four focus on much longer periods of time. On the other hand, both one and four commence with Anna Pavlovna Scherer's receptions. Instances of repudiation of strict temporal structures occur throughout the novel. For example, Pierre sees the 1812 comet in 1811. The novel concludes with Nicholas Bolkonsky's ruminations about his father Andrey, Pierre, and Nicholas Rostov, which recall the origins of *War and Peace* in *The Decembrists;* on the basis of the correspondence between his thin neck and that of Vereshchagin, one may assume that young Nicholas's project to please his father will in fact be death in the Decembrist movement of 1825. In part six, Tolstoy has advanced Andrey's activities so far that he must return to Pierre with the statement, "Nearly two years before this, in 1808, Pierre. . . ."

A fine instance of Tolstoy's sustained attention to spatiality in order to reverse time appears in parts ten and eleven, which recount the wounding of Andrey at Borodino.

"Can this be death?" thought Prince Andrey, looking with a quite new, envious glance at the grass, the wormwood, and the streamlet of smoke that curled up from the rotating black ball. "I cannot, I do not want to die. I love life—I love this grass, this earth, this air."

Immediately Andrey is carried to a dressing station "pitched at the edge of a birch wood." These instances, however, are replete with reversing detail. Andrey's thoughts parallel those of Nicholas Rostov before Schon-Grabern:

"In myself alone and in that sunshine there is so much happiness; but here . . . groans, suffering, fear, and this uncertainty and hurry. . . . There—they are shouting again, and again are all running back somewhere, and I shall run with them, and it, death, is here above me and around. . . . Another instant and I shall never again see the sun, this water, that gorge!"

The birches of course recall Andrey's reflections before the battle: "He looked at the row of birches shining in the sunshine, with their motionless green and yellow foliage and white bark. 'To die . . . to be killed tomorrow. . . . That I should not exist. . . . That all this should still be, but no me.'" In part eleven, Tolstoy halts the reader's temporal concern for Andrey by having him heard of by other characters until his reunion with Natasha. For instance, Pierre hears that he has died, and one is left uncertain whether this ultimate temporal event has occurred or whether a different temporal structure, persistence in the same wounded state, prevails. Later Andrey is lodged at the Rostovs' house for one night; Sonya and the Countess, but not Natasha, learn of his presence. The narrative then reverts to Pierre and the incident with Vereshchagin, Moscow burns, Natasha goes to Andrey, and only then one learns of Andrey's experiences up to this reconciliation. If *War and Peace* seems timeless, it is partially because of these achronic devices, which suggest a narrative not yet written (Nicholas Bolkonsky) or a written narrative constructed atemporally (Andrey's wounding and reconciliation with Natasha). This is the result of Tolstoy's belief that the "focus should not be capable of being completely explained in words." It is on this account that James Curtis may speak of the novel as having "no linear movement" within it, and that Reginald Christian may declare that it is "not a finished work," and has "no real ending" and "no obvious climax." Because of this atemporal quality, the characters in *War and Peace* reach a "higher stage" of development which is nevertheless "not final and irreversible." Boris Eichenbaum's statement about the experimental nature of *Childhood* is descriptive of *War and Peace* as well: "*Childhood* is linked together not by a movement of events which form a plot, but by a sequence of diverse scenes. . . . Here time plays the role of an external plan only; its movement therefore is not felt."[14]

Eichenbaum's recognition of this linkage, however, suggests the importance of *enfilage* in the novel. Tolstoy himself recognized this principle in a letter to Strakhov in 1876:

In everything, in almost everything that I have written, the necessity of collecting thoughts linked among themselves for expressing myself has guided me, but every thought expressed separately loses its meaning, [and] is frightfully degraded when it is taken from the linkage in which it is located. The linkage itself is composed not of thought, I think, but of something else, and to express the basis of this thought is possible only indirectly—by describing images, actions, positions in words.

An entire series of devices emphasizing location and linkage comprises the spatial secondary illusion of *War and Peace*. If one recalls Todorov's "Categories," it is apparent that many of the practices he recognizes in *Dangerous Liaisons* appear in *War and Peace*. Both antithesis and parallelism are particularly evident in the *histoire*. Shklovsky felt: "The oppositions among certain characters or certain groups of characters in the novels of Tolstoy represent a most complex form of parallelism." He emphasized particularly the relations between Napoleon and Kutuzov, and Pierre and Andrey, to which one may add those between Natasha and Hélène or Petya Rostov and Nicholas Bolkonsky. The simplest variation is evident, however, when one considers that among the women the principal character Natasha is the axis between Hélène and Princess Mary, while among the men it is her brother Nicholas, not the principal male figure, who is the axis between the two male protagonists. Tolstoy's characters change by confrontation with this opposite figure, and yet they "remain in the camp to which they have always belonged." The same parallelism appears in the structuring of the family groups in the novel, with the Bolkonskys and the Rostovs representing the moral fiber of Russia in contrast to the Kuragins and the Drubetskoys; Russia stands morally superior to the invading French. This parallelism extends as well to the links or connections between situations that serve a persistent reversing function in the novel. In vastly different moods, Andrey Bolkonsky sees the oak tree twice; he observes "the sky to which Pierre had pointed, and for the first time since Austerlitz saw that high, everlasting sky he had seen while lying on that battlefield." Pierre observes the comet twice, once after saving Natasha from eloping with Anatole Kuragin and again when the French have taken Moscow. Such parallels may occur between characters as well. For example, Nicholas Rostov before Schon-Grabern and Andrey Bolkonsky before Borodino have the same reactions to life and death. The process of reversal is carried even further, as Shklovsky observed, by repeated instances in which the expected in fact does not occur. There is a fine illustration of this technique when Pierre hears Andrey is dead; the reader discovers only much later, when Andrey is brought to the Rostov home during the evacuation, that he still lives. The evacuations themselves, first of the Russians from Moscow (part eleven) and then of the French from Russia (part fourteen), include within the story itself the reversal motif.[15]

The *discours* or narration of *War and Peace* verifies that it was constructed rather than written. Tolstoy's extensive and peculiar use of repetition in the novel is particularly important as a reinforcement of geometric parallelism. Shklovsky observes that it is not so much accretive or additive as "defamiliarizing," isolating outside time. The repetition of a gesture or detail may be of two types; in one case the item receives a new emphasis by virtue of its new context, and in the other its valuation remains the same. Characterization of Princess Lise by her lip is of the former type, and that of Hélène by her marble shoulders is of the latter. Christian has analyzed the varieties of this device in the novel in considerable detail. Tolstoy, for instance, has his own favorite expressions conveying a moral attitude: "peculiar to," "natural," and "as is always the case" convey his idea that the best people are unaffected, and that individuals are both unique and universal. In many instances a phrase is reiterated within a passage to indicate not progression but intensification, often with shame or guilt. Thus, Pierre thinks of Hélène:

> "But how often I have felt proud of her, proud of her majestic beauty and social tact," thought he; "been proud of my house, in which she received all Petersburg, proud of her unapproachability and beauty. So this is what I was proud of!"

Extreme parallelism appears in the structure of paragraphs and sentences, particularly tripartite structures erected on nouns, adjectives, verbs, and prepositions:

> On his return to Moscow from the army, Nicholas Rostov was welcomed by his home circle as the best of sons, a hero, and their darling Nikolenka; by his relations as a charming, attractive, and polite young man; by his acquaintances as a handsome lieutenant of hussars, a good dancer, and one of the best matches in the city.

Within a single brief paragraph Tolstoy effects a metonymy of disparate attitudes, producing a simultaneous impression of the returned soldier.

In addition to these forms of repetition, however, Tolstoy also makes extensive use of alternation, a technique which is very evident in the structure of the four volumes. In the first volume, for example, part one takes place in peace and part two in war (Schon-Grabern); part three takes place first in peace and then in war (Austerlitz). The two battles themselves are contrasted as relative victory and absolute disaster. Volume two is devoted to activities during relative peace, while volumes three and four are preoccupied with persistent war. The volumes vary in their beginnings and endings as well. Christian observes that volume one begins with peace and ends with war, but that the succeeding volumes begin and end in the same state—volume two, peace; volume three, war; volume four, peace. The principle of contrast in characterization is therefore well supported in the narration by antithesis and alternation.[16]

Because of this alternation between spatial lines, the reader receives no complete account of the nature of the characters or of their fates. For instance, after Andrey is wounded at Borodino, one learns only indirectly of his subsequent experience through other characters (Pierre, Sonya, the

Countess, and finally Natasha). Boris Eichenbaum could defend the "digressions" in the novel as part of this technique of discontinuity; they constitute a structural device, providing intentional discontinuity, atemporal reflection, and *ralentissement*. Such discontinuity, Christian states, even appears in sentence structure, as Tolstoy frequently inserts an extensive adjectival or participial expression between an adjective and its noun. V. V. Stasov commented on the technique of alternation leading to discontinuity in a letter apropos of the interior monologue in *War and Peace:*

Nearly all authors write monologues which are absolutely correct, consistent, streamlined, polished, ultra-logical, and consistent.... But is this the way we really think? Of course not. I have only met one exception up to now—Count Lev. Tolstoy. He is the only person who in his novels and dramas gives us real monologues with all their irregularity, fortuitousness, incompleteness, and jerkiness.

The protagonists in this novel reflect much more within themselves by interior monologue, that is, outside time, than with other persons in actual conversational dialogue. [17]

Tolstoy's opposition of France and Russia in *War and Peace* shows another variation of the formal use of geometric line in the novel, the use of two contrasting geographic locations along which to "line" the protagonists. In *Moby Dick* Ahab declares: "Ye two are the opposite poles of one thing; Starbuck is Stubb reversed, and Stubb is Starbuck; and ye two are all mankind; and Ahab stands alone." [18] Starbuck with his ruthless rationality and Stubb with his jovial fatalism are constructive poles in *Moby Dick*. Relatively easy oppositions of geography, which in turn reflect spiritual orientation, include London and the country, in the eighteenth century, in *Evelina, Humphry Clinker, Joseph Andrews,* and *Tom Jones*. Walter Scott contributed in the early nineteenth century to the spiritual loci of this psychological linearity. In *The Heart of Midlothian*, Jeannie Deans struggles from Edinburgh to London, from Calvinistic austerity to Hanoverian splendor. Scott is more profound in *Rob Roy*, a novel with little of the fairy tale quality of *Midlothian*; Frank Osbaldistone is placed to choose between the mercantile world of Lowland Glasgow and the primitive clans of the Highlands, neither of which is completely satisfactory. Tempering his mercantilist tradition with a renewed sense of an older order, he becomes an early protagonist with two historical burdens. Jane Austen is striking in her use of the city-country opposition; in *Emma* she shows a small community breaking open before the entrance of the London intruder Frank Churchill and the Bath intruder Mrs. Elton. Charlotte Brontë, an early strategist of the European-English conflict in *Villette*, presents Lucy Snowe encountering an alien religion, language, and love in Brussels. The legacy of these polarities includes the American-European opposition in James's work, the Anglo-Indian situation in Forster's novel *A Passage to India*, and the Slavic-Western opposition in Conrad's *Under Western Eyes*. Many different methods are used to present these polarities, but all basically involve, particularly after the eighteenth century, the stasis of one location and the importing of the other by a representative. Such representatives include, for example, Frank Churchill from London in *Emma*, Mrs. Moore from England in *A Passage to India*, Razumov from Moscow in *Under Western Eyes*, and Mordecai from Palestine in *Daniel Deronda*.

In addition to the method of the geometric loci, the novelist may employ as well what Gérard Genette, analyzing Proust's methods, has called the "palimpsest." As a variation of geometric line, the spatializing palimpsest permits two planes of language to exist simultaneously:

As a matter of fact, the most characteristic trait of the Proustian representation is without doubt, with the intensity of their material presence, this superposition of objects simultaneously perceived which permits one to speak in this connection of "surimpressionism."

Likewise, Todorov's theory of approaching the stories of Henry James, "superimposing the different works one on the other," suggests the importance of an atemporal reading of a single author's entire oeuvre. Todorov in "How to Read?" emphasizes several important elements of the plane. For example, the unique quality of interpretation, the relation of the novel to the external world, rests on the palimpsest:

The term *interpretation* refers here to every substitution of another text in place of the present text, to every step which seeks to uncover, through the apparent textual tissue, a second more authentic text.... The conception of the text as palimpsest is not alien to reading; but instead of replacing one text by another, this last term describes the relation of the two. For the act of reading, the text is never (an-) other, it is multiple.

The process of reading itself involves two methods, those of *superposition* and *figuration*. A reading by superposition, for instance, involves the correlation of linguistic structures with thematic intentions, accomplished by Eichenbaum's examination of Gogol's *Overcoat* (included in *The Theory of Literature*). By figuration, all the works by one author may be analyzed in their relation to one another. In this latter instance, each work is conceived as a single plane read as a transparency to another work.[19]

A particularly distinguished application of the theory of line as several superimposed planes occurs in Cervantes's *Don Quixote*. These planes constitute a palimpsest which includes not only past romances, as ur-texts over which Cervantes wrote, but also potential texts which were written after Cervantes's own text. This is to say that the novel *Don Quixote* then becomes the ur-text over which such works as *Joseph Andrews* (1742), *The Female Quixote* (1752), and *The Spiritual Quixote* (1772) will be written. There is only one central image in *Don Quixote,* and that is the mirror. This mirror implies that *Don Quixote* contains within itself not only texts preceding it but also those succeeding. The text embodies its past as well as its future. *Don Quixote* cannot stand alone.

First of all, it needs itself. This fact is striking and absolute. How many novels are *Don Quixote?* Dorothy Van Ghent perceived two, that of 1605 and that of 1615. In reality, however, there are three, which may be represented by the equation "romance" : 1605 text :: 1605 text : 1615 text. This equation expresses constant contrasts. For instance, Don Quixote governs part one, and Sancho part two; the 1605 section with its inn and highway is rural, while the 1615 section with its castle and city streets is urban. The 1605 version contains five interpolated tales which are themselves contrasted; and Don Quixote and Sancho are as split as the book, in contrast not only to each other but within each other. There are other oppositions which suggest mirrors. Gerald Brennan and Erich Auerbach have commented on Cervantes's own attitude toward his protagonist; Harry Levin remarks that *Don Quixote* is "an overt act of criticism" of the genres which preceded it; E. C. Riley states, pursuing Levin's point, that if *Don Quixote* is a parody of romances, it likewise contains the object of its parody. If the two protagonists mirror each other, each likewise embodies mirrors, as does the larger structure of the work which embodies him. Furthermore, Cervantes creates the putative editor Cid Hamete, who recounts the tale of *Don Quixote;* Cervantes : Cid :: Cid : *Don Quixote,* as Leo Spitzer has declared.[20] Or is it that Cervantes creates "Cervantes" who creates Cid who...?

Don Quixote is a novel written against itself. In at least three ways, according to Spitzer, *Don Quixote* has negative being, as counternovel, antinovel, and antiromance. It is negative, but embraces its negatives. Lowry Nelson, on the other hand, declares that it *is* three things: antiromance, pastoral, and epic (which might extend to picaresque). Moreover, the 1605 Don Quixote and Sancho have become quite different in 1615, since in 1615 they have an existence clearly independent of their lives in part one. As Américo Castro has well observed, there was nothing like it until Pirandello and the *teatro dello specchio.* It is hardly an accident that so many critics speak of perspective when discussing *Don Quixote,* or that its associations with painting would eventually be noted, as, for example, by Gerald Brennan in his remarks about Zurbarán and Ribera, and by Helmut Hatzfeld in his association of *Don Quixote* with Velásquez's *Las Meninas.* For in the novel, as often as truth opposes lies, nearly as often lies equal truth; particularly in part two, the Duke and Duchess seem as mad as either Sancho or his master. Cervantes confutes the categories of truth and falsity. Nevertheless, as Erich Auerbach notes, he manages to do this without ever identifying Don Quixote's wisdom with his madness, a most essential point that finds its complement in the image of distorting mirrors, where the distortion and distinction of one from the other is as paramount as the meager "reflection." We do not have the one without the other, but they are not each other. Dorothy Van Ghent felt compelled in the beginning of her essay on the novel to return to the etymology of "paradox" and "parody," both of which embrace the simultaneous existence of two separate entities.[21] One may extend her idea to say that paradox and parody embrace each other in this novel. A paradox turns on itself and a parody on something outside itself, but in *Don Quixote* the outside term of the parody is within (what it is not, it is, call it pastoral, epic, romance, picaresque), while the paradox must depend on what it is not, the parody. *Don Quixote* is both parode and palinode.

As Thomas Mann so well realized, the result of these techniques is that *Don Quixote* is a novel unlike any other. In particular, as he noted, in this novel "space will have its time," since time is "naturally bound up with it." Still, while reading *Don Quixote* on his transatlantic voyage Mann wondered: "Are we then going back in time whilst we press forward in space?" He has focused on a significant truth, that *Don Quixote* is atemporal as well as more conventionally "timeless." Lowry Nelson's study of its incremental repetition, echoes, and juxtapositions proves that these devices detemporalize Cervantes's text to bring together but not to merge separate entities.[22] *Don Quixote* is the perennial critique of itself, presuming the existence of previous texts and also embodying future texts that will be created according to its paradigm. There are, then, three planes of texts in *Don Quixote*. The ur-text of the novel is a romance like *Amadís de Gaula;* as a putative representation of the world, it may be called the "real" text. The second plane, the "actual" text, is the novel entitled *Don Quixote.* The third plane, the text which is the paradigm of future novels, is the "paradigmatic" text. The three planes are presided over, respectively, by Cid Hamete, Cervantes, and "Cervantes."

Concerning the reality of *Don Quixote*, that is, the part of it which represents but is not actuality, one must invoke Borges's insight about Franz Kafka: "Every writer *creates* his own precursors." The province of romance in *Don Quixote* is essentially that of the ur-text, written not by the chivalric chroniclers but by Cid: the novel *Don Quixote* is its own precursor. It confounds time, negates it: the protagonist Don Quixote "looks back from the future upon events which have yet to take place." The quality of the events in *Don Quixote* becomes, therefore, atemporal in two ways: its future is already known prior to its presentness, and its reality is created through the declaration of its opposite, the romance. Its present exists before its past. This atemporal quality, for instance, marks Dulcinea:

As the story goes, there was a very good-looking farm girl who lived near by, with whom he had once been smitten, although it is generally believed that she never knew or suspected it. Her name was Aldonza Lorenzo, and it seemed to him that she was the one upon whom he should bestow the title of mistress of his thoughts. For her he wished a name that should not be incongruous with his own and that would convey the suggestion of a princess or a great lady; and accordingly, he resolved to call her 'Dulcinea del Toboso,' she being a native of that place.

Her present existence as Aldonza exists before her past as "Dulcinea," but her future as Dulcinea was there before her present; so too was the man Quijada before "Don Quixote" but after Don Quixote. In "Perspectivism in *Don Quixote*," Leo Spitzer has noted the polyonomasia in the novel, as in the names of the protagonist and his lady; polyonomasia is of course spatial in its simultaneity. As José Ortega y Gasset observes, "The real is not so much what is seen as foreseen." The incident of the windmills illustrates the point. Cid Hamete's chronicle reveals that "thirty or forty windmills" are standing on the plain: here is already the end result of the adventure, which ceases to be one because the debate about the reality of the windmills occurs before that reality is tested, not after. Clearly the ur-text connotation of "giants" is created after the fact. Sancho's question, "What giants?," follows Cid's statement that the objects are windmills. As Borges has observed, "The *Quixote* is less an antidote for those fictions than it is a secret, nostalgic farewell."[23] Gérard Genette in *Figures III* has called this atemporal structure the *prolepse* ("anticipation"), by which the result of forthcoming action is revealed prior to its presentation. It is particularly important because it violates the linearity of the novel, bringing the narrative (*histoire*) into conflict with the narration (*discours*). Adventure in *Don Quixote* is not, as it is in other fictions, something essentially expected. It is much more something past, something evaluated before it occurs. The real is foreseen, the precursor created, the event a reaction before it is an action. One is going back in time as one presses forward in space.

The realm of the actual, as opposed to the a posteriori real, is that of Cervantes. In his "Parable of Cervantes and the *Quixote*," Borges remarked: "Vanquished by reality, by Spain, Don Quixote died in his native village in the year 1614. He was survived but a short time by Miguel de Cervantes."[24] Cid Hamete Benengeli does not appear in the novel until the ninth chapter of part one. Until that point, there is a narrator closely identified with Cervantes but not at all identified with "Cervantes," the paradigmatic, not actual, author. The appearance of Cid Hamete is accompanied by an *ekphrasis*, an artistic representation of its verbal contents. This picture, invoking framing or *encadrement*, places the Cid and his narrative in perspective:

> No sooner had I heard the name Dulcinea del Toboso than I was astonished and held in suspense, for at once the thought occurred to me that those notebooks must contain the history of Don Quixote. With this in mind I urged him to read me the title, and he proceeded to do so, turning the Arabic into Castilian upon the spot: *History of Don Quixote de la Mancha, Written by Cid Hamete Benengeli, Arabic Historian.* It was all I could do to conceal my satisfaction and, snatching them from the silk weaver, I bought from the lad all the papers and notebooks that he had for a half a real. . . .
>
> In the first of the books there was a very lifelike picture of the battle between Don Quixote and the Biscayan, the two being in precisely the same posture as described in the history, their swords upraised, the one covered by his buckler, the other with his cushion. As for the Biscayan's mule, you could see at the distance of a crossbow shot that it was one for hire. Beneath the Biscayan there was a rubric which read: "Don Sancho de Azpeitia," which must undoubtedly have been his name; while beneath the feet of Rocinante was another inscription: "Don Quixote." Rocinante was marvelously portrayed: so long and lank, so lean and flabby, so extremely consumptive-looking that one could well understand the justness and propriety with which the name of "hack" had been bestowed upon him.
>
> Alongside Rocinante stood Sancho Panza, holding the halter of his ass, and below was the legend: "Sancho Zancas." The picture showed him with a big belly, a short body, and long shanks, and that must have been where he got the names of Panza and Zancas by which he is a number of times called in the course of the history. There are other small details that might be mentioned, but they are of little importance and have nothing to do with the truth of the story—and no story is bad so long as it is true.

In the prologue Cervantes calls himself Don Quixote's "stepfather," implying he supports but does not create Don Quixote. In chapter six the curate and the barber cull Don Quixote's library, jettisoning the romances and chivalric tales, until they come upon Cervantes's own *La Galatea:*

> "But what is that one next to it?"
>
> "*La Galatea* of Miguel de Cervantes," said the barber.
>
> "Ah, that fellow Cervantes and I have been friends these many years, but, to my knowledge, he is better versed in misfortune than he is in verses. His book has a fairly good plot; it starts out well and ends up nowhere. We shall have to wait for the second part which he has promised us, and perhaps when it has been corrected somewhat it will find the favor that is now denied it. Meanwhile, keep it locked up in your house."

Later in the narrative the manuscript of *Riconete and Cortadillo*, also by Cervantes, is found:

The curate thanked him and, opening the manuscript at once, he saw that the title was *The Story of Riconete and Cortadillo,* from which he gathered that it was a work of fiction; and since *The One Who Was Too Curious* had afforded such pleasant reading, he assumed that this must also be an interesting tale, as there was a possibility that they were by the same author, and so kept it with the intention of reading it later when he had an opportunity.

Cervantes exists actually as the author of all the works previous to the *Don Quixote,* and appears as the stepfather, or editor, of Cid Hamete's manuscript. The result of these presentations of the actual Cervantes in *Don Quixote* is a severe analepse; that is, information prior not only to any event in the novel but prior to the writing of the novel itself is included. This method, described in Genette's *Figures III,* means that Cervantes is like his novel, containing the things it rejects. Cervantes is the author of *Don Quixote* only by writing against himself. His actuality is an analeptic rejection of his actuality as the author of romances and pastorals. By becoming the narrator-editor of *Don Quixote,* Cervantes has forced his previous actual work into the realm of reality, the realm of Cid Hamete. The relation of reality to actuality in *Don Quixote* suggests Julian Marias's observation that for Ortega y Gasset, "Reality is seen in foreshortening. . . . The decisive factor is the discovery of reflections and connections of things *in* the thing being considered."[25] The reality of Cid Hamete is given perspective by Cervantes, who is its perfect commentator.

What makes *Don Quixote* such an achievement, however, is its second part. Here a new character is created, "Cervantes." In the third chapter Don Quixote and Sancho listen as the young scholar Sanson Carrasco recounts their existence in a book, now not by Cervantes or Cid Hamete, but by "Cervantes," who thus becomes the paradigmatic author, whose text will be a palimpsest for succeeding authors, including the imitator Alonso Fernandez de Avellaneda. Sancho, Don Quixote, and Cervantes have passed into the realm of potentiality; they have become paradigms. Depth in literature, Ortega y Gasset claims, comes in two ways, in what the work is "materially," in reality and in actuality, and in what it is in its future paradigmatic life. Borges's story, "Pierre Menard, Author of the *Quixote,*" analyzes this fact: Pierre has written the ninth and thirty-eighth chapters of part one, but "he did not want to compose another *Quixote*— which is easy—but *the Quixote itself.*" Thus "the *Quixote* is a contingent book," contingent in the sense that its virtual life is its most significant element.[26] Did Menard believe what he wrote? He had the "resigned or ironical habit of propagating ideas which were the strict reverse of those he preferred." The text by "Cervantes" is the paradigm of all the delusive works Cervantes meant to vanquish. The episode of the "Knight of the

Mirrors" in part two verifies this conclusion. Don Quixote vanquishes a knight known as the Knight of the Wood, who turns out to be the Knight of the Mirrors, none other than the scholar Sanson Carrasco, the person who first informed Don Quixote of his potential paradigmatic existence.

At the beginning of this episode Don Quixote and Sancho have a discussion about a gold crown:

> "The crowns and scepters of state emperors," remarked Sancho, "were never known to be of pure gold; they are always of tinsel or tinplate."
>
> "That is the truth," said Don Quixote, "for it is only right that the accessories of a drama should be fictitious and not real, like the play itself. Speaking of that, Sancho, I would have you look kindly upon the art of the theater and, as a consequence, upon those who write the pieces and perform in them, for they all render a service of great value to the State by holding up a mirror for us at each step that we take, wherein we may observe, vividly depicted, all the varied aspects of human life; and I may add that there is nothing that shows us more clearly, by similitude, what we are and what we ought to be than do plays and players.

"What we are and what we ought to be." "What we are" is composed of the reality (what we are not) and the actuality (what we are) presided over by Cid Hamete and Cervantes; what "we ought to be" is governed by "Cervantes" or the successive Pierre Menards who have succeeded him, whether in a *Female Quixote* or *Spiritual Quixote*, whether they be Fielding or Dickens. The paradigmatic "Cervantes" has an existence far more substantial than the actual. As E. C. Riley has observed, if Cervantes, like Velásquez in *Las Meninas,* "has contrived to be simultaneously outside and inside his subject," it is in this way that he is both actual and potential.[27] The trick of the Knight of the Mirrors is so powerful that both Sancho and Don Quixote refuse to believe it is Carrasco. Carrasco, one is sure, was led to his scheme by the paradigmatic Sancho and Don Quixote, who already during Cervantes's lifetime were pursuing the legacy of "Cervantes" in being written about by other authors. Proposing to conquer the fictions by enacting them and showing their falsity, Carrasco verified their existence.

In *On the Theory of Prose* Victor Shklovsky has noted that the second part of *Don Quixote* is "more a mosaic than the first," and that the "thread of the action is everywhere frayed and constantly broken." Both of these observations indicate how spatial is the achievement of *Don Quixote.* Shklovsky enumerates many examples of the inlaid, recessed narratives comprising the work. The importance of these narratives, however, lies once again in their spatial nature. Spitzer declares that, contrary to the principal *histoire,* where one may distinguish the real before the unreal (as in the windmills), in the tales the unreal is presented first and only much later is the real clarified. These broken threads, these encadred tales reversing the principal narrative, these devices of *ralentissement,* indicate the atemporal strategy that governs the novel. The three levels of the work, the real, the actual, and the paradigmatic, constitute the fundamental nature of its "mosaic." It is a novel not only about its own composition, but also containing its own precursors and descendants. In his *Meditations on Quixote,* Ortega y Gasset spoke of an incident in the *Symposium:*

Socrates argued against Agathon, the young author of tragedies, and Aristophanes, the comic writer, that the poet of tragedy and of comedy ought to be one and not two different men. This episode has not been satisfactorily explained but I have always suspected, when I read it, that Plato, a soul seething with intuitions, was planting here the seed of the novel. If we prolong the attitude taken by Socrates in the *Symposium* in the pale light of dawn, it will seem as if we come up against Don Quixote, the hero and the madman.

Cid Hamete, Cervantes, and "Cervantes" accomplished what Socrates had in mind and what Plato had in Socrates' mind.[28] *Don Quixote,* by its geometric plane, is thus ur-text, text, and palimpsest simultaneously, a Platonic construct. As in the *Symposium,* so in *Don Quixote* three persons participated, producing a work not only in search of time past but in fulfillment of its own future.

If one explores the inner structure of certain novels, it becomes evident that geometric spatiality is a major form of their construction. For example, in *The Princess of Clèves,* the use of dances, points forming geometric patterns, symbolizes the complex relationship among the Princess, her husband, and the Duc de Nemours. A novel using a complex structure, the spiral, characterizes Flaubert's extraordinary text of geometric spatiality, *The Sentimental Education,* a work of the deepest probing of spatial point and line.

Albert Thibaudet declared that "the exposition of *Madame Bovary* was an exposition in time," but that in *The Sentimental Education* Flaubert "made it pass from time into space." More than any other novel of the nineteenth century, as Gérard Genette has declared, *The Sentimental Education* anticipates the twentieth-century novel, and does so on the basis of its spatiality. Flaubert criticized his novel precisely for the failure of its spatial elements. Writing to Joris-Karl Huysmans about *The Vatard Sisters* in March 1879, Flaubert criticized it along with *The Sentimental Education:* "*The Vatard Sisters,* like my *The Sentimental Education,* lacks the *illusion of perspective.* There is no dramatic development. At the end of the book, the reader has the same impression as he had at the beginning. Art is not nature." In October 1879 he wrote to Mme. Roger des Genettes, repeating the same response:

Why did not the book have the success I expected?... It is too lifelike and, aesthetically speaking, it lacks the *illusion of perspective*. The plan has been so well coordinated that it disappears. Every work of art should have a point, a peak, should be shaped like a pyramid, or have the light strike it on the tip of the dome. Now there is nothing like that about life. But Art is not Nature!... As for its conclusion, I confess that I have continued to resent all the stupid remarks it gave rise to.

Yet this mood of explanation and resignation was not obtained easily, for five years earlier he had written to Turgenev: "What does depress me is the failure of *The Sentimental Education*. I am really astonished that people have not understood that book." It goes without saying that Flaubert's statements about *The Sentimental Education* are not consonant among themselves nor with his earlier statements about other literature. For example, he remarked that "what is stupendous about *Don Quixote* is the absence of art," and that what is finest about *Les Fleurs du mal,* as he wrote to Baudelaire in 1857, "is that Art comes first." "You sing of the flesh without love of it in a sad and detached way.... You are as hard as marble and as penetrating as an English fog."[29]

The Sentimental Education, a work Flaubert wrote more than once, elicited one final statement from its author. As recounted by Henri Céard, Flaubert declared: "The book is not constructed like this (joining hands by fingertips upraised). The public wants works which praise its illusions, where *The Sentimental Education*—." It is important to note that Flaubert considered that the novel had a plan which disappeared in the work; Flaubert was also certain that the plan was not a pyramid, as is clear both from his own statement and from the anecdote recounted by Céard. But what was the plan? It is logical to assume that the products of art should be like the pyramid, that is, according to Flaubert, one should experience there a climax which life never exhibits. One may assume from Céard's account that *The Sentimental Education* is the reverse of the pyramid, the inverted pyramid, or more properly, a descending spiral. What Flaubert did not realize about his own work is that it has a climax, but it is far more like that of the funnel of the *Inferno* than of the objects he witnessed in Egypt. In the years 1849 to 1851 Flaubert did such things as stand on the pyramid of Cheops to see the sunrise, and the pyramidic influence is strong in the *First Education.* When, therefore, Flaubert claimed that *The Sentimental Education* was not a pyramid, he implicitly isolated two central aspects of the work. First, it was more like life than art perhaps should be; and second, it was a world removed from the young man who thought that a sunrise from the top of a pyramid was the climax to any sort of life at all. In short, Flaubert in *The Sentimental Education* repudiated his old self and the falsity of ascending climactic art. But the seed was already there, even on the Egyptian journey. Passing through the prostitutes' quarter at Kena, he recorded: "I abstained deliberately, in order to preserve the sweet sadness of the scene and engrave it deeply in my memory. In this way I went away dazzled, and have remained so."[30] Almost two decades before he wrote it, Flaubert recorded the "climax" of *The Sentimental Education* when Frédéric exhibits the same insight, not from the top of a pyramid now, but from the last level of his inferno:

Frédéric suspected that Madame Arnoux had come to offer herself to him; and once again he was filled with desire, a frenzied, rabid lust such as he had never known before. Yet he also had another, indefinable feeling, a repugnance akin to a dread of committing incest. Another fear restrained him—the fear of being disgusted later. Besides, what a nuisance it would be! And partly out of prudence and partly to avoid degrading his ideal, he turned on his heel and started rolling a cigarette.

In his "Silences of Flaubert," Genette has noticed the atemporal quality of the interruptions in the narrative of *The Sentimental Education*. They are atemporal in two respects: first, the characters cease speaking to listen to their dreams; second, this interruption of dialogue and action stops the discourse of the novel itself, "in a kind of interrogation without voice." The famous imperfects and adverbs, eloquently noticed by Proust in "The Style of Flaubert," constitute "silences," spaces as vast as the desert minus the pyramids. As Jean Prévost has said of Flaubert's style, the result is "the most singular petrifying fountain of our language . . . which renders everything immobile." André Malraux has called Flaubert's texts "beautiful paralyzed novels." This "paralysis" is not, it is important to note, frozen. Declaring that Flaubert did not write his novel about nothing nor his novel without a subject, Genette states that Flaubert cast over his subjects "this heavy thickness of petrified language, this 'smooth pavement' as Proust said, of imperfects and adverbs which could only *reduce them to silence*." His achievement resulted in making *The Sentimental Education* the masterpiece of its time for ours.

Flaubert found *The Sentimental Education* aesthetically deficient, from a default of action, of perspective, of construction. He did not see that this book was the first to effect this *dedramatization*, one wishes almost to say *denovelization*, of the novel from which began all modern literature, or rather he felt as a defect what is for us the major quality. From *Bovary* to *Pécuchet*, Flaubert did not cease writing novels *repudiating*—without knowing it, but in their essence—the exigencies of novelistic discourse. It is this refusal which matters to us, and the involuntary trace, almost imperceptible, of ennui, of indifference, of inattention, of forgetfulness, which he left on a work apparently strained to a useless perfection, and which remains for us admirably imperfect, and as if *absent from itself*.

This achievement has a perspective, one which Georges Poulet has called an awareness of "depth of duration," "a depth that is glimpsed through a

descending perspective" by a "retrospective movement" in an abyss of
moments fused by recollections but separated by the fact that past experiences eventually become another life. As a result, duration finally ceases,
movement ceases to exist. There is no better description than Poulet's of
Frédéric's experience. It is a falling, a slipping, for which the perfect
image is the descending spiral, at first so gradual that direction cannot be
ascertained as down or up, but eventually by its "fissures" assuming an
irreversible downward motion. Flaubert supplied the perfect image of
this experience in the opening scene, where the smoke from the funnel of
the *Ville-de-Montereau*, instead of projecting the ashes upward, drops its
soot on the passengers below. The image is reinforced by the fact that
Frédéric is first presented motionless, gazing at the spires of the Cité and
Notre Dame; there the ascending spire and the descending funnel stand
before him as he enters his "first circle," so nearly level that he cannot
perceive it is the motion of descent. It is hard to believe that the Seine is
not the first river of hell. The spiral is present, as Poulet notes, as the
perfect image of "the operation of memory in Flaubert."[31]

After the composition of the *First Education* in 1845, Flaubert traveled
in Brittany, worked on the first *The Temptation of Saint Anthony*,
traveled in the Orient, and returned in 1851 to work on *Madame Bovary*.
Around April 1852 he wrote a sketch entitled *The Spiral* (not published
until April 1958, in *La Table ronde*), a work describing, in Victor Brombert's words, the "permanent somnambulism of a hallucinated madman."
Both Brombert and E. W. Fisher interpret the work as a document
recounting the liberation from the self by an escape toward infinity:

But this title is evidently symbolic, or if one wishes, even metaphysical. The word
is often found in the work of a writer, and one could say he loves it. The image of
these circles rising always higher, higher, and disappearing into the infinite,
charmed him: it had become, one could even say, an *idée fixe* for him.

In *Memories of a Madman*, Flaubert had written: "Oh! the infinite! the
infinite! immense chase, spiral which rises from the abyss to the highest
regions of the unknown." Of a friend's work he wrote: "Its general idea is
the whirlpool, the infinite spiral; everything which strikes us is explained." Fisher concluded:

Therefore, it seems to me that the image of the Spiral was a kind of symbol for the
author, a symbol for the deliverance from myself, for an intellectual ascension, for
a soaring toward the infinite and the beyond. Thus interpreted, the title accords
well with the life of the protagonist—a life which is only thought and which ends
in a surrealist world of illusions.

In short, the spiral indicates a desire to "pass beyond the limits of terrestrial existence of the individual."[32]

Is this interpretation of liberation from the self accurate? Such an assertion is easy when the avowed protagonist is a madman. Whether there is a
successful "liberation" is in such a case indeterminable. If Fisher's date of
1852 for *The Spiral* is correct, the major portions of the work reveal the
influence of the trip to the Orient during the previous two years. The
work seeks to prove that happiness is in the imagination, that as "the
dream has a vital moralising influence on life, so does life have an imaginative influence on the dream." This theme is illustrated by the ambitions of
a young dreamer who loves a married woman and experiences the pains of
acquiring money and of jealousy and hostility, which are followed by
intense experiences in "la vie fantastique." The concluding section is
important in associating the spiral with imagination:

The spiral—of successive experiences.

The conclusion is that happiness consists in being mad (or what people call so),
that is to say to see the truth, the totality of time, the absolute—

He considers as present the past and the future. He talks with gods and sees
their types.

He is enclosed in a madhouse—and there he sees no alteration—so elevated is
he that he speaks the truth about society, in speaking to each of the madmen who
represent one of the different professions. The one who thinks he's a king thinks
like a king—the musician is as much a musician as any musician.

He is therefore in the truth and the moral is that happiness is in the imagination.

But he has been a long time getting there—he has lacked experience and
education.

The concluding part is, rather than being a liberation from the self, a
seizure of the self, the "finer madness" of the prophets which approaches
God himself in his comprehension, his isolation, and his individualism.
The "madman" is not so much in truth as the truth.[33]

"Real" life and the imaginative life, by being first reciprocal, have
become indistinguishable. The last section of the manuscript indicates
that it is the novel of a suicide; when the appropriate occasion arises, "the
action is taken." The final element of the plan is action. Finding that
oneself is mad, that the madhouse is a true descent into the maelstrom,
suggests that this spiral is a descent into the self, not a transcendence of it.
The vista seen by the madman is surely that of Flaubert himself surveying
his age, and of Frédéric seeing his Madonna become flesh during the final
interview with Madame Arnoux. By lighting a cigarette Frédéric opts for
the happiness of the imagination, of the untainted potential, rather than
the disenchantment of consummation. One may speak here of a climax,
but it is not that of ordinary art. It is Godlike life, comprising the ultimate
Godlike quality of being the only person alive and yet still using the

subjunctive. This is the heart of the reverse egotism of the madman, of Flaubert and of Frédéric, the voice of the descending spiral, life itself, gasping, for all the imagination may be worth, "Let there be dark." In this way, as Gérard Genette notes, Frédéric is very different from Emma Bovary. While both have the capacity for dreaming, Frédéric "is not Bovarystic; he is an erratic dreamer but, at bottom, lucid."[34]

To a phenomenologist like Gaston Bachelard, the image of the spiral is highly ambiguous. On the surface, it seems close to the image of the staircase, which may ascend and transcend toward the attic or lead to the diabolic cellar. This dwelling is associated, furthermore, not only with staircases but also with shells, again of equivocal moral meaning. Flaubert illustrates Bachelard's idea that the spiral is a life image:

Actually, however, life begins less by reaching upward, than by turning upon itself. But what a marvelously insidious, subtle image of life a coiling vital principle would be! And how many dreams the leftward oriented shell, or one that did not conform to the rotation of its species, would inspire!

Flaubert, in the anecdote recounted by Céard, was saying exactly this: life is a spiral which might appear momentarily to ascend but is actually convoluted about itself, very closely approximating the situation of Frédéric in *The Sentimental Education*. As it is life emerging from form, the spiral is the image of form. Life, emerging from shells, reaches into its past, an attitude related to *The Spiral* with its evocation of the previous Oriental trip and to Frédéric by his having a past before even having lived, as in his imagined orgies: "The things in these daydreams became so real that in the end they made him feel as miserable as if he had lost them." One meaning of the subtitle *Story of a Young Man* is that an individual is forever half-in, half-out, hanging back in a "hesitation of being." Bachelard states: "The spiraled being who, from outside, appears to be a well-invested center, will never reach his center." The spiral verifies man as a "half-open being," the image of what Victor Brombert has remarked about *The Sentimental Education:* "The entire book seems to be conceived under the ambiguous sign of continual motion and stasis, which correspond to Frédéric's contradictory need to escape outside his solipsistic self and yet to seek refuge, to dissolve within it." Flaubert's protagonists as far back as *November* are rent by this inner scission. As torn as the individual may be in himself, extension into another being is equally disturbing. Such penetration, as Jean-Pierre Richard observes, becomes a hemorrhage leading to the "dissolution of one's being," as is indicated by the images of oozing and permeability in the novel.[35] Fear of dissolution is another explanation for Frédéric's decision not to possess Madame Arnoux during their final interview.

This act of descending to a point or drop, a movement comprising both horizontal contraction and vertical descent, has serious metaphysical consequences. The spiral, while it may constitute a descent into the self, also reaches an abyss. The abyss has frequently been described as the true subject of *The Sentimental Education*. In his study of this abyss in the nineteenth century, Robert Adams has noted Flaubert's own declarations that he inhabited the "objective void entire" (*néant objectif*). Adams argues that the voyages in the novels are both into nothing and culminate in nothing, a nothingness of supreme meaning. One of Flaubert's favorite poems, Leconte de Lisle's "Midi," concludes with the phrase "le néant divin." It is the understanding that nothingness is divine that constitutes an education; one must disagree with Martin Turnell, who claims that there is no education. Flaubert used the image of the abyss when he declared in a letter of 16 January 1852 (the year of *The Spiral*) that he wrote between the "two abysses of lyricism and vulgarity," and that he was two persons, one transcendent, one terrestrial. The same letter contains a famous paragraph:

What seems beautiful to me, what I should like to write, is a book about nothing, a book dependent on nothing external, which should be held together by the strength of its style, just as the earth, suspended in the void, depends on nothing external for its support; a book which would have almost no subject, or at least in which the subject would be almost invisible.

Brombert has called *The Sentimental Education* a study of a "permanent vocation for nothing," a prostitutional "propensity for selling-out," a "contemplation of universal nothingness" whose central verb is *anéantir*. [36]

This nothingness is associated with the spiral, with spatiality. In *The Nature of Space*, I. Rice Pereira has investigated how this experience of the abyss and the void arises from a spatial, not a temporal, dislocation. In the Renaissance, space was conceived as distance in which man could project figures from a spherical onto a plane surface, with himself looming very large. In the nineteenth century the machine had destroyed distance, moving man to a minute point on the horizon. The result was frightful:

At the vanishing point, his size is diminished to nothing. What he feels, he can no longer accept as real because his reality has been limited to only measurable distance.... When there is no longer an object or thing in the distance, the sensation of physical space vanishes, and man is confronted with the unknown.

The development of a society depends on its ability to participate in space. If there is no participation, humanity remains in an undeveloped state and retrogresses to an instinctual level. If there is too much expansion horizontally, a society will expand materialistically and there will be very little or no creative activity. If the vertical becomes too extended, man will lose his balance and have no sense of reality in relation to the world he lives in.

When there is nothing left in the distance, the external world-view breaks down at the vanishing point, and man is confronted with the vast space of the infinitely large.... Unless man is able to make his inner experience of the three-dimensional world solid, and establish frames of reference for the unknown, there will be a contraction of space (spiral) in his mind, objectified by a vacuum. What he perceives as reality is 'nothing' because what he feels is a 'void.'

However cynical Proust was in declaring the blanks the most satisfying part of *The Sentimental Education,* he was not wrong to notice them. The spaces, the void, and man at the vanishing point, diminished to nothing, are hallmarks of the novel, and are consequences of spatial disorienta-tion. [37]

Henry James observed a peculiarity of *The Sentimental Education:* "An indefinable shrinkage has overtaken it in the execution." In light of Pereira's statements, it appears that the book reflects a central nineteenth-century experience, the diminishing to the vanishing point. The inverted pyramid become spiral has peculiarly this strange quality of "shrinkage." Rudolph Arnheim has demonstrated that the relation of the cortex to the retina, of object to observer, is essentially cubistic. This cube, however, may be transformed into a spiral.

But now imagine one side of the cube shrinking to the size of a point and thus moving from infinity to a finite distance. The result will be an infinitely large pyramid.... Such a world would be non-Euclidean. All the usual geometric criteria would hold, but they would lead to startling results. Parallels issuing from the side that had shrunk to a point would diverge in all directions. Objects would be of equal linear size if their distances from the peak were proportional to their sizes. An object moving toward the peak would shrink without becoming smaller and slow down while maintaining a constant speed. If an object changed its spatial orientation, it would change its shape and retain identity of shape at the same time.

Flaubert reproduces this cube in *The Sentimental Education* by having four men and four women constitute the "top" and "bottom" of it.

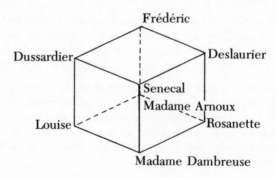

The text begins as a cube. However, by locating the central consciousness in Frédéric, Flaubert achieves the shrinkage of the cube to a point, which correlates with the "drop" image. The world, like Arnheim's cube, can diminish without moving, slow down while remaining constant, effects which give rise to the slowness, almost the immobility, of the novel. It is Flaubert's image of the world as the spiral. The use of a central perspective "makes space appear as a pointed flow, entering the picture from the near sides and converging toward a mouth at the distance." Flaubert's cube is compressed to the point of Frédéric through his connection with the four women of the novel. With each of them Frédéric imagines he is expanding horizontally. As the novel "progresses," however, the paradoxical ability of the collapsed cube to both move and be unmoved appears through a terrifying contraction. Imagining he is expanding, Frédéric is in reality slipping in a spiral.

Frédéric

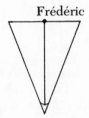

The beginning of the epilogue of *The Sentimental Education* reflects this contraction. Jean Ricardou observes how its events, its "fiction," have shrunk to nothingness even as its "narration" or recounting continues. The structure of the text itself undergoes *enlisement* ("shrinking").

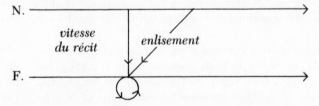

At the beginning of the epilogue, therefore, Flaubert gives the paradigm by which the entire spatiality of this novel may be grasped, an architecture of absolute correlation between content and form, the spiral seen as the mirror of the nineteenth-century experience of nothingness, and the spiral as the form of that nothingness in *The Sentimental Education*. [38]

The structure of the text reinforces this spiral. The numbers of chapters in its three parts reflect both the oozing and the falling elements of the spiral. While the first two parts contain six chapters, the third has seven. If, on the other hand, one considers the final two chapters an "epilogue," the structures maintain both the oozing and the falling off, by the pattern six-six-five. In this way the entire novel reflects the famous adverbs at the ends of sentences and the famous short sentences at the ends of paragraphs.

Each part of the novel exhibits this reduction to the point of the spiral by using an illusory climax. In part one Frédéric, having become an heir, appears to have reached a peak. In reality, this experience is one of his greatest descents, seemingly horizontal in its prosperity but in fact a vertical decline. At the conclusion of part two, Frédéric, with no illusions, takes Rosanette to the home prepared originally for Madame Arnoux, while the shooting begins on the Boulevard des Capucines:

> It was the fusillade on the Boulevard des Capucines. "Ah! They're killing off a few bourgeois," said Frédéric. For there are situations in which the kindest of men is so detached from his fellows that he would watch the whole human race perish without batting an eyelid.

The conclusion to part three, the return to the brothel visited in 1837, is the final point of the spiral.

The same tendency toward collapse appears throughout the chapters in the novel. Nothing better demonstrates this falling than part three, chapter one, in which one moves from the Revolution to Fontainebleau to the Revolution. The chapter opens with the entry of the mob into the Palais-Royal, with convicts rolling in the princesses' bed and a prostitute standing like a statue of liberty. Later Frédéric goes with Rosanette to Fontainebleau, where Rosanette is more impressed by the fish pond than the tapestries depicting Diane de Poitiers as Diana. Frédéric then returns to the city as the Revolution continues. The last image is of old Roque having shot a young soldier imprisoned in the Tuilleries: "There was a tremendous howl, then nothing. Something white remained on the edge of the grating."

Like paragraphs, sentences grind to a point: "Quand elle eut déposé au bord de la cheminée un petit portefeuille de velours grenat, elle s'assit" ("After placing a little red velvet wallet on the edge of the mantelpiece, she sat down"), or "Mais les ors et les blancs, qui se détachaient au milieu des ténèbres, l'attirèrent" ("But the golds and the whites, standing out in the midst of the shadows, attracted her attention"). Terminal adverbs or adjectives appear with the same falling rhythm. Frédéric declares to Madame Arnoux, now that all is over: "Est ce que j'y pensais, seulement!" ("It is that I have thought of, only!"). Frédéric hears of Rosanette: "Elle est veuve d'un certain M. Oudry, et très grosse, maintenant, énorme." ("She's the widow of a certain Monsieur Oudry, and very fat now, enormous"). [39]

Flaubert's use of the imperfect tense (*il y avait*) has the same effect. The imperfect prolongs the past indefinitely; Proust could call it "éternel imparfait," trailing its own time behind itself, trying to emerge from its pastness, from its spiral, and never doing so. The past indefinite (*il y a eu*) and the future anterior (*il y aura eu*) that likewise characterize *The Sentimental Education* can neither terminate an action nor begin it independent of its past. To no other work is Sartre's statement so applicable: "The author's style is directly bound up with a conception of the world."[40] There is only the respiring fall, or the imperfectly begun or continued. The spiral is the quintessential symbol of Flaubert both as thinker and artist. *The Spiral* indicates that, within a year of standing on the pyramid to watch the sunrise, the young Flaubert had realized that life is much more a descent; once one slides from the womb at birth, the plunge is absolute. In its structure and in its recognition of this "divine nothingness," the spiral of *The Sentimental Education* ironically makes the novel a pinnacle of geometric spatiality in the history of the novel.

The geometric spatiality of the novel, including its emphasis on point, line, and superimposed planes, demonstrates how central spatial secondary illusion is to this temporal art form. In an epistolary novel, such as *Dangerous Liaisons* or *Humphry Clinker*, the recipient of the letters functions as a spatial point; in the organic novel, such as *The Ambassadors, Henry von Ofterdingen*, or *Remembrance of Things Past*, spatial point constitutes the essence of novelistic form. George Eliot's *Adam Bede*, by using spatial point as a formal method, reflects her ethical conception of moral consequences as radiating from a point of action.

Thomas Hardy's recognition of "line of perspective" in the preface to *The Hand of Ethelberta* isolates the second crucial geometric illusion in the novel, the line. Henry James's *ficelle*, Shklovsky's *enfilage*, and Todorov's emphasis on parallelism and antithesis show how essential such geometric line is to the novelist; in *War and Peace* spatial line becomes the secondary illusion generating the entire novel. The geometrized loci of such works as Walter Scott's *The Heart of Midlothian* or *Rob Roy*, Charlotte Brontë's *Villette*, or Jane Austen's *Emma* or *Persuasion* reveal that geometric spatiality may function as an ethical system. Todorov's conception of the act of reading as superimposed planes, while indicating that critical interpretation is spatial, also suggests the power of spatially superimposed planes in Cervantes's *Don Quixote*. In Flaubert's *Sentimental Education*, the spiral is the key spatial illusion by which form becomes ethical. The geometric spatiality of parallelism, superimposition, palimpsest, geographic lines, and organic word demonstrates the crucial spatial illusion of the temporal art of the novel. Spatial illusion, however, assumes a more complex form when one examines the function of pictorial, sculptural, and architectural space in the novel. This type of spatiality, called "virtual" spatiality after one of Proust's observations in *Swann's Way,* concerns the role of the plastic arts in the structure of the novelistic text.

CHAPTER THREE

The Virtual

> Another Combray person whom I could discern virtual
> and typified, in the Gothic sculptures of Saint-André-
> des-Champs was young Théodore, the assistant in
> Camus's shop.
>
> Proust, *Swann's Way*

In *Swann's Way*, Marcel Proust called the relation between sculpture
and characterization *virtuel*. The word *virtual* may be used to designate
the form of spatial secondary illusion in the novel, which involves the
literary text and its relation to the spatial arts of painting, sculpture, and
architecture. This form of spatiality—virtual spatiality—concerns the appearance of spatial artistic properties in the novel, including the relation
of scene to painting, characterization to sculpture, and structure to architecture. Since the primary meaning of "virtual" is "potential," virtual
spatiality describes those qualities of the spatial arts which are in a secondary, that is potential, state in the text. Of all the forms of virtual
spatiality in the novel, the most evident is the association of the pictorial
with scene and place. Place is a significant constant: its function is preeminently spatial in this constancy, but it differs in several respects from
"scene." As Susanne Langer has noted in *Feeling and Form*, scene is the
essential quality of painting, "a space opposite the eye and related directly
and essentially to the eye."[1]

In the theory of the novel, on the other hand, "scene" is a moment
dramatized in a specific location in place and time. Dramatization, however, is not sufficient to produce scene; there must be a location, and thus
it is that scene in the novel, whether in the "pictorial" sense of background or setting in the specialized sense of "dramatized in location," is
eminently spatial by this reliance on location. In contrast to place, scene is
never anthropomorphized. Scene, even in a pictorial sense, has direction,
which distinguishes it from the nondirectional nature of place. Scene,

whether as setting or as dramatized moment, invites entrance, not only contemplation. Furthermore, there seems to be what can be called a "grammar" of locations throughout the history of the novel, such as the house, the window, the staircase, the prison, the room; these locations recur, one may argue, not only because human beings inhabit them (setting) but because certain actions occur there (dramatized moment, scene). That scene is eminently functional is evidenced by the fact that dialogue is not relevant by itself, but is made so by the setting in which it occurs (Isabel Archer on the stair; Natasha Rostov at the dance; Andrey Bolkonsky at the window). When the narrator declares in *Adam Bede* that "the dairy was certainly worth looking at," one asks not so much why but how?

Russian Formalist criticism is particularly apposite in illustrating the complex nature of scene, especially its momentary aspect (in contrast, once again, to the constancy of place). In "Thematics," for example, Boris Tomashevsky presented his well-known theory of the motif, which he defines as "an irreducible part of a work." Tomashevsky restates Shklovsky's distinction in his essay on *Tristram Shandy* between "plot" and "story." While both deal with the same events, "story is, in fact, only material for plot formulation." Shklovsky adds: "As a composition of motifs, such a treatment would be proper." Expanding this idea, Tomashevsky distinguishes "bound" and "free" motifs. Bound motifs are those "which cannot be omitted," while "those which may be omitted without disturbing the whole causal-chronological course of events are *free motifs*." Bound motifs are crucial to "the actual chronological and causal order of events," which is the story; free motifs "sometimes dominate and determine the construction of the plot" and may include details or digressions. Shklovsky also notes a second dichotomy, between "dynamic" and "static" motifs. Free motifs are usually static, including "descriptions of nature, local color, furnishings, characters, their personalities, and so on.... The actions and behavior of the main characters are typically dynamic motifs." "Dynamic motifs are ... central to the story and ... keep it moving; in the plot, on the other hand, static motifs may predominate."[2]

Scene, therefore, with its pictorial elements of two-dimensional, one-point perspective, may be a static motif, that is, an element of plot, conceived as "description." The contrast between scene and place is very clear: scene could be omitted, but place, never. For example, in any instance where a title is a place, like *Petersburg, Mansfield Park,* and *The Heart of Midlothian,* or where the place remains constant, as does the Petersburg of *The Idiot* and the provinces of *Madame Bovary,* place is a *bound motif.* Tomashevsky's caution, however, is important: "Free motifs are usually static, but not all static motifs are free." While some static motifs may be free, not all are. This static motif is the origin of recurring locations in the novel—the kitchen, the window, the staircase, the prison—which cannot be dispensed with. There is thus an important sense in which scene may be dynamic and bound. Lubomír Doležel, in "Toward a Structural Theory of Content in Prose Fiction," declares: "Scene is an aggregate of dynamic motifs presenting certain constituent features. These features can be of various kinds, such as a certain place of action (setting), a certain time-span of action."[3] As soon as one must say, "Then he sees her walking near Pemberley," rather than "Then he sees her," one is discussing a scene that is dynamic and bound. There is one clearly spatial concept involved in each of these pairs of key terms: *static* and *free*, *dynamic* and *bound.*

Tomashevsky's theory of motifs has an interesting correlation with the system developed by Heinrich Wölfflin in *Principles of Art History.* Generally speaking, he saw the main progress of painting as from the "linear" to the "painterly": a linear painting, such as a work of Albrecht Dürer, is characterized by an emphasis on line, with individual objects isolated from each other; composition is by the plane (a series of planes); the work is "closed" (that is, it does not extend beyond the picture space); its unity is that of a multiplicity of individual objects; its clarity is absolute; its appeal is tactile; it is the representation of being. On the other hand, a painterly work, such as a canvas by Rembrandt, emphasizes the merging of individual objects; it emphasizes depth recession, particularly by diagonal lines (contrapposto), rather than the plane. Its surface tends to end beyond the physical picture space; it is a composite unity with relative clarity, an appeal to the visual rather than the tactile. It is an image of becoming rather than being. Wölfflin's concepts of "closed" and "open" correspond to Tomashevsky's "bound" and "free," while "being" and "becoming" correspond to "static" and "dynamic." These correspondences point to the pictorial elements in the Formalists' thinking about scene, and this connection between scene and painting has a clear spatial consequence. In his "Frontiers of the Récit," Gérard Genette has observed: "Description . . . because it lingers over objects and arrangements considered in their simultaneity, and because it envisages these processes themselves as spectacles, seems to suspend the course of time and contributes to spread the narrative in space."[4]

The first aspect of free and static scene has the cerebral qualities of the painterly. In many instances, the effect of being "beyond the frame" is so extreme that the reader is encouraged to feel he has entered a picture. In *The Mayor of Casterbridge*, for example, Henchard and Farfrae "sat stiffly side by side at the darkening table, like some Tuscan painting of the two disciples supping at Emmaus; Elizabeth-Jane, being out of the frame and out of the group, could observe all from afar." In *Felix Holt* both Mrs.

Transome and her son Harold are frequently associated with portraits. Harold is like a painting by Lawrence; Mrs. Transome, confronting Jermyn, appears thus: "The brilliant smiling young woman above the mantelpiece seemed to be appearing at the doorway withered and frosted by many winters." "I notice you can't pull yourself away from that painting of the Fall of Troy. Well, I'll try and interpret its subject in verse," declares a character in *The Satyricon*. Novelists have frequent recourse to these static and free conceptions, invoking space beyond the canvas in painterly fashion.[5]

A static but bound scene is an extension of the portrait. This practice pursues the painterly with a different emphasis, that of locating every object in the totality of the scenic surface. George Eliot in *Adam Bede* uses this technique extensively. When she writes, "Evidently that gate is never opened," we are decidedly in a scene of recessed depth, indicated above all by "that" and the sentences which follow: "It would be easy enough, by the aid of the nicks in the stone pillars, to climb over the brick wall with its smooth stone coping; but by putting our eyes close to the rusty bars of the gate, we can see the house well enough, and all but the very corners of the grassy enclosure." There is an immediate shift to a constant present tense: "It is a very fine old place." The ultimately static quality of this scene, nevertheless bound because of its symbolic nature, is obvious. "The house must be inhabited, and we will see by whom; for imagination is a licensed trespasser: it has no fear of dogs, but may climb over walls and peep in at windows with impunity. Put your face to one of the glasspanes in the right-hand window: what do you see?" Then follows the description of Mrs. Poyser's kitchen.

Scenes which are static and either free or "almost bound" demonstrate the strong potential of the painterly to achieve powerful effects in the narration. Shklovsky, writing of *Little Dorrit*, notes that the mystery technique of the novel is "built around several simultaneous actions" linked by a common character or "through locale." These "simultaneous actions whose interrelationship is not immediately specified by the author" serve as "plot impediment," and in that fashion show clearly the value of "relative clarity," unity (simultaneity), recession, and particularly "becoming." The painterly free static scene becomes a cornerstone of the mystery novel, whose emphasis is ever on "becoming," the process of knowing.[6] In an epistolary novel, each letter becomes a recessed narrative drawing the reader into itself, as in *Dangerous Liaisons*.

There is a highly specialized form of this pictorial static element in the frame narrative. In "The Space of the Novel," Butor notes: "Planting his easel or his camera at one of the points of the space evoked, the novelist will discover all the problems of framing, of composition, and of perspective encountered by the painter." The practice of framing, called by Todorov *enchâssement* and by Shklovsky *encadrement*, not only emphasizes the spatial-pictorial quality of the plot (in Tomashevsky's sense) but also functions in another atemporal manner, as a "delay." As Shklovsky observes, in the *Decameron* this framing constitutes the delay which is the point of the tales themselves, to eclipse time during the plague. What Todorov calls "the inclusion of one story at the interior of another" becomes not so much an element of the narrative as of the narration. Such enclosures serve the presentation of "simultaneous actions," as Shklovsky observed in Dickens.[7]

When an author uses the device of *encadrement* or *enchâssement*, the spatial element of one narrative is obvious as it becomes a background, a recessed element of a larger narrative. In an early narrative like *The Golden Ass*, an interpolated tale, such as "Cupid and Psyche," obviously serves as an impediment to the narrative. A complex form of this spatialization appears in Charles Maturin's *Melmoth the Wanderer*. The inability of any character to escape the horrors recounted is wonderfully reinforced by the enclosed structure, which simultaneously creates terror because of the delayed certainty of being engulfed.

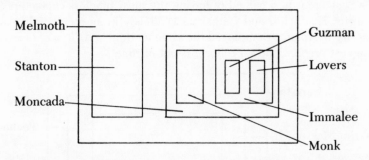

Similar effects are achieved by framing in Mary Shelley's *Frankenstein*, where such enclosure, by distancing the Creature's story, also provides delay to insure that Walton and the reader believe it.

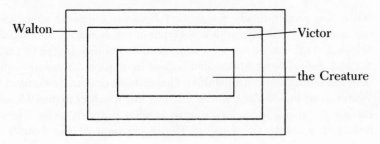

The enclosure in *Frankenstein* also shows structurally Walton's internalization of Victor's fearful story, which he does to such an extent that he decides to abandon his explorations. Walton's letters to his sister demonstrate an interesting element of the epistolary novel, because each letter is a small inlaid narrative, attempting to negate time by making its content simultaneous with its formation, as in *Pamela* or *Dangerous Liaisons*. In *Wuthering Heights*, this spatialization produces a simultaneous existence of content and narration.

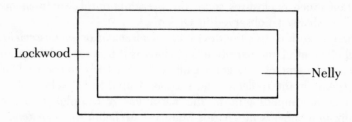

The pictorial structure therefore completes what Emily Brontë is at pains to clarify immediately in the book, the present knowledge of Heathcliff and Lockwood about each other. In *Wuthering Heights* and *Frankenstein* the advantage is also gained of having the most timeless characters (the Creature, Heathcliff, and Catherine I) already in an atemporal relative obscurity. Lermontov employed the same method in *A Hero of Our Time* to suggest precisely how Pechorin is out of time.

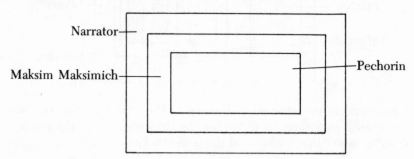

When the reader finally encounters Pechorin's journal narrative, this recession has made Pechorin archetypal of the Romantic estranged individualist. At the same time, he is made approachable by the fact that the narrator and Maksim Maksimich appear first, such distancing supplying both authenticity and probability. The same device has been used by Sir Walter Scott in *Rob Roy*, where the long introductory material lends Rob Roy an atemporal legendary stature in what purports to be a temporal, historical account. The Custom House segment of *The Scarlet Letter*

serves to emphasize the parabolic function of the tale of Hester and Dimmesdale. Conrad was to apply this practice later in both *Lord Jim* and *Victory*. Such framing, extremely pictorial by its recession, draws the reader into the becoming not of the narrative, but of the atemporal narration.[8]

The framing technique appears early in the history of the novel, most conspicuously in Longus's *Daphnis and Chloe*, where there is also an ekphrasis in the prologue. The tradition of the ekphrasis, in Murray Krieger's words "the imitation in literature of a work of plastic art," is indeed an old one. Early examples of it include the shield of Achilles (*Iliad* 18), the tapestry of Catullus (poem 64), the walls of Carthage (*Aeneid* 1), and the shield of Aeneas (*Aeneid* 8). The ekphrasis of Longus is unusual, however, because this prologue is also the "outer frame" of the novel.

When I was hunting in Lesbos, I saw, in a wood sacred to the Nymphs, the most beautiful thing that I have ever seen—a painting that told a love-story. The wood itself was beautiful enough, full of trees and flowers, and watered by a single spring which nourished both the flowers and the trees; but the picture was even more delightful, combining excellent technique with a romantic subject. It had become so famous that crowds of people used to go there even from abroad, partly to pray to the Nymphs, but mainly to see the picture. In it there were women having babies and other women wrapping them in swaddling clothes, babies being exposed, sheep and goats suckling them, shepherds picking them up, young people plighting their troth, pirates making a raid, enemies starting an invasion.

After gazing admiringly at many other scenes, all of a romantic nature, I was seized by a longing to write a verbal equivalent to the painting. So I found someone to explain the picture to me, and composed a work in four volumes as an offering to Love and the Nymphs and Pan, and as a source of pleasure for the human race—something to heal the sick and comfort the afflicted, to refresh the memory of those who have been in love and educate those who have not. For no one has ever escaped Love altogether, and no one ever will, so long as beauty exists and eyes can see. But as for me, I hope that the god will allow me to write of other people's experiences, while retaining my own sanity.

The crucial phrase *antigrapsai te graphe* ("to write a verbal equivalent to the painting") indicates the method necessary to interpret *Daphnis and Chloe*, a recognition of its central quality as a literary explication of a pictorial representation.[9]

This ekphrastic prologue is interesting in itself, but it has the additional function of bounding the narrative as well as of initiating it. The boundary encloses a series of frames that are as critical as the existence of the ekphrasis itself. The prologue, a verbal painting, introduces the sequence of frames that comprises the structure of the novel. The result is a clear example of *encadrement*.

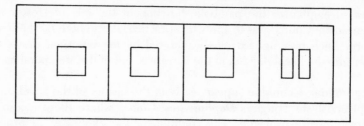

With the prologue-painting serving as the outer structure, each book becomes its own frame as well, and within its individual frame contains an
additional inlaid narrative. In book one there is the tale of the dove, in book
two the story of the pipe, in book three the tale of Echo, and in book four
Lamon's account of Daphnis and Dryas's account of Chloe. The tension of
pictorial and literary, therefore, is maintained throughout the novel.

The first function of the pictorial frame is to provoke an instant bounded
particularity. The setting is localized to Lesbos and Mytilene, and the
time compressed to a year and a half. Through pictorial space and
chronological time, Longus builds detail to provide psychological plausi-
bility for the awakening sexual consciousness of the protagonists. Even if
the spatial frame served no other function, it enforces spatial order within
temporal dynamics. Longus's technical achievement is in striking contrast
to the excessive diffusion of stories like Xenophon's *Ephesian Tale*.

The gradual evolution of consciousness in *Daphnis and Chloe* indicates
the pervasive influence of spatial reflexive ordering. There are several
points at which interior monologue provides a halting point for reappraisal
on the part of either Chloe or Daphnis, with an intriguing interior dialogue by Daphnis. These moments, albeit temporal, nevertheless suspend time both to summarize and to anticipate action. This crucial
spatiality, furthermore, is completely realized when the motif of
metamorphosis is introduced with Dorcon's disguise as a wolf, for here
the ambivalent nature of love as both longing and hunting is mirrored
many years before Freud's "wolf-man." Immediately after this transformation, Daphnis recounts the first of the inlaid tales, whose motif is the
metamorphosis of a woman into a bird. The paradigmatic transformation
of spatial to temporal in the prologue is here explicitly amplified. The
inlaid narrative of book two recounts the metamorphosis of Syrinx; book
three tells of the transformation of Echo. Book four opens with the temple
of Bacchus and its wall paintings, among which is one recounting the
transformation of the Tyrrhenian mariners: the two inner narratives of
book four detail the metamorphoses of the protagonists themselves.

The final spatial direction of the narrative is contained in the closing
sentence: "Chloe realized that what had taken place on the edge of the

wood had been nothing but childish play." Her life at the beginning contained its end. The transformation of a spatial to a temporal art form in the prologue is now reversed as the temporal art form assumes spatiality. This is not a picaresque travelogue, filled with random incidents, but rather a causally related narrative that finds its completion in its beginning. The work is a "spot of time" which, as Murray Krieger notes, is "precisely the union of spatiality and temporality."[10] Longus's use of *antigrapsai* means literally to "write back."

As the spatial ekphrasis bounds the dynamics of the narrative formally, the use of space also elicits the ethical or moral, as well as the aesthetic significance of this text. As the spatial form causes the gradualness in the temporal narrative, so too does it mirror the ethical standard of the work, which may be summarized as the necessity of equating desire with need. One must bound temporal desire by restricted need as spatial form bounds temporal movement. The formal spatial boundary has become a moral boundary as well, forbidding either escapism or indulgence. In book four, Dionysophanes urges Lamon "to tell the truth instead of inventing fairy-stories." A work of realism like *Daphnis and Chloe* may include such a statement, but no romance can afford to indict its bases in such a fashion. Ethical and aesthetic space underlies the entire novel. This is not a modern idea but only a modern rediscovery. One recalls Paul de Man's emphasis: "Movement does not take place as an actual sequence in time; to represent it as such is merely a metaphor making a sequence out of what occurs in fact as a synchronic juxtaposition." The pattern of inlaid narratives evolving from the ekphrasis proves this is so. The ekphrastic frame of *Daphnis and Chloe*, while serving both an aesthetic and an ethical function in the novel, likewise explains the appeal of the work itself. In *The Poetics of Space*, Gaston Bachelard has noted the importance of inlaid and recessed drawers and boxes as gratifying our "need for secrecy" and "intimate space."[11] This tendency leads ultimately to our becoming our own hiding places. The final idea extolled by the spatial ekphrasis of *Daphnis and Chloe* is the inviolability of the self.

Because a pictorial frame does not permit extension of its own space, the use of a "centre," as in James, is peculiarly suited to creating the novel's pictorial illusion. *The Portrait of a Lady*, published in 1881, is, in fact, preeminently about pictorial illusion. The concept of a portrait remained with James throughout his career. In the early *Roderick Hudson* (1876), the protagonist, although a sculptor, evokes by his name the painting of the Hudson River School of Cole; in *The American* (1877), Newman and Mlle. Nioche meet in the Louvre; in the late *Wings of the Dove* (1902), James depicts Milly Theale finding a great revelation before a Bronzino portrait. In *The Ambassadors* (1903), Strether sees his quarry and its lure indelibly framed on the river Seine. In the preface to *The Portrait of a Lady,* James calls Dickens, Scott, and Stevenson "painters"; he adds that the settings of Florence, and in particular of Venice, provided the "true touch for my canvas." Discussing the "germ" of the novel, he recalls Turgenev's remarks about the "fictive picture" and wonders about the problem of the "setting," the place, in relation to architecture. Almost immediately after this statement, James adds an architectural image to the pictorial one; it is also one of the central images of his novel:

The house of fiction has in short not one window, but a million—a number of possible windows not be reckoned.... These apertures, of dissimilar shape and size, hang so, all together, over the human scene that we might have expected of them a greater sameness of report than we find. They are but windows at the best.... They are not hinged doors opening straight upon life.... But they have this mark of their own that at each of them stands a figure.

James describes his emblem: the scene before the window is the subject; the aperture is the literary form; the watcher is the "consciousness of the artist." The novel is no longer seen as merely pictorial; the *donnée* is the "small corner-stone," and the novel "a square and spacious house ... put up round my young woman while she stood there in perfect isolation."[12] In terms of spatial criticism, this preface is extraordinary for such a shift, or rather an amalgam, of the pictorial to the architectural. It is this amalgam which creates the artistic tension of *The Portrait of a Lady,* permitting neither a "freestanding" young woman nor, on account of the frame, the admission of an outside architectural structure of a house. One has something framed but not freestanding, albeit with strong tendencies toward that state. One has, in Isabel Archer, a character of high relief. It is in this sense that James's work is a portrait.

Dorothy Van Ghent's statement, that the problem in James's fiction is that of "surface against depth," surely implies that in *The Portrait of a Lady* "sight is insight," and that the *ficelle* of Henriette Stackpole serves as " 'relief' in that sense in which the lower level of a relief provides perspective for the carved projections." Marion Montgomery has pointed out that the "blueprint" for the novel was all too faithfully followed by James, particularly in "his desire to foreshorten climax so that rising action equals falling action." But in the context of the spatiality of the novel, it is not the climax but its foreshortening that is the concern. The "second portrait" of Isabel, following her marriage, is "unveiled; but we have not seen it painted as we did the first." Whether *The Portrait of a Lady* is interpreted as a study of the loss of innocence, a study of puritanism, an analysis of free will and determinism, an exposé of egotism, a treatment of the international theme or of the isolated American, or as a use of the mythic quest motif, its central element remains its portrait nature.[13]

The clearest evidence of the importance of the title lies in the early rumination of Isabel's cousin, Ralph Touchett. Isabel's arrival is the revelation of "a real little passionate force to see at play."

"It's finer than the work of art—than a Greek bas-relief, than a great Titian, than a Gothic cathedral. It's very pleasant to be so well treated where one had least looked for it. I had never been more blue, more bored, than for a week before she came; I had never expected less that anything pleasant would happen. Suddenly I receive a Titian, by the post, to hang on my wall—I receive a Greek bas-relief to stick over my chimney-piece."

Here Isabel begins by being finer than the relief but ends by becoming it, amid some architectural confusion. This early in the novel Isabel is already an art work, as she will be later for Osmond, and as Prince Amerigo became the Ververs' prize acquisition in *The Golden Bowl*. Isabel found, though she never needed it, an avenger in Maggie Verver.

One's initial impression of Isabel Archer is inevitably of independence, inevitably in the sense that the female archer evokes Diana, the goddess of the hunt (and hints of James's debt to Gwendolyn Harleth in George Eliot's *Daniel Deronda*). She has an aim. In the first volume of the novel, James underscores this impression. She is "quite independent," "fond of her liberty." Isabel rejects Warburton for this reason. "She couldn't marry Lord Warburton; the idea failed to support any enlightened prejudice in favour of the free exploration of life that she hitherto entertained or was now capable of entertaining."

And yet one need not have hindsight, only foresight, to see already a different Miss Archer. James is careful to distinguish Isabel both from Ralph Touchett, who has independence and indifference, and from Henrietta Stackpole, who represents that "a woman might suffice to herself and be happy." These are not Isabel's forms of independence; when she refuses to attend the Dutch House school in Albany she is given her freedom, but it is "an incident in which the elation of liberty and the pain of exclusion were indistinguishably mingled." It is this fear of exclusion that even as a child marks her for less than the independent person she thinks herself. Much later, Isabel tells Warburton that she cannot be happy "by separating myself . . . from life," as marriage to him supposedly would cause her to do. She makes her greatest declaration of liberty in refusing the self-made Caspar Goodwood: "I like my liberty too much. If there's a thing in the world I'm fond of . . . it's my personal independence." "I try to judge things for myself; to judge wrong, I think, is more honourable than not to judge at all. . . . I wish to choose my fate and know something of human

affairs beyond what other people think it compatible with propriety to tell
me." Nevertheless, one has learned much earlier from the narrator that
the "deepest thing" in Isabel's soul was "a belief that if a certain light
should dawn she could give herself completely." It is this sentence, more
than any other, that makes one recall that the third word in the novel is
"circumstances." And it is Madame Merle who clarifies the meaning of
"circumstances" to Isabel: "When you've lived as long as I you'll see that
every human being has his shell and that you must take the shell into
account. By the shell I mean the whole envelope of circumstances."

It is indeed ironic, and very calculated by James, that it should be Ralph
who delivers a decisive pronouncement about Madame Merle and about
Isabel as well. Of Madame Merle, he twice declares that she is "complete," "too complete, in a word." This is nearly to say that she is too
finished, or, to use her own words, not a self and a shell but a shell only.
She is all circumstances, or as Ralph puts it, "she's the great round world
itself." Yet this criticism of Madame Merle must be put next to Ralph's
own pronouncement about Isabel: "You want to see, but not to feel." It is
here that Isabel's difference from Ralph and especially from Henrietta is
evident. Much earlier in the novel, Isabel has been confused about the
relation of liberty to "giving oneself completely." Another disturbing
element is expressed in something she declares to Ralph's father: "I like
more unexpectedness." Unexpectedness, surely, is not liberty but rather
circumstances, the shell, "to see, but not to feel." Isabel fails to remember her own early intuition that "the importance of what had happened was out of proportion to its appearance." The question becomes
what is wrong with the "proportion." Henrietta tells her:

"The peril for you is that you live too much in the world of your own dreams.
You're not enough in contact with reality—with the toiling, striving, suffering, I
may even say sinning, world that surrounds you. You're too fastidious; you've too
many graceful illusions. Your newly-acquired thousands will shut you up more
and more to the society of a few selfish and heartless people who will be interested
in keeping them up."

A reader may be more specific. While Isabel is not in contact with reality,
that is not because reality is to be equated with the "world that surrounds
you." That world in fact is what Isabel is in contact with, what will "shut
her up." How did she "see" "out of proportion" and become "shut up"?

It is hardly accidental that in chapter twenty-two, after Henrietta and
Ralph have clarified Isabel's dangerous interpretation of "liberty," James
begins to refine his portrait. Osmond is visiting the convent where Pansy
has been placed. Thus, there exists "a small group that might have been
described by a painter as composing well" of the father, daughter, and

two nuns. The villa is described: "The windows of the ground-floor, as you saw them from the piazza, were, in their noble proportions, extremely architectural; but *their function seemed less to offer communication with the world than to defy the world to look in*" (italics added). The room is filled with "those angular specimens of pictorial art in frames," and in front of one (much like the later Milly Theale in *The Wings of the Dove*) stands Pansy, "looking at the picture in silence." The two sisters are in an "attitude" of "final reserve." Such words as "window," "specimen," and "attitude" will be central for the remainder of the novel. At this time Osmond "was the elegant complicated medal struck off for a special occasion." It is striking that James advises the reader that this is a picture "composing well." The girl is in front of yet another picture, the nuns are in an attitude, and the father is a "medal." The whole occurs inside windows which "defy the world to look in." The crucial meaning of the episode is driven home when Osmond remarks to the nuns, "You're very complete."

When Isabel surveys Osmond's own gallery, she stands before a picture which he then brings into more light: "She looked at the other works of art, and he gave her such further information as might appear most acceptable to a young lady making a call on a summer afternoon. His picture, his medallions and tapestries were interesting; but after a while Isabel felt the owner much more so." Later the themes of art and freedom are brought together. "It was her present inclination, however, to express a measured sympathy for the success with which he had preserved his independence. 'That's a very pleasant life,' she said, 'to renounce everything but Correggio!'" The relation to frame and independence, and to the meaning of James's title, rests here. In the second volume, Isabel stands before the *Dying Gladiator* in the Capitoline Museum and recounts her refusal of Lord Warburton. Osmond reacts: "He perceived a new attraction in the idea of taking to himself a young lady who had qualified herself to figure in his collection of choice objects by declining so noble a hand." Osmond, "fond of originals, or rarities," sees Isabel as a specimen to be added to the gallery.

That gallery becomes the frame for her portrait.

As the months elapsed, she had followed him further and he had led her into the mansion of his habitation, then, *then,* she had seen where she really was . . . the house of suffocation. Osmond's beautiful mind gave it neither light nor air; Osmond's beautiful mind indeed seemed to peep down from a small high window and mock at her.

The mansion, the window. Clearly she had regarded Osmond in time rather than in space. She had first "mistaken a part for the whole," and only later had his mocking comment hit home. The spatial element is present, almost but not quite too late. As the thought comes back, she will go back. "She had thought it a grand indifference, an exquisite independence. But indifference was really the last of his qualities." Osmond cannot live without the world: "He was unable to live without it; and she saw that he had never really done so; he had looked at it out of his window when he appeared to be most detached from it." Osmond's mind, a house unlike the house of fiction, has only one window.

The frame, the boundary, is the reason that she does return, for James espouses an aesthetic morality that may be summarized by the aphorism "nothing in excess," particularly nothing in excess of the original form. Later Strether will reject Maria Gostrey so that he will not bring anything in excess back to Wollett after his failed mission. Isabel much earlier in the second volume had begun to be the painter; when she returns to the Palazzo Roccanera she goes to her room, and then to the drawing room:

Just beyond the threshold of the drawing-room she stopped short, the reason for her doing so being that she had received an impression. . . . The soundlessness of her step gave her time to take in the scene before she interrupted it. . . . Madame Merle was standing on the rug, a little way from the fire; Osmond was in a deep chair, leaning back and looking at her. Her head was erect, as usual, but her eyes were bent on his. What struck Isabel first was that he was sitting while Madame Merle stood; there was an anomaly in this that arrested her.

This portrait is nearly all, everything. The tendency to perfect form, which Isabel develops as a strategy for survival, begins here. Isabel, after declaring she cannot "publish" her error, becomes aware that she is her own portrait already; she confesses to Henrietta: "You're all looking at me; it makes me uncomfortable." The desire for self-containment grows, until Osmond appeals to her "honour," and she responds: "He spoke in the name of something sacred and precious—the observance of a magnificent form." "It came over her that in his wish to preserve appearances he was after all sincere, and that this, as far as it went, was a merit." When Isabel returns to Gardencourt, she walks "into the library and along the gallery of pictures." "She envied the security of valuable 'pieces' which change by no hair's breadth, only grow in value, while their owners lose inch by inch youth, happiness, beauty."

Isabel cannot become any other art form than a painting, something which has no coextension, no volume, no mass; her story is, therefore, a portrait, a fine relief but surely not the rounded figure. This is the meaning of the kiss. Goodwood puts his arms around her and kisses her "like white lightning," but she remains aware particularly of "each aggressive fact of his face" in this "act of possession." Unlike a statue, she refuses to be encompassed; "there was a very straight path" which was as much a boundary as a direction. Here is the form, the portrait, the picture as aesthetic morality, celebrating self-containment, nothing in excess, nothing loose. This portrait is the window, the window of the house of Osmond, which forbids rather than permits access. It is here that the Jamesian theory of the centre is carefully illustrated. The irony above all is that the first adjective applied to Goodwood—"straight"—describes the one-point perspective.

And yet the window, the house, and the portrait take one back to the preface to this novel, for these three elements are as much a part of the process as of the product. Isabel becomes the painter in the famous tableau scene, but just as she becomes this in the presence of Osmond, the collector, so too does another collector inhabit her life, the 'I' narrator: "It was one of her theories that Isabel Archer was very fortunate in being independent"; "The effect she produced upon people was often different from what she supposed"; "I do not know whether it was on this occasion or on some other"; "These reflexions . . . are presented in a cluster for the convenience of the reader"; "I am bound to confess, though it may cast some discredit on the sketch I have given"; "according to the rule I have hinted at. . . ." The all-important word is "sketch." There was, then, someone in the window frame of Isabel's centre other than herself; her morality of self-contained "magnificent" aesthetic form was as inevitable as it once appeared to be chosen. By exploiting the centre James gives us but the one-point perspective of a painting, and we cannot obtain multiple views (as one might of a freestanding sculpturesque character). Mrs. Touchett's and Ralph's dislike of Isabel's marriage "served mainly to throw into higher relief the fact, in every way so honourable, that she married to please herself." It is not coincidental that "honour" and "relief" appear in company with "please herself"; portraiture is the process and the product of the novel. Its creator had sketched; this *Portrait of a Lady* was inevitable.

An alternative mode of spatial characterization in the novel exists in sculptural volume. There are three well-established ideas in the tradition of criticism about sculpture. These are that statues could speak and are "alive," that sculpture involves a temporal secondary illusion, and that characters in literature have an overt relation to sculptured objects. C. M. Bowra observes in *The Greek Experience:* "The Greeks . . . maintained to a late date an early, almost animistic idea that statues are in some sense alive." Diodorus Siculus noted that Daedalus could create figures which moved by themselves, and Homer in *Iliad* 18 described Hephaestus similarly. In *The Sister Arts*, Jean Hagstrum observes that "the mute statue was given a voice and the silent form was endowed with the power of speech." Although it is "silent," Keats's Grecian urn can speak its cryptic aphorism. Epitaphs on tomb sculptures are for this reason in the first person. In effect, this belief in the ability of statues to speak suggests the great temporal secondary illusion created by this spatial art. In Donatello's *David*, the figure of the hero stands on the head of Goliath while still holding his stone; the same sculptor's *Judith* depicts a sword raised not only in preparation to slay Holofernes but already attesting to her triumphs by its gesture. At a later date François Rude's *Ney* will demonstrate the same quality, for the scabbard is held for the sword already drawn to be drawn. It is not surprising, therefore, that the novelist creating characters sought the complementary process in his temporal art. Hagstrum remarks that ancient biography attests to the correlation of characterization with sculpture: "Varro called his seven hundred prose biographies of Greek and Roman celebrities *Imagines* [likenesses, statues] and is said to have illustrated each with a portrait." Xenocrates of Sicyon, a sculptor, "is thought to have written works of iconic prose on art objects in which he attempted to outdo in verbal form what had been achieved in graphic form in his subjects." Such a practice was also pursued by Callistratus, who described statues in prose, and Philostratus, who considered "paintings literary." In the romance *Clitophon and Leucippe*, Achilles Tatius used descriptions that were "pictorial, not natural"; he was "as much interested in 'rendering' an artifact, an *object d'art*, a painting, or a statue as he was in 'rendering' a natural scene." The culmination of this tendency is the ekphrasis of *Daphnis and Chloe*, a novel "viewed as a series of tableaux."[14]

Thomas's *Tristran* occupies an important place in the history of fiction because of its clear recognition of the sculptural secondary illusion underlying character. In the section "The Hall of Statues," Tristran recreates all the characters in *imagines:*

One day Tristran overcame a giant in a forest just beyond the boundary of the Duke's domain and accepted the monster's homage. The following day Tristran commanded him and his minions, who were skilled carpenters and goldsmiths, to make a hall in a cavern and to fashion lifelike statues of Queen Ysolt and Brengvein. When these were finished, the image of Ysolt held in its right hand a sceptre with a bird perched on it that beat its wings like a live bird; in its left the image held a ring on which were inscribed the words which Ysolt had uttered at the parting. Beneath Ysolt's feet lay the image of the Dwarf who had denounced her to Mark in the orchard, while beside her reclined Peticru, modelled in pure gold and as the dog shook its head, its tiny bell jingled softly. The statue of Brengvein held a vial, around which ran the legend: "Queen Ysolt, take this drink that was made for King Mark in Ireland."

Whenever Tristran visits the image of Ysolt he kisses it and clasps it in his arms, as if it were alive. . . .

By means of the image Tristran recalls the delights of their great loves, their troubles and their griefs, their pains and their torments. When he is in a gay mood, he kisses it a great deal; but he vents his rage when he is angry, whether because of thoughts or dreams, whether because he believes lies in his heart to the effect that she is forgetting him or has some other lover; or that she cannot help loving another whom she has more to her pleasure.... He fears that, not having her desire, she will take what she can, that, unable to have Tristran, she will take another lover.

When Tristran imagines such maddening things he vents his hatred on the statue; he does not wish to look on her, not to see or speak to her.... He made this image so that he might tell it what is in his heart—his right thinking and mad aberration, his pain, his joy of love; for he did not know to whom to reveal his longing or desire.

The central myth underlying Thomas's technique is that of Pygmalion, which here, however, is reversed. The images derive from actuality rather than become it. Nevertheless, when the story resumes, Thomas does not clearly indicate whether it is the images or the character whose activities are being described.[15]

The legacy of these procedures in the *Iliad, Clitophon and Leucippe,* and *Tristran* for the history of the novel appears in Balzac's *Cousin Bette,* where the author explains not only Valérie Marneffe but also her creation: "Valérie is a sad reality of existence, modelled from life, correct in every particular." The business of the novelist derives from both Prometheus and Pygmalion. Balzac continues:

One can copy a model and the work is done; but to impart a soul to it, in the representing of a man or woman to create a type, is to snatch fire from heaven like Prometheus.... One statue is enough to make a man immortal, just as it took only Figaro, Lovelace, and Manon Lescaut to immortalize Beaumarchais, Richardson, and the Abbé Prévost.

Mary Shelley titled her novel *Frankenstein: A Modern Prometheus,* which may be read on one level as a myth of the creation of character in the novel. At nearly the same time as the publication of *Cousin Bette, Vanity Fair* appeared in England. Although its original subtitle, "Pen and Pencil Sketches of English Society," already suggested a spatial element, Thackeray explicitly expressed the connection between characterization and sculpture at the beginning of chapter fifteen: "Every reader of a sentimental turn (and we desire no other) must have been pleased with the *tableau* with which the last act of our little drama concluded; for what can be prettier than an image of Love on his knees before Beauty?"[16]

The consequence of statements like Balzac's in *Cousin Bette* appeared in subsequent criticism and creation of fiction. Writing of *Madame Bo-vary*, Sainte-Beuve stated:

At certain moments and situations in this book, the author could easily have superimposed a coating of idealism over his implacable realism. By so doing he could have "patched up" a character and rounded it off—that of Charles Bovary, for example. A few more pats, and the clay the novelist was molding could have turned out a noble and touching figure instead of a vulgar one.

Later Sainte-Beuve was to describe the chapter of *Salammbô* as "ta-bleaux." Harry Levin has referred to "the Rodinesque energy with which [Zola] symbolizes issues" in *Germinal* and *Nana*. In the Théâtre des Va-riétés, Nana is "enthroned Venus in the gutter by the pavement-side." She becomes the statue the Second Empire erects to itself on its way to ruin in the Franco-Prussian War:

In the background Vulcan's forge glowed like a setting star. Diana, since the second act, had come to a good understanding with the god, who was to pretend that he was on a journey, so as to leave the way clear for Venus and Mars. Then, scarcely was Diana alone, than Venus made her appearance. A shiver of delight ran round the house. Nana was nude. With quiet audacity, she appeared in her nakedness, certain of the sovereign power of her flesh. . . . It was Venus rising from the waves, with no veil save her tresses.[17]

This sculptural element of characterization is frequently found in other novels. In *Barchester Towers*, Trollope entitles the chapter recounting Mrs. Proudie's domination of her husband "Mrs. Proudie Victrix," as if she has singlehandedly carved her own memorial. So important is this fact to Trollope that he expands it in *The Last Chronicle of Barset*, where Mrs. Proudie when dressed appears more armored than decorated, and when dead is more an effigy than a person to her husband, who is anguished not at her death but at his relief. The sculpturesque appears in the tale of Dalrymple, and in the combat over whether Clara Van Siever or Mrs. Dobbs Broughton will be Sisera in his sculpture. D. H. Lawrence, who recognized the power of a protagonist as "victrix," coupled it to the bibli-cal method of *The Rainbow* in the brilliant chapter "Anna Victrix," calling to mind Pygmalion as Anna Lensky, exulting at the birth of Ursula Brangwen, claims herself as "Anna Victrix" to her overwhelmed husband. Lawrence, in the cancelled and suppressed prologue to *Women in Love,* states Birkin's fascination at the "plastic form" of men. Flem Snopes is described in William Faulkner's *The Hamlet:*

A thick, squat soft man of no establishable age between twenty and thirty, with a broad still face containing a tight seam of mouth stained slightly at the corners with tobacco, and eyes the color of stagnant water, and projecting from among the other features in startling and sudden paradox, a tiny predatory nose like the beak of a small hawk. It was as though the original nose had been left off by the original designer or craftsman and the unfinished job taken over by someone of a radically different school.[18]

By such techniques the creation of character is integrally related to the myth of Pygmalion. Pip at his forge, Jude at his carving, or Victor Frankenstein in the laboratory suggest the myth.

Nathaniel Hawthorne's novel *The Marble Faun* is particularly involved with sculptural secondary illusion. Hawthorne uses a conflict of sculptural ideas as a structure to demonstrate that spatial form can be a reflection of spiritual transcendence. Henry James, in *Hawthorne* (1879), recognized the importance of formal spatiality as spiritual transcendence in the novel.

The plastic sense was not strong in Hawthorne; there can be no better proof of it than his curious aversion to the representation of the nude in sculpture. . . . He apparently quite failed to see that nudity is not an incident, or accident, of sculpture, but its very essence and principle.

The work bears the name of *The Marble Faun*. . . . It completely fails to characterise the story.

In *Transformation (The Marble Faun)* he has attempted to deal with actualities more than he did in either of his earlier novels.

The fault of *Transformation* is that the element of the unreal is pushed too far, and that the book is neither positively of one category nor of another.

This is the trouble with Donatello himself. His companions are intended to be real . . . whereas he is intended to be real or not, as you please. He is of a different substance from them; it is as if a painter, in composing a picture, should try to give you an impression of one of his figures by a strain of music.

Nearly all the norms are provided here for Hawthorne's intention, though not to the conclusion that in fact Hawthorne intended. James isolates not only the conflict of "actualities" with "the unreal," but also the attempt of the painter to weld time to his spatial art. However, James fails to connect his observations to the two opening chapters of the novel, or to its English title, *Transformation*. In effect, Hawthorne knew absolutely what he was about in calling the work *The Marble Faun;* few works have attacked more directly the problem of spatiality in the temporal art of the novel. When James claims that Donatello may be "real or not," he is close to the question of spatiality. No one ever used the concept of secondary illusion with more illusion than did Hawthorne. If the title *Transformation* was forced on him by the English publishers, it nevertheless reveals the essence of the book, which is not exclusively about the fall into evil, guilt, penance, and expiation, but is also about spatiality and temporality. In it Hawthorne studied the reverse of the normal relation between life and art, as he moves from the *Faun* of Praxiteles to Donatello, rather than from the being to the statue. In this sense *The Marble Faun* remains one of the few novels about Pygmalion ever written. Seen in conjunction with Hawthorne's attempts to produce the "actualities" recorded in *The Italian Notebooks*, the novel reveals that for him the "possible" of romance was none other than the secondary illusion. James wondered about the painter incorporating music; Hawthorne wrote about the novelist confronting sculpture.[19]

On a simple level, the confrontation is instantly manifested in the names associated with the protagonist, the *Faun* of Praxiteles and Donatello. By using the names of two sculptors with such contrasting styles, Hawthorne invoked his problem. Praxiteles' achievement in the evolution of ancient sculpture is, in a word, naturalism. Gods are seen as men, and therefore a living model is justifiable; the beauteous Phryne, for example, was the model for the *Aphrodite of Cnidus*. This naturalism is immediately evident in Praxiteles' other most famed work, the *Hermes and Dionysus*, in the distinguishing S-curve of the body, with its resultant cool dynamism, in the realism of the drapery, in the tree trunk, and in the right arm breaking the experience of mass. In the *Aphrodite* itself, the S-curve appears again, as well as the contrast of smooth skin and folded garment. More than any artisan of his time, Praxiteles conceived his art free of architecture, the famed curve defying any building to embrace it. In the *Faun* one sees the curve, the trunk, the remnants of a pipe, the overripe languor, and the deep folds of the animal skin, all suggesting the sensuous naturalism that Hawthorne so obviously felt in this nude work. If Hawthorne was repelled by such nudity, it is only because in Praxiteles it was so definitely natural.[20]

However, the pieces of Donatello the sculptor contrast strongly with a work like the *Faun* of Praxiteles. Of first significance is that Donatello was, after a few brief "realistic" pieces like *Saint Mark*, a decidedly abstract sculptor. The turning point in his work was unquestionably *Lo Zuccone*, the figure of a prophet in the realm of abstraction, his body neglected, a conception of the human being in terms not of the probabilities of this earth but of the possibilities of the next world. The famous *David* depicts an intellectual rather than physical, a spiritual rather than corporeal, victory over Goliath. In the later *Magdalen*, *Saint John the Baptist*, and even *Judith and Holofernes* (all mentioned in *The Marble Faun* by name if not by specific art work), Donatello moves to greater levels of abstraction. One should note that the murder in *The Marble Faun* precisely reverses the order of the *Judith*, for the man Donatello kills for the woman Miriam, whereas Judith slew Holofernes for the soldiery of Bethulia. Finally, in the figures on the pulpit of San Lorenzo, and especially in the figure of Christ, Donatello resorts, as Anthony Bertram observes, to the "medieval system of symbolic scale," with Christ larger than the other figures, but also tattered as if emerging "from the chambers of the Gestapo." Only with Michelangelo's and Bernini's *Davids* do we have a departure from the "idealized" *Davids* of Donatello and Verrocchio.[21] In short, while Hawthorne's references to the *Faun* of Praxiteles recall his creator's naturalism, it is Donatello's name that invokes the abstraction of his sculptor namesake. Thus Hawthorne indicates the first element of his conflict, the conflict between naturalism and abstraction, or, as James would have it, "real or not."

Richard Chase's contention that characters in romance are "abstract and ideal" embraces the basic tendency of Donatello the sculptor. In addition, however, James's statement in the preface to *The American* that the province of romance is "disconnected and uncontrolled experience" expands this conception of abstraction; it is furthered when he declares that in *The Marble Faun* "the story ... is dropped and taken up again," which suggests the ellipsis, an inherently abstract method. One chapter of *The Marble Faun* is called "Fragmentary Sentences" for this reason. But James feels that "the unreal is pushed too far," with the result that "the book is neither positively of one category nor of another."[22]

A reader of the opening two chapters of *The Marble Faun* experiences the feeling of sculptural coextensive volume absolutely realized. Hawthorne has made the secondary illusion visible by aligning his actual and his sculptural Faun, and depicting precisely the activity of volume. This is to say that he has brought into the temporal art the very process of sculptural secondary illusion characterization. The statues in the Capitoline Museum seem to Hawthorne to have "an ideal life," which is presumably a reference to their timelessness rather than to their inherent naturalism. In the realm of this sculpture "the present moment is pressed down or crowded out, and our individual affairs and interests are but half as real here as elsewhere. *Viewed through this medium, our narrative* — into which are woven some airy and unsubstantial threads, intermixed with others, twisted out of the commonest stuff of human existence—may seem not widely different from the texture of our lives"(italics added). This passage is indeed extraordinary. Hawthorne's contention that the story must be viewed through the medium of sculpture is truly revolutionary and he immediately follows it by an open admission of the amalgam of real and unreal which James criticized but which Hawthorne obviously intended. Finally, he also uses the image of line, "threads," which is decisive in the interpretation of the novel.

This concern with sculpture is not fanciful, as Miriam points out to Kenyon:

"You never chiseled out of marble, nor wrought in clay, a more vivid likeness than this. . . . The portraiture is perfect in character. . . . If it were a picture, the resemblance might be half illusive and imaginary; but here, in this Pentelic marble, it is a substantial fact, and may be tested by absolute touch and measurement. Our friend Donatello is the very Faun of Praxiteles."

The likeness in portraiture would not only be "imaginary" but would clearly be impossible without the coextensive volume of sculpture to embrace, in effect, the persons in the room. After Donatello assumes the pose of the statue, Hawthorne attempts to describe the *Faun*, "however inadequate may be the effort to express its magic peculiarity in words." Hawthorne declares: "[Its] form . . . has a fuller and more rounded outline, more flesh, and less of heroic muscle than the old sculptors were wont to assign to their types of masculine beauty." He acknowledges its "softened marble," which is to say that he recognizes the naturalistic quality of the statue. As Miriam later observes of Donatello: "He is not supernatural, but just on the verge of nature, and yet within it." She clearly perceives that volume is not only itself but also embraces, incorporates the space surrounding it. Donatello's ignorance of time and his birth "is equivalent to being immortal on earth," another correlation between him and the *Faun*. In the subsequent discussion of the *Dying Gladiator*, when Kenyon claims that "moments . . . ought not to be incrusted with the eternal repose of marble," Miriam declares that painting may include time, but Hawthorne himself disagrees with Kenyon: "Why should not each statue grow warm with life!" In his preface Hawthorne claims that he did not take Kenyon's personal qualities from sculptor friends (Akers, Story, Rogers), "his own man of marble being entirely imaginary." Hawthorne does align "this medium" of sculpture with "our narrative." Likewise, the appellation "man of marble" may be extended to include nearly all the characters.

As if to reinforce this connection of characterization with sculpture, at the end of the second chapter the model appears, haunting Miriam "as if he might just have stepped out of a picture." During the visit to the Catacombs, he appears again, reminding Kenyon of "similar figures . . . reclining on the Spanish steps, and . . . waiting for some artist to invite them within the magic realm of picture. Nor . . . could Kenyon help wondering to see such a personage shaping himself so suddenly out of the darkness." At the moment of the murder on the Tarpeian rock, Hawthorne clearly has this idea of volume in mind. "In the basement wall of the palace, shaded from the moon, there was a deep, empty niche, that had probably once contained a statue; not empty, either; for a figure now came forth from it and approached Miriam." Miriam, Donatello, and the model all have one quality in common: they appear to have emerged from works of art. Miriam indeed paints herself and bears a remarkable likeness to a portrait of Beatrice Cenci. Earlier she had observed that Donatello might "dance out" of any picture in which he found himself. Given the number of such allusions, it appears that Hawthorne is at the very heart of his own theory of the novel, the problem of the statuesque invoked by Praxiteles and Donatello.

With this in mind, one need only look at the chapter "The Sylvan Dance," which takes place at the Villa Borghese, the location of Bernini's dynamic sculptures, *Pluto and Persephone, David,* and *Apollo and Daphne.* Nowhere does Hawthorne indicate better his true understanding of sculpture than when Miriam and Donatello assume the attitudes and positions of nymphs and fauns in the woods. Indeed, the *Apollo and Daphne* has come to life.

Here, as it seemed, had the Golden Age come back again within the precincts of this sunny glade, thawing mankind out of their cold formalities, releasing them.

It seemed the realization of one of those bas-reliefs where a dance of nymphs, satyrs, or bacchanals is twined around the circle of an antique vase; or it was like the sculptured scene on the front and sides of a sarcophagus.

There was an analogy between the sculptured scene on the sarcophagus and the wild dance which we have been describing.

It is quite possible that in invoking the bas-relief Hawthorne is thinking of Donatello's own *Second Cantoria* in the Duomo in Florence.

Murray Krieger has observed that "Hawthorne gives to Kenyon . . . a similar artistic problem" to his own of writing a novel.[23] The problem is clearly defined during Miriam's visit to Kenyon's studio: "The figure is embedded in the stone, and must be freed from its encumbering superfluities." To Miriam, "the features . . . seemed to be struggling out of the stone. . . . It was impossible not to think that the outer marble was merely an extraneous environment; the human countenance within its embrace must have existed there since the limestone ledges of Carrara were first made." Finally she makes the correlation explicit, drawing Hawthorne into the process as well: "As these busts in the block of marble . . . so does our individual fate exist in the limestone of time. We fancy that we carve it out; but its ultimate shape is prior to all our action." Surely here are all the well-known stories surrounding Michelangelo's *David* and the *Tomb Figures* or *Captives.* Somewhat contemptuously, Miriam declares to Kenyon: "It is so difficult . . . to compress and define a character or story, and make it patent at a glance, within the narrow scope

attainable by sculpture!" Her statement seems, however, to be Hawthorne speaking of his own material. Later, when Kenyon attempts a bust
of Donatello, the problem is "how to make this genial and kind type of
countenance the index of the mind within." As he tries to embody Donatello's "personal characteristics," he thinks it is "his difficult office to bring
out from their depths, and interpret them to all men, showing them what
they could not discern for themselves, yet must be compelled to recognize
at a glance, on the surface of a block of marble."

In despair, Kenyon alters the clay model before Donatello himself,
seeking the "inner man," and finally leaving the studio. But he "would
have done well to glance again at his work; for here were still the features
of the antique Faun, but now illuminated with a higher meaning, such as
the old marble never bore." In effect, this figure *is* the novelistic Faun
created by Hawthorne himself, but by the technique of random flashes,
by the dropping and the resuming, as James noted, of the story itself. This
fragmentariness is ultimately preserved, for Kenyon never finishes the
bust. "Most spectators mistake it for an unsuccessful attempt towards
copying the features of the *Faun* of Praxiteles." Hawthorne had quoted
Bertel Thorvaldsen's analogies: clay model, life; plaster cast, death;
sculptured marble, resurrection. Could Hawthorne have been more
explicit?

Hawthorne welds the specific backgrounds of Miriam, Donatello, Kenyon, and Hilda to his sculpturesque notion of characterization. Miriam
has her painting studio in the tower, Donatello his villa, Kenyon his
studio, and Hilda her combined shrine and dovecote. In three of these
cases, the specific settings are the famous towers. When Donatello visits
Miriam in her studio, Hawthorne emphasizes the one element that over
all unifies them: their constant affiliation with art. Donatello appears to
leap from pictures; Miriam puts herself in them through self-portraits. In
the next chapter Hawthorne describes Hilda's tower, "The Virgin's
Shrine," when Miriam visits it. The contrasting temperaments, sensuous
and ascetic, of the two women are obvious, but in this chapter Hawthorne
puts moral constructs on verticality. From the tower Hilda can "descend
into the corrupted atmosphere of the city beneath." To Miriam she seems
"partly ideal," but she is like Donatello and Miriam in that she appears
"like an inhabitant of picture land," "the counterpart in picture of so many
feminine achievements in literature." Finally, the Owl Tower at Monte
Beni takes on spiritual significance. "Your tower resembles the spiritual
experience of many a sinful soul, which . . . may struggle upward into the
pure air." The vision at the summit prompts Kenyon to note: "It is a great
mistake to try to put our best thoughts into human language. When we
ascend into the higher regions of emotion and spiritual enjoyment, they

are only expressible by such grand hieroglyphics as these around us." The emphasis on the tower, however, becomes crucial at the moment in which the light of Hilda's dovecote is extinguished. "For the first time in centuries, the consecrated and legendary flame, before the loftiest shrine in Rome, had ceased to burn." This of course represents Hilda's "descent" into the experience of guilt, her suffering before reaffirmation of life.

Gaston Bachelard's *Poetics of Space* is a gloss on the entire novel in this respect. Bachelard contends that we "experience the house in its reality and in its virtuality" such that a house not only may but must be "read" in its two dimensions of the vertical and the central. In the vertical, there is the tension between attic and cellar, between the "aerial and the terrestrial," which Hawthorne alluded to in the periodic descent of Hilda to the corrupted atmosphere of Rome. Centrality, however, is preeminently represented by the image of the lamp in the window. "A lamp *is waiting* in the window, and through it, the house, too, is waiting. The lamp is the symbol of prolonged waiting." If "our soul is an abode," we have here a topoanalysis of our intimate life, the house being a chrysalis, symbolic both of repose and of flight. The conflict in the residence between centrality and verticality is complicated by the idea of line. Discussing the poetry of André Lafon, Bachelard observes: "In his literary 'prints,' the house welcomes the reader like a host. A bit more and he would be ready to seize the chisel and engrave his own reading." For Bachelard, the house in literature does not remain a mere "representation." "Its lines have force and, as a shelter, it is fortifying." Readers become sculptors working on the house. "When I speak the image sincerely, I suddenly feel a need to underline. And what is *underlining* but *engraving* while we write?" This underlining, however, is horizontal, and we are brought again to the question of boundary, whether between naturalism and abstraction, realism and romance, or life and art, to the problem of the line between them, or, as the English title of the novel would have it, *Transformation*. [24]

What Hawthorne has accomplished is not only to place his sculpturesque notion against line, but against vertical line. Verticality and horizontality are, of course, simultaneity and continuity respectively; they represent, furthermore, lack of causality (what Hawthorne called "latitude"), abstraction and naturalism, romance and realism. The movement of *The Marble Faun* is decidedly horizontal and sequential, but its ideas are vertical in that they do not rely on development for their validity. One line, the "path of movement" in the novel, is decidedly horizontal, but also decidedly impersonal, for the horizontal, as Bachelard demonstrates, cannot be "intimate." Hawthorne has underscored, engraved, underlined his own work. The characters, however, are decidedly the vertical, representing as they do the abstraction of spiritual regeneration, the possible.

Their line is the graph of their intentions, their edges, but not their bodies. To Hawthorne, the temporal art of the novel is inevitably horizontal, but its intentions are those of its own secondary illusion, space; for him it is romance, with its wider latitude, that can more thoroughly realize this space than can the novel. The paradox remains perfect in the titles of the first and of the last chapters, where both are the same (vertical) although movement (horizontal) has taken place. The spatiality of the novel is for Hawthorne its spiritual possibility. The emphasis on verticality, timelessness, and lack of causality, which are the elements of this spatial secondary illusion, become supremely ethical in *The Marble Faun.* It is perhaps the only work of literature that exploits the secondary illusion for its own spiritual purposes. The longing of the temporal art for the spatial is the longing of temporal man for the timeless. That is why, ultimately, the four central figures are constantly associated with statues, submerging into or emerging from paintings and niches and ascending and descending towers.

The four characters also constitute the four corners of the frame that is *The Marble Faun.* The square becomes the perfect paradigm of the union of horizontal and vertical; it is easy, therefore, to separate the novel into four sections which do not have any causal connection with each other, as is appropriate to its spatiality. The series of spiritual regenerations does not occur because of the interaction of the characters with each other, but precisely in that "disconnected and uncontrolled" method of the romance as James saw it. This is made possible by the illusion of linear and sculptural timelessness, a welding of the vertical and horizontal, the spatial and the temporal, the romantic and the realistic. *The Marble Faun* is neither the one nor the other. Hawthorne's intuition about the *Faun* of Praxiteles and his own Faun Donatello are validated: it is neither the atemporal naturalism of Praxiteles nor the temporal abstraction of Donatello, but the two together.

The utility of sculpture for the novelist rests, above all, on the property which distinguishes it from the pictorial art of two-dimensional, one-point perspective. Sculpture, as Susanne Langer claims, is a "virtual space," a created space whose purpose is "to make tactual space visible." As a creation, spatial art is "not only a shape in space, but a shaping of space." This latter property Mrs. Langer calls "volume," the ability of a statue not only to occupy its own space but also to *in*fold, incorporate, its surroundings into itself. A painting hung on a wall does not organize its surroundings as does a statue; it has, properly speaking, no volume at all. Sculpture, by its volume, "fills" a room in the sense that it "absorbs" it into itself. Such a phenomenon explains, scientifically, the validity of Keats's experience before his Grecian urn. The idea of coextensive volume, therefore, is at the heart of all great sculpture. Displays of sculpture, such as the approach to the *David* in the Academy in Florence, reinforce rather than create this effect. The importance of inner and outer in sculpture becomes apparent, the balancing of the internal life of the statue against its exterior surroundings. This same balance forms the essence of the novel, the balancing of the individual against his society, of "man and his surroundings." The concept of point of view has been distorted by the failure to include in it the idea of volume. Elizabeth Bowen's remark about Elizabeth Bennett of *Pride and Prejudice*, that it is impossible not to believe she has entered the room, exactly illustrates the reaction to volume rather than to point. [25] This sculptural coextensive volume is one method by which a novel demonstrates what Butor in "The Book as Object" calls its *volumen*.

In order properly to understand the concept of sculptural volume as it occurs in the novel, it is necessary to examine briefly some representative statements about characterization in fiction. For example, in *Character and the Novel*, W. J. Harvey uses the terms of sculptural art as well as the concept of perspective, while claiming these effects result from mimesis. He observes, for instance, that irony rests not only on "perspective of range" (one's knowledge of the situation) but also on "perspective of depth" (the degree to which certain characters "stand out from, or are immersed in, a world of other human beings"). Yet these ideas are discussed without established relation with sculptural or pictorial art. E. M. Forster's statements about character in *Aspects of the Novel* likewise focus on a sculptural conception: "We may divide characters into flat and round. Flat characters were called 'humorous' in the seventeenth century, and are sometimes called types, and sometimes caricatures. In their purest form, they are constructed round a single idea or quality." Forster, after analyzing Dickens's characters, praises their opposite in the method of Jane Austen: "She is a miniaturist, but never two-dimensional. All her characters are round, or capable of rotundity. . . . All the Jane Austen characters are ready for an extended life." [26] Between Forster's declaration and Harvey's explications the basic confusion appears, the failure to grasp the implication of the origin of the terms *flat, round, extended, perspective, viewpoint,* and *depth.*

What is needed is an explanation of this language, the terminology proper to sculptural art. Harvey errs in declaring that a character must not be aware of his function, but even more strangely, he says that the "reader must not be too conscious of the formal patterns." His standard would thus exclude several masterpieces of the twentieth century, such as *The Counterfeiters,* or works such as *Frankenstein,* and all first-person narratives, in which the writer-protagonist-narrator is always conscious of his function. Forster's reference to the "extended" life of Jane Austen's characters can invoke only sculpture, which by its volume does "extend." Writings on the novel, for example by D. H. Lawrence, cannot avoid the language of sculpture. Lawrence begins a treatise on the novel by invoking the volume, the roundedness of Cézanne's apples; there is an unavoidable conflict between characterization and the extension required for interpretation unless one acknowledges sculptural volume. In *Dead Souls*, Gogol declares that his connection of characterization to sculpture comes from nature itself, not only from art.

In short, it was all beautiful, as neither nature nor art could contrive, but as only happens when they unite together, when nature's chisel puts its final touch to the often unintelligently heaped up labour of man, relieves the heavy masses, destroys the all too crudely palpable symmetry and the clumsily contrived gaps through which the unconcealed plan reveals itself so nakedly, and imparts a wonderful warmth to everything that has been created by the cold and carefully measured neatness and accuracy of human reason.

Faulkner declares of Joe Christmas in *Light in August*: "Save for the rise and fall of the stick and the groaning respirations of the animal, they might have been an equestrian statue strayed from its pedestal."[27]

There are three tensions which may account for the operation of sculptural secondary illusion on characterization. These are the tensions between inner and outer, subsuming the issue of point of view and volume; between relief and statue; and between carving and modeling. All three have been apparent to novelists. Flaubert, replying to Sainte-Beuve's review of *Salammbô*, first defended the historical accuracy of his portrait of the Hannibalic wars and the formal location of scenes in the novel, and then summarized the faults of the work, pointing out: "The pedestal is too large for the statue. Now as 'too much' is never a transgression, but 'not enough' is, one hundred pages more would have been needed, relating to Salammbô alone." These are arresting sentences, particularly when one considers they were echoed by Conrad in *Lord Jim* about his protagonist: "He was like a figure set up on a pedestal, to represent in his persistent youth the power, and perhaps the virtues, of races that never grow old." Later Marlow adds: "I don't know why he should always have appeared to me symbolic." The reason in retrospect is clear: Marlow is a novelist looking at his characterization, unable to avoid the secondary illusion. What Flaubert suggested is amply fulfilled by Conrad.[28]

The opposition of inner and outer is of course the operative heart of sculptural volume. A statue in effect involves two spaces, one which it occupies and one with which it is coextensive. In two important passages from *Dead Souls*, Gogol indicates that the sculptural ideal is based as much on nature as on art. Chichikov realizes, when looking at Sobakevich, that the man's face is one of "many faces in the world over the finish of which nature has taken no great pains, has used no fine tools, such as files, gimlets, and the like. . . . The eyes gouged out with a great drill, and without smoothing it, nature thrusts it *into the world* saying: 'It will do'" (italics added). One's figures originate in the outside world. In *Moby Dick*, Dagoo declares: "Who's afraid of black's afraid of me! I'm quarried out of it!" This dichotomy of inner and outer is an ethical as well as an aesthetic relation, as for instance in Kate Chopin's *The Awakening*, when Edna Pontellier realizes that "at a very early period she had apprehended instinctively the dual life—the outward existence which conforms, the inward life which questions." The problem of the "absorption" of outward existence by inward life demonstrates that the problem of this duality is common to both a character and his characterization. George Eliot states in *Middlemarch:* "There is no creature whose inward being is so strong that it is not greatly determined by what lies outside it." The ethical concept of interrelatedness is likewise a formal method of characterization by sculptural secondary illusion, or, as Eliot declared in *The Mill on the Floss:* "The tragedy of our lives is not created entirely from within."[29]

French works, for example André Gide's *Counterfeiters*, have enhanced one's awareness of the importance of sculptural character, particularly coextensive volume, to the novel. In the chapter "Edouard Explains His Theory of the Novel," Gide states that the entire problem of characterization rests in "how to express the general by the particular—how to make the particular express the general," and the solution becomes clear a few moments later. "To arrive at this effect . . . I invent the character of a novelist, whom I make my *central figure;* and the subject of the book, if you must have one, is just that very struggle between what reality offers him and what he himself desires to make of it." Gide declares that the underlying subject of his book is "the rivalry between the real world and representation of it which we make to ourselves." This "rivalry" is sculptural. In the *Journal* to his novel, Gide clarifies this fact. "The poor novelist constructs his characters; he controls them and makes them speak. The true novelist listens to them and watches them function; he eavesdrops on them even before he knows them." In other words, he encounters them by their coextensive volume, by their ability to permit him access rather than he them.[30] The principle of coextensive volume, therefore, validates such encounters between creator and character as that between Tolstoy and Anna Karenina, who permitted him access to herself.

The work of D. H. Lawrence is central to the concept of sculptural coextensive volume, particularly in its concern with "equilibrium" and "otherness." Recognized only as a novelist, Lawrence was nevertheless a painter in watercolor and oil for twenty-five years (roughly 1903–28) and a critic of the artistic doctrines and movements of his time, especially those of futurism, significant form, and postimpressionism. During the production of his novels, therefore, Lawrence maintained a continuing interest in art, both as theoretician and practitioner. The implications of this parallel concern with spatial art in the greatest of the novels, *Women in Love* (1920), and to a lesser extent in its important predecessor, *The Rainbow* (1915), are extensive. Even in the early *Sons and Lovers* (1913), Lawrence makes Paul Morel, his autobiographic protagonist, a painter, not a novelist.

Lawrence's art criticism established principles by which he evaluated his own painting. In "Introduction to These Paintings" (1929), he began by indicting the Anglo-Saxon sensibility as so fearful of the physical that its deadened intuition permitted at best only a "cerebral excitation" for art. It was only with Cézanne, Lawrence claimed, that the bloodless trend in painting was reversed, for contrary to the "purely optical" effects of the Impressionists, Cézanne resurrected the idea "that matter *actually* exists." "Cézanne's apple is a great deal, more than Plato's Idea," Lawrence continued, for it generated a movement toward physicality and wholeness which even the "tombstone" doctrine of significant form (Roger Fry's and Clive Bell's reversions to cerebrality) could not overwhelm. In the most important paragraph in the essay, Lawrence wrote:

For the intuitive apperception of the apple is so *tangibly* aware of the apple that it is aware of it *all around,* not only just of the front. The eye sees only fronts, and the mind, on the whole, is satisfied with fronts. But intuition needs all-roundedness, and instinct needs insideness. The true imagination is for ever curving round to the other side.

Artistic perception for Lawrence rests on this "wholeness of being" of the apple.[31]

This wholeness is for Lawrence likewise the aim of the novel. In "Morality and the Novel," he begins by discussing Van Gogh; in both his criticism and his letters he characteristically thinks of the novel in spatial terms. Van Gogh's sunflower exists "only in the much-debated fourth dimension. In dimensional space it has no existence."

It is a revelation of the perfected relation, at a certain moment, between a man and a sunflower. It is neither man-in-the-mirror nor flower-in-the-mirror, neither is it above or below or across anything. It is in between everything, in the fourth dimension.

And this perfected relation between man and his circumambient universe is life itself, for mankind. It has the fourth-dimensional quality of eternity and perfection. Yet it is momentaneous.

That which exists in the non-dimensional space of pure relationship is deathless, lifeless, and eternal. That is, it gives us the *feeling* of being beyond life or death.

All great art is concerned with this timeless moment between man and his universe. "Morality is . . . that delicate, for ever trembling and changing balance between me and my circumambient universe, which precedes and accompanies true relatedness." His belief that "the novel most of all demands the trembling and oscillating of the balance" is crucial. It is the novel that seeks to fulfill the spatial property of balance, but with a wholeness that is its own, for "only in the novel are *all* things given full play," as he claims in "Why the Novel Matters." In Lawrence's criticism about fiction, the originating idea is always a spatial concept. Ideal creation in the novel welds wholeness to the equilibrium of man and his surrounding universe. In chapter nine of *Lady Chatterley's Lover* (1928), Lawrence reiterated this theory with the inevitable metaphor: "The novel . . . can reveal the most secret places of life . . . where the tide of sensitive awareness needs to ebb and flow."[32]

Lawrence's correspondence about the genesis of *The Rainbow* and *Women in Love* is startling. They were to have been one novel, a fact interesting in itself, but their clearly experimental nature is much more significant. In 1913, Lawrence wrote to Edward Garnett: "It is *very* different from *Sons and Lovers:* written in another language almost." "Another language"? In less than a year, Lawrence had found its nature. He told Garnett that "something of what I am after" was to be found in the theories of the Futurist Marinetti. "That which is physic—non-human, in humanity, is more interesting to me than the old-fashioned human element." He emphasized that his concern was with the "physiology of matter." "You musn't look in my novel for the old stable *ego* of the character."[33]

Three days before, Lawrence had written to A. W. McLeod, discussing at greater length the Futurist experiment and its connection with his two novels. He admired the Futurist destruction and purging of old forms. Filippo Marinetti, in the *Futurist Manifesto* (1909), decreed, "Exalt the aggressive gesture," and spoke of the "fervor of the primordial elements." There was "no more beauty except in struggle." In his letter, however, Lawrence dissociated himself from the methods, not the aims, of the Futurists, for he felt they would "progress down the purely male or intellectual or scientific line."

They will even use their intuition for intellectual and scientific purpose. The one thing about their art is that it *isn't* art, but ultra scientific attempts to make diagrams of certain physic or mental states. It is ultra-ultra intellectual.

Their failure, as Lawrence saw it, rested in the abstract, nonphysical quality of their perception. It is crucial that the formative stages of *The Rainbow* and *Women in Love* were simultaneous with Lawrence's attention to painting and to art criticism. [34]

The Futurists were preoccupied, to return to Lawrence's phrase, with the equilibrium "between man and his circumambient universe," which is "life itself." This conception of characterization is eminently sculptural in its concern with a figure and its surrounding location. Lawrence's decision to approach characterization in this fashion is the major new dimension of these novels, and he owes much of it to Futurist theory. Futurist principles—to express a "plastic dynamism, the absolute vitality of matter" (Severini), to "open up the figure or shape and fill it full of the environment in which it has its being" (Boccioni), "the more we get inside the object, the less it closes in on itself" (Bazaine)—stirred Lawrence during the writing of *The Rainbow* and *Women in Love*. [35] As he was to say in *Lady Chatterley's Lover*, the novel had to "reveal the most secret places of life," and "plastic dynamism" would be the perfect method to accomplish this aim. In the temporal art of the novel, therefore, he conceived a spatial method of sculptural characterization. The volume of sculpture, with its unique power to be coextensive, not only to occupy its own space but also to incorporate into itself the "circumambient universe," was a great force for him.

Lawrence devotes so much attention to spatial art forms in *The Rainbow* that his use of the medium as a method in the novel needs little delineation. The marsh is enclosed like a picture; natural description veers into impressionism in passages such as that describing Tom Brangwen's return from proposing to Lydia Lensky or that which occurs just before his son's birth. "The evening arrived later very beautiful, with a rosy flush hovering above the sunset, and passing away into violet and lavender, with turquoise green north and south in the sky, and in the east, a great, yellow moon hanging heavy and radiant." [36] But whatever pictorial effects occur in *The Rainbow*, it is to sculpture that the book owes its power. The very introduction of Will Brangwen, Anna Lensky's husband and the father of Ursula and Gudrun of *Women in Love*, is marked by the interest he takes in sculpture and architecture. He has a strong interest in ecclesiastical architecture. "The influence of Ruskin had stimulated him to a pleasure in the medieval forms," but beyond this is a lifelong interest in sculpting, first as a hobby and later as a profession. It is important that he moves from early carving, of figures like the phoenix and Eve, to later modeling, like the head of Ursula.

But the sculptor is himself sculpted, and here the motif of sculpture reveals the heart of two things—Lawrence's conception of the relationship between man and woman, and his parallel conception of characterization itself. The formal analogy becomes an ethical idea. "He let her do as she liked with him, and shone with strange pleasure. She was to dispose of him as she would. He was translated with gladness to be in her hands." "In her hands": we sculpt each other. Women, furthermore, have the ability to sculpt themselves, as the chapter "Anna Victrix" reveals. This woman, in bearing Ursula, has made herself into the perfect Pygmalion, conceiving and bringing to actuality a human being. She is therefore given the name of a statue in her moment of triumph. At the end of *The Rainbow*, Ursula can think of her lover Skrebensky as someone "she had created . . . for the time being."

Architecture also plays an important part in *The Rainbow*, for it represents the realm of the ideal, timeless equilibrium that Lawrence advocated in his theoretic treatises. Will reflects about Lincoln Cathedral:

Here the stone leapt up from the plain of earth . . . away from the horizontal earth, through . . . the whole range of desire, through the swerving, the declination, ah, to the ecstasy, the touch, to the meeting at the consummation, the meeting, the clasp, the close embrace, the neutrality, the perfect, swooning consummation, the timeless ecstasy. There his soul remained, at the apex of the arch, clinched in the timeless ecstasy, consummated. And there was . . . only this, this timeless consummation . . . the apex of the arch.

But it is not everything, as Will recognizes when he hears a bird outside the cathedral. Will is flawed, for "in spirit, he was uncreated." Lawrence uses the tight integration of the cathedral plan as a principle of construction in *The Rainbow*, with its carefully strategic chapters alternating between old and new, eclipsing generations within them, and then expanding during the final half with the chronicle of Ursula's first love affairs. But as Lawrence himself came to recognize, the element of Will's "uncreated spirit" is in the book; the theory of chapter itself is not formed, leading finally to a lack of equilibrium that reflects the uncertainty of a novel which stops rather than concludes. However, the achievement of *The Rainbow* vis-à-vis *Women in Love* is that it establishes two demands for the next text: to realize the implications of a sculptural ethical and aesthetic conception of character and to embody this conception in an architecture of chapters.

F. R. Leavis has declared: "The conception of art expressed by Loerke doesn't stand by itself, unrelated; it has its part in the comprehensive examination of the nature and function of art that the reader, once alerted, will find to have been performed in the course of *Women in Love*." In *Women in Love* one is concerned not only with the art in the novel but the art of the novel. In *The Rainbow* Lawrence had already anticipated the women in the later work. Gudrun, a child of fancies and

irresponsibility, draws indifferently but is a fine sculptress of little ani-
mals. Ursula, aware that art has a snob appeal, is critical of exclusive
theoreticism in the arts, its tendency to enshrine what is not life. These
attitudes are maintained in *Women in Love*, proof that the two novels are
not so disconnected as the tradition of Lawrence scholarship has made
them appear. [37]

All the characters in *Women in Love* react to space; in fact, in no other
novel are the protagonists so conscious of distance, polarity, and bound-
aries. Gudrun affects Ursula by the "enclosure" of her presence at the
novel's beginning. Gudrun herself always has a tendency to turn actual
people into art objects. Observing the Crich wedding, "She saw each one
as a complete figure, like a character in a book, or a subject in a picture, or
a marionette in a theatre, a finished creation." But this process is also
personal, for one does "create oneself" inevitably, whether by one's own
laws or by the world's. From the beginning Gudrun is conscious of
Gerald's limiting effect on her, which drives her to a sense of her own
negation. Gerald, a true Futurist creature of motion, has a fear of boundedness which he tries to counteract by obsession with centre and point.
Like Gudrun (and this is a characteristic that attracts them to each other),
he regards people as art works. Halliday, for example, is like Christ in a
pietà. In the chapter "Death and Love," Gudrun, overwhelmed by
Gerald's "beauty," embraces him, thinking: "Enough now—enough for the
time being. There were all the after days when her hands, like birds,
could feed upon the fields of his mystical *plastic form*" (italics added). [38]

But she is not the first to react in this manner to Gerald. In "Gladiator-
ial," Birkin contemplates Gerald's naked body and remarks: "Yes. You
have a northern kind of beauty, like light refracted from snow—and a
beautiful, plastic form." This sculpturesque notion of character is reinforced by the canceled prologue to *Women in Love*, in which Birkin
thinks: "Why was a man's beauty . . . so vivid and intoxicating a thing to
him . . . ? He thought women beautiful purely because of their expression.
But it was plastic form that fascinated him in men, the contour and
movement of the flesh itself." [39] While both Gudrun and Gerald are concerned with boundedness, space for Birkin and Ursula emphasizes itself
as distance. Birkin feels that between men and women this distance is
manifested as "otherness."

But I, myself, who am myself, what have I to do with equality with any other man
or woman? In the spirit, I am as separate as one star is from another, as different in
quality and quantity. Establish a state on *that*. One man isn't any better than
another, not because they are equal, but because they are intrinsically *other*, that
there is no term of comparison.

Birkin, "normally distant," tells Ursula: "What I want is a strange conjunction with you . . . not meeting and mingling . . . but an equilibrium, a pure balance of two single beings." This is to say that if the one is the "man" of Lawrence's conception, the other person is "the circumambient universe." The ideal, quite obviously, is that of a statue and its surroundings, that it remains itself while incorporating, without negating, the "circumambient universe" by its coextensive volume. This ethical posture is of the essence of sculpture: to stand alone, but to dwell with, fulfillment without negation. "And he wanted to be single in himself, the woman single in herself." The concept of polarized distance in Lawrence, therefore, is sculptural, the achievement of union without loss of individuation.

But how could he embody this sculptural ethic into a novel? This was the challenge for Lawrence in *Women in Love*. The crucial concept of coextensive volume, by which Birkin's "conjunction" may really occur in sculpture, had to be achieved through novelistic methods. Lawrence's "Making Pictures," in which he discusses his own career as an artist, suggests something about his approach to the problem. One day Maria Huxley left four canvases at the house near Florence. "I sat on the floor with the canvas propped against a chair—and with my house-paint brushes and colours in little casseroles, I disappeared into that canvas." What strikes one immediately is that "disappearing" is not at all a painterly reaction, but a sculptural one. By coextensive volume a statue may produce such an effect, but a painting, bounded and lacking volume, cannot. No one would deny, as Harry Moore notes, the painterly nature of Lawrence's prose, and Lawrence himself admits it. "All my life, I have from time to time gone back to paint, because it gave me a form of delight that words can never give." But the result of this conflict of reactions, painterly and sculptural, needs no other verification than Lawrence's own paintings. In every one in which bodies appear, as in *Resurrection, Flight back into Paradise, Spring, Renascence of Men,* or *Contadini,* the figures are elementarily distorted. The reason is clear: they are statues inhabiting canvases, their massiveness poorly executed for their space, their ponderous stasis (abhorred by Birkin in *Women in Love*) suggesting not previous movement, but no movement at all. They are figures longing to break their painterly two-dimensionality to acquire the coextensive volume of three-dimensional sculpture but failing, and failing because of Lawrence himself. One's knowledge that Lawrence never worked from a nude live model suggests but does not explore the problem.

Lawrence left a clue to the flaw when he declared: "I decided I couldn't paint. Perhaps I can't. But I verily believe I can make pictures, which is to me all that matters in this respect. The art of painting consists in making pictures." Surely this is not so. Lawrence, in his great appreciation of Cézanne, failed to recognize that the sense of volume in Cézanne is organic, not visual. The attempt to show all rarely succeeds; it in fact always produces its opposite, incompleteness, and, worse yet, fragmentation. One does not quarrel with Lawrence's statement, again sculpturesque, that "intuition needs all-roundedness" in "Introduction to His Paintings."[40] It is strange, however, that the two vehicles of "resolution" in *Women in Love*, Ursula and Birkin, present the best indictment of Lawrence's methodology. In *The Rainbow*, Ursula Brangwen watches Skrebensky bathe:

His body was beautiful, his movements intent and quick, she admired him and she appreciated him without reserve. He seemed completed now. He aroused no fruitful fecundity in her. He seemed added up, finished. *She knew him all round, not on any side did he lead into the unknown.* Poignant, almost passionate appreciation she felt for him, but none of the dreadful wonder, none of the rich fear, the connection with the unknown, or the reverence of love [italics added].

The crux of the problem is that this very knowledge in the round is never achieved by its own self, by roundedness. One must have distance for the sculptural coextension to operate, even to achieve the longed-for equilibrium advocated by both Lawrence and Birkin. In revealing to the reader the most "secret places," the great aim of the novel as stated in *Lady Chatterley*, Lawrence forgot that the reader also needs the distance, just as do the men and women of Birkin's ideal "conjunction." The reader must be able to experience this volume as well as the characters. Lawrence failed the reader; he supplied the "man" but not the distance implied by "circumambient universe." What Ursula thinks of Skrebensky one thinks of Lawrence's characters. One knows them all round, but all round from the beginning; "not on any side" do they "lead into the unknown." This exposure is only nakedness, primitiveness, and not completeness, not roundness.

In other words, these figures are not the sculptural ideal. They become instead figures in *tableaux vivants*, figures of throbbing high relief crying to gain total volume but restricted by their author. "What a snare and a delusion, this beauty of static things. . . . [It is] an intolerable confinement," Birkin thinks of Breadalby. A statue may be three-dimensional, but it is not completely seen from any one angle. Rather, it is felt to be complete by its volume. The demand for succession in the temporal art form of the novel compels recognition that the encounter with the "circumambient universe" must be continuous. Lawrence did not by such total exposure give us the distance for complete exposure. Paul de Man has observed: "The writer remains so closely involved with action that he can never free himself of the temptation to destroy whatever stands between him and his deed, especially *the temporal distance that makes him dependent on an earlier past"* (italics added). [41]

Throughout *Women in Love,* Lawrence's characters cry to be "beyond" it. As Susanne Langer says:

Great sculpture, no matter how intimately relating to a building, is not an architectural element. The created place . . . must give it room. . . . The two art forms are, in fact, each other's exact complements: the one, an illusion of kinetic volume, symbolizing the Self, or center of life—the other, an illusion of ethnic domain, or the environment created by Selfhood. Each articulates one half of the life-symbol directly and the other by implication. . . . In highly ideal creations sculpture and architecture often have to supplement each other.

Her words echo Lawrence's own categories of "man" and "circumambient universe." The architectural element of *Women in Love* has not "given room" to these creations. Lawrence thwarts the longing for beyond by removing time as a constructive element of the chapters in *Women in Love,* in total contrast to his method in *The Rainbow.* The chapters themselves are isolated units, paralleling rather than complementing the persons in the novel. They are, to use Mark Schorer's word, "spectacular," but with all its literal implication—they are spectacles, living pictures. [42]

Unlike Birkin, Lawrence did not realize that "you have to be like Rodin, Michael Angelo, and leave a piece of raw rock unfinished to your figure. You must leave your surroundings sketchy, unfinished, so that you are never contained, never confined, never dominated from the outside." It is a devastating moment in *Women in Love* when Birkin utters these words. They are the writing on the wall Lawrence aesthetically erected around his longed-for nondimensional space. His aim, "almost another language," of a conjunction of art and literature was decisive for fiction, and that is his triumph. But it is Birkin's, as in the moment he crashed out at Breadalby, that he got "beyond" to tell the tale.

Elizabeth Bowen's idea that it is impossible to believe Elizabeth Bennet is not in the "room" of *Pride and Prejudice* leads to another important concept, the idea of point of view and its relationship to volume. It is clear that much of what has been attributed to point is in reality a product of the coextensive volume existing between reader and character. W. J. Harvey discusses the balancing of the self and the world as a fundamental "polarity," without recognizing that this has nothing to do with point and everything to do with volume. His discussion of Sartre's *pour-soi* ("self") and *en-soi* ("other"), which rests on the problem of volume rather than point, is inadequate without comprehension of volume. Thus he is compelled to speak of "variety of perspectives," "variety of viewpoints," or even *"angle* of mimesis." [43]

Sartre's *Nausea* confirms the importance of volume over point: "The

Nausea is not inside me: I feel it *out there* in the wall, in the suspenders, everywhere around me. It makes itself one with the café, I am the one who is within *it.*" Roquentin's utterance points clearly to "around," to being "within," and certainly not to any "angle." Gide in the *Journal* quotes Albert Thibaudet at the suggestion of Martin du Gard: "The authentic novelist creates his characters according to the infinite directions of his possible life; the false novelist creates them from the single line of his real life. The genius of the novel makes the possible come to life: it does not revive the real."[44] Harvey focuses on what Thibaudet cites as the "false" method of the "single line," for which one may almost read single point of view, single mimetic "angle." Volume alone permits the option of "infinite directions."

Point of view implies volume, if for no other reason than that the point itself occupies and is surrounded by space. Following James's enunciation of the value of the centre, or filtering intelligence, Percy Lubbock in *The Craft of Fiction* (1921) declared point of view to be the basic structural problem of the novel, elevating the third person limited to the highest status amid the hierarchy of possible points. However, it is Wayne Booth's *Rhetoric of Fiction* (1961) that remains the most important text on point. His book analyzes point according to such criteria as reliability (collaboration or deception), degree of knowledge, agency, self-consciousness, power of observation, effacement or intrusion, neutrality, dispassion, or impartiality. The central element of volume appears in Booth's discussion of the impossibility of the novel attaining to "pure literature," its inability to be totally divorced from the (implied or mirrored) outside world. Point must have volume to exist at all, whether in first person observer, first person protagonist, third person limited, third person omniscient, or the ubiquitous implied author, an elusive figure.

"Sculpture" includes two obvious forms, "relief" and "statue." Relief is sculpture which is "not freestanding," with varying depths of projection, such as *alto-relievo,* or high relief, through *mezzo-relievo* to *basso-relievo.* The problem of dimensionality in the two forms of relief and sculpture rests on the degree of depth. In *alto-relievo* the figures are so raised that one almost obtains a freestanding conception of the work, which is to say the relief is nearly statuesque. On the other hand, as Kenneth Clark among others has shown, frequently a freestanding statue may exhibit a peculiar frontality, as does the *Apollo of the Tiber,* Donatello's *David,* or Verrocchio's *David.* Bernini provides an interesting example of movement from this relief aspect to rotundity in the sequence of *Aeneas and Anchises, Apollo and Daphne,* and his *David,* the last of which, far from being frontal, reaches out to involve the spectator in a true concrete illustration of sculptural volume. In Bernini's *David,* coextensive volume has become a theme as well as a technique in making its essence its ethic.[45]

The technique of relief in fiction contains an essential element—"relief characters" are inseparable from their backgrounds. There is no finer illustration of this technique than in Hardy's *Return of the Native*. "There the form stood, motionless as the hill beneath. Above the plain rose the hill, above the hill rose the barrow, and above the barrow rose the figure. Above the figure was nothing that could be mapped elsewhere than on a celestial globe." Eustacia Vye is therefore accurately called, in the sixth chapter, "The Figure against the Sky." At the end of the novel Clym has become a silhouette on the heath, occupying the place in relief once inhabited by Eustacia. This is Hardy's first description of Clym and his countenance: "Should there be a classic period to art hereafter, its Phidias may produce such faces." Hardy reiterates the background on which, for all their individualized grandeur, Clym and Eustacia remain relieved. This frontality provides their distinction but also their anonymity; both are set into terrifying relief by the heath. Clym is thus seen by his mother cutting furze, "a mere parasite of the heath."[46]

In an entirely different way, a novelist like Zola also preserves his characters against a background, forcing them into relief rather than statue. An example is shown in the figure of Gervaise in *L'Assommoir*. Although characters in relief may have life and power, it is evident that one tends more to study than to experience such figures. Frequently the focus of direction is extremely controlled; it is not necessarily limited to one view, but nevertheless it is so governed by the presence of the narrator that the character does not have an extended life. In the case of James's Isabel Archer in *The Portrait of a Lady*, where the word "portrait" leads one to relief, this result is intentional. But in Zola's work, although he is much more desirous of our experiencing Gervaise's misery, one encounters only observation. In the opening sentence of the novel, Gervaise is awaiting Lentier in the window; soon Gervaise fades into the background of the crowded street, as she will do in the inferno of the apartment house. This tendency is so strong in Zola that Gervaise's son Étienne Lentier, in the opening of *Germinal*, cannot even see the roadway in the intense darkness. More significantly, neither can we distinguish him from the milieu in which, once again, we will study rather than experience him. The fact that Zola assigns names to the gin mill in *L'Assommoir* or to the mine in *Germinal*, and that they absorb their victims, instantly locates the relative depth of the human figures against these backgrounds.

Whereas Zola and Hardy begin their works with figures etched against the sky, Balzac's method in *Père Goriot* is to move from the *basso-relievo* of the Maison Vauquer, with its figures nearly indistinguishable from the walls: "Her whole person, in short, provides a clue to the boarding-house, just as the boarding-house implies the existence of such a person as she is." The *alto-relievo* of Rastignac's challenge to Paris at the end of the novel inexorably implies his permanent relieved quality. He is, to use Balzac's own classification of the works that make up *The Human Comedy*, one of the "Studies of Morals," with all this category implies. Balzac never permits freestanding persons; never, for example, is one in doubt. The character in relief, however high, provokes great curiosity but never doubt. [47]

"Rotundity," the statuesque, may leave one only as knowledgeable as relief. The statesque character has one distinguishing feature, which is not his potential for change, for many characters of relief have it also, but rather his particular potential to change himself, to be the agent of his own alteration. This quality frequently takes the form of being able to reflect with himself before, not after, a crucial moment. It is seen in Nostromo's awareness before the sinking of the silver, in Pierre Bezukhov awaiting execution, in Mme. de Clèves before the final interview with Nemours, and in Fabrice del Dongo in *The Charterhouse of Parma*:

"Ah! If I reasoned like Conte Mosca," thought Fabrice, "when he assures me that the risks a man runs are always the measure of his rights over his neighbors, I should blow out this servant's brains with a pistol-shot, and, once I was mounted on the thin horse, I should laugh aloud at all the police in the world. As soon as I was safely in Parma, I should . . ."

Similarly, Natasha Rostov reflects in *War and Peace*:

"Is it possible no one will ask me, that I shall not be among the first to dance? Is it possible that not one of all these men will notice me? They do not even seem to see me, or if they do they look as if they were saying, 'Ah, she's not the one I'm after, so it's not worth looking at her!' No, it's impossible," she thought. "They must know how I long to dance, how splendidly I dance, and how they would enjoy dancing with me."

Andrey Bolkonsky comes up, having been asked to do so by his friend. Tolstoy demonstrates, however, that this action was motivated on Andrey's part. After hearing the still unknown Natasha at the window he had thought:

"It is not enough for me to know what I have in me—every one must know it: Pierre, and that young girl who wanted to fly away into the sky, everyone must know me, so that my life may not be lived for myself alone while others live so apart from it, but so that it may be reflected in them all, and they and I may live in harmony!"

This is a character of coextension advocating a coextensive effect on those around him. The sculpturesque character, to cite Stendhal in *The Red and the Black* describing Julien Sorel, is "moved, like a writer of plays, by his own story." The sculptural volume, belonging according to Stendhal to the happy few characters in fiction, appears completely only when the agonist is capable of being moved by his own story. This situation has little to do with point of view, but all to do with volume. When Maria Gostrey remarks to Strether in *The Ambassadors*, "You're complete," she is noting that he is a figure of relief, not of sculpture. The contrast is in the difference between "Yes I will Yes Yes" of Molly in *Ulysses* or "All right, then, I'll *go* to hell" in *Huckleberry Finn* and "It was the devious-cruising Rachel, that in her retracing search after her missing children, only found another orphan" of *Moby Dick*. In Ishmael's case, the relief bears out two things: that he can only be an orphan if the readers cut off from him, and that that is how he wanted it when he said, "Call me Ishmael."[48]

The novelist who models is perhaps best exemplified by Balzac, with his theory of characterization by types. The concept of study frequently influences this notion; a figure is selected because its essence is entire from the beginning. Such characters are frequent in the novels of Balzac, Fielding, and Zola. Valérie is a Laïs, Sophia Western of *Tom Jones* is a "heroine," and Coupeau of *L'Assommoir* is "a drunkard." The novelist who models is indicated by additional rather than refining detail, by a general reliance on the third person omniscient point of view or on Norman Friedman's "multiple selective omniscience." The carved character, comprising most first person narrators and third person centres, is illustrated by another of Stendhal's comments about Julien Sorel: "This is, to my mind, one of the finest traits in his character; a human being capable of putting such constraint on himself may go far, *si fata sinant*."[49]

The key word here of course is "constraint." A simple form of such restraint is offered by Jane Austen in *Pride and Prejudice*, whose opening chapter is a paradigm of the method of carving. The Bennets are presented before their explanation in the final paragraph. A complete explanation of them occurs much later in the novel. "Her father captivated by youth and beauty, and that appearance of good humour, which youth and beauty generally give, had married a woman whose weak understanding and illiberal mind, had very early in their marriage put an end to all real affection for her. Respect, esteem and confidence, had vanished forever."[50] The method of carving is by subtraction. The *donnée* does not so much expand as annihilate itself in the process of "growth": carved characterization moves toward reduction rather than addition. The modeled character will, like the novel, move forward by addition in time; the carved character, on the contrary, exists in opposition to the forward momentum of its medium, assuming "negative direction" in its refinement. The conclusion of *The Charterhouse of Parma* is the essence of this methodology, where the vanishing of Fabrice del Dongo into the

monastery is his ultimate explanation. Stendhal correctly titled the work
from an incident that occupied only the penultimate paragraph of the
novel. Protagonists who accumulate genuine self-knowledge, accomplished by a casting off rather than an accretion, satisfy carving. Heyst in
Victory, Natasha in *War and Peace,* Levin in *Anna Karenina,* Raskolnikov
in *Crime and Punishment,* or Quentin Compson in *Absalom, Absalom!*
verify the reductive nature of the carved character. His completion arises
from his subtraction, his "constraint on himself," as opposed to the addition of the modeled character, constrained by his creator or by others.
Whether characterization is achieved by carving or modeling, however,
the novel requires its architectural spatiality.

As early as 1929, Jurij Tynianov in "On Literary Evolution" used architectural terminology in evaluating the development of the novel.

The evolutionary relationship of function and formal elements is a completely
uninvestigated problem. An example is given above of how the evolution of forms
results in a change of function. There are also many examples of how a form with
an undetermined function creates or defines a new one, and there are also others
in which a function seeks its own form.

The relationship between form and function is not accidental. The variability of
the functions of a given formal element, the rise of some new function of a formal
element, and the attaching of a formal element to a function are all important
problems of literary evolution.

Investigation must go from constructional function to literary function; from
literary function to verbal function. It must clarify the problem of the evolutionary
interaction of functions and forms.

According to Tynianov, a function is the "interrelationship of each element with every other in a literary work and with the whole literary
system as well." There are two types of functions, an "auto-function,"
which is the interrelationship of an element with similar elements in other
works, and a "syn-function," which is the relationship of an element with
a different element in the same work. The interrelationship is the function; the form is the method of interrelationship. This close connection of
literary to architectural theory may be seen in Susanne Langer's definition of architecture as "functional form." For her, as for Tynianov in
literature, form neither follows function nor does function follow form; the
emphasis is on the interrelationship. The domain of architecture is "the
sphere of influence of a function"; architectural space, whether in a building or a novel, is self-contained and yet expressive of the world which
surrounds it. It is "a total environment made visible." Like that of a
building, the architecture of the novel "both excludes and forms the
external world." Langer's words recall Tynianov's "auto-function" and
"syn-function."[51]

The central element of architecture is this relation of exterior to interior. When Proust speaks of the church at Combray in *Swann's Way*, he is of course speaking of his novel.

All these things made of the church for me something entirely different from the rest of the town; a building which occupied, so to speak, four dimensions of space—the name of the fourth being Time—which had sailed the centuries with that old nave, where bay after bay, chapel after chapel, seemed to stretch across and hold down and conquer not merely a few yards of soil, but each successive epoch.

Richard Macksey has observed the extent to which Proust resorted to architectural metaphor to define his role: "I had wanted to give each part of my book the title: Porch, Stained glass of the apse, etc." Benjamin Cremieux defended Proust as a genius in handling "rose-window composition," which led, in the true architectural sense, to the creation of "a dialectic between inside and outside," the quest for an "interior space," as Macksey notes. Gérard Genette has remarked of architecture in "Literature and Space" in *Figures II:* "The art of space, par excellence, architecture, does not speak of space: it would be truer to say that it makes space speak... in itself and... of itself." Michel Butor has noted the presence in Balzac's *Human Comedy* of architecture of a type which results in the reader being himself an architect: "Balzac's *Human Comedy* ... provides the example of a work conceived in distinct blocks which each reader, in fact, approaches in a different order."[52]

The extent to which a novel is an edifice has been particularly well clarified by Butor in "The Book as Object." He notes that the book is a volume by virtue of its superimposed structure, which it reveals in a "simultaneous exposure to our eyes of what our ears can grasp only sequentially," especially as the written word is "permanent" in contrast to the spoken. "The book... is therefore the arrangement of the thread of speech in three-dimensional space according to a double module: length of line and depth of page." It has the spatial asset of making "looking back easy." The page is spatially arranged, including the vertical, horizontal, and oblique. Body type, margins, and edges are also spatial elements. All books when opened are diptychs. In "On the Page," Butor quotes Claudel's observation that pages are like constructive stages in a Japanese garden.[53]

Tzvetan Todorov's "Categories" and Shklovsky's "Construction of the Short Story and of the Novel" contain considerable architectural material. Shklovsky discusses two central methods of constructing a literary work: *en boucle* ("in a shield," "circular") and *en paliers* ("in stages"). These strategies include three particular methods: repetition by superposition, parallelism (different characters, similar situations or same character, different situations), and contradiction. Furthermore, to Shklovsky the locations of these devices in the text serve important functions. They may produce *ralentissement* ("slowing") of the narrative; *débats par contes* (thematic opposition by stories), *emboitage* ("joining") by focus on a single character, as in *Gil Blas*, or *enfilage* ("linking"). *Enfilage*, Shklovsky argues, is of two types; first, where the action and the agent are not linked, as when the protagonist undergoes adventures he did not seek; and second, where the action and the agent are linked, as when Lucius's curiosity leads to the exploits of *The Golden Ass*. In "The Categories," Todorov isolates three methods of repetition of actions in the narratives themselves: antithesis (as in the alternating letters of *Dangerous Liaisons*); gradation (development by increment); and parallelism. There are three methods of constructing the narrative: *enchainement* (the juxtaposition of different stories); *enchâssement* (the enclosure of one story within another); and *alternance* (going back and forth between stories), as in *Bleak House* or *The Old Wives' Tale*.[54]

The similarity of these ideas to the principles of architecture is obvious. Repetition, parallelism, *enchâssement, ralentissement, encadrement,* gradation, and antithesis are properly speaking among the oldest of architectural principles. Of particular significance are the concepts of unity, scale, rhythm, proportion, and sequence. Unity, for example, emphasizes not merely the integrity of the structure itself but the importance of uniting with the observer's awareness. Of all the arts, architecture most takes into account the observer, the necessity of confronting him with the structure's wholeness. Scale facilitates "the orientation of the observer with regard to the structure." As a temporal element of architecture, rhythm is especially conceived as repetition (including parallelism), as for example of columns, or "the repetition of elements whose *differences* progress uniformly."[55] Rhythm may involve a major rhythm, as of columns, with a secondary rhythm of windows, statues, or panels, with balances resulting from symmetry and asymmetry. Since rhythm is concerned with distances between elements, the "speed" of a building is rhythmic.

On the other hand, proportion, "the interplay of principal subordinating parts," is concerned with the composite result of function, materials, scale of object, and time, while sequence deals with the control of passage, toward, into, through, and from, "not merely distance, nor even measured time, but how long each event seemed to take." Sequence is especially concerned with progression and climax. The distinction between "composition," the controlled pattern to a climax, and "construction," the use of materials leading to the climax, is close to the Formalist distinction between story and plot, or method of narration. As Boris Eichenbaum expresses it in "The Theory of the Formal Method," plot is a "compositional element rather than a thematic concept."[56]

Architectural methods in the novel are well summarized by Gérard Genette in "Literature and Space" in *Figures II*. The first is "a spatiality . . . of language itself . . . where each element is qualified by the place which it occupies in a total picture and by the vertical and horizontal relations which it maintains with the related and adjoining elements." The location of words in a sentence becomes "a mode of being of language that must perforce be called spatial." The second spatiality is clearly demonstrated in a written text. "The manifest spatiality of writing can be taken as a symbol of the profound spatiality of language. At the very least, for us who live in a civilization where literature is identified with the written work, the spatial mode of its existence cannot be considered accidental or negligible."[57]

As does Michel Butor, Genette observes that since Mallarmé we have "rediscovered the visual resources of writing and of page layout and the existence of the *book as a kind of total object*." This "change of perspective" has increased our awareness "of the spatiality of writing, of the atemporal and reversible ordering of signs, words, phrases, of the discourse, in the simultaneity of what one calls a text." Proust's technique of the "telescope" called attention

to relationships . . . which are established between episodes very much separated in the temporal continuity of linear reading (but peculiarly close, let us note, in the written space, in the paginal depth of the volume), and which require for consideration a type of simultaneous perception of the total unity of the work, a unity which does not reside only in horizontal relationships of proximity and succession but also in those relationships called vertical, or transverse, of those effects of expectation, recollection, response, symmetry, perspective, in the name of which Proust compared his own work to a cathedral.

A third form of spatiality, Genette argues, exists in the word itself as a sign. The relation of the *signifiant* ("literal word") to the *signifié* ("extended meaning") in the sign is for him a "simultaneity [which] establishes style as semantic spatiality of the literary discourse." This third form of spatial architecture, of the figure, is of course marked by the difference between what Todorov called the *sens* and the *interprétation*. The *sens* "of an element of the work is its potential to enter in correlation with other elements of this work and with the entire work"; *interprétation*, on the other hand, depends on the historical or ideological orientation of the critic.[58]

The scriptive, what concerns the book as a written object, involves the larger units of its construction. There are two, sometimes three, large elements—those of chapter, and book or volume, which have the function of arranging the narrative itself. The chapter is the most important architectural unit for the novel, since it is the method by which the functions of antithesis, gradation, and parallelism are expressed. These functions, of course, to return to Tynianov's distinction, occur both as auto-functions and as their own syn-function within a work. In many novels the book or volume may be the major rhythm, with the chapter the secondary. Although he was not the first to speculate about the function of the chapter, James noted, in the preface to *Roderick Hudson,* the necessity of design in fiction: "Really universally, relations stop nowhere, and the exquisite problem of the artist is eternally but *to draw, by a geometry of his own,* the circle within which they shall happily appear to do so" (italics added). "To draw, by a geometry of his own, the circle," is as clear a statement as one could wish of the architectural nature of the chapter. In addtion to this rhythm of the chapter, Philip Stevick has noted in "The Theory of Fictional Chapters" how "one responds to the form of a novel by responding to its chapter." This idea corresponds to that of architectural scale, which Henry Hope Reed has gone so far as to define as "the relation of the parts of a building to the human figure," permitting man "to measure a building, to find a place to rest, and to attain the security of constant reference." Stevick tends to interpret chapter units as methods of working with the human desire to make patterns, and he claims there are four methods of handling data in a chapter for its enclosure: (1) close the data in an expected way; (2) close the data in an unexpected way; (3) provide data which suggest but do not effect their enclosure; (4) provide data "which suggest an ambiguity of enclosures." However, Stevick's emphasis on enclosure obscures the rhythmic progressive function of the chapter.[59]

Fielding, in a statement about the chapter in *Joseph Andrews,* notes: "Those little spaces between our chapters may be looked upon as an inn or resting-place. . . . I would not advise [the reader] to travel through these pages too fast." His remark suggests that the chapter is more than simply a halting place; it recalls Reed's statement of function, "to find a place to rest." Assuming that Fielding is speaking without great irony, the phrase "travel through" supports the view that the function of the chapter is architectural, not only in providing a halting place but also in controlling the sequence of passage through the novel. And, as Shklovsky noted, a chapter in *Joseph Andrews* such as "to divert the reader" is clearly a slowing device (*ralentissement*), a function of rhythm. One may further see an indication of scale here, when Fielding declares that stating the contents of a forthcoming chapter alerts the reader to pass it by if he wishes or enter it. That is, he may adjust its scale to accommodate, in Reed's words, "the parts of a building to the human figure."[60]

The functions of rhythm, scale, and sequence may be seen by examining some examples of chapter architecture. In *enchainement,* where two chapters of the *discours* serve the function of juxtaposition, one finds a simple architectural rhythm. In *Emma,* for example, volume one, chapter fifteen concludes with the heroine in turmoil after an unexpected proposal; chapter sixteen opens: "The hair was curled, and the maid sent away, and Emma sat down to think and be miserable.—It was a wretched business indeed!" But this juxtaposition is also for gradation in the *histoire:* the protagonist sits to ruminate over the failure of her plans and her "own misjudgment." "How she could have been so deceived!" The situation extends beyond Stevick's assertion that here is the "beginning. . . a new episode"; there is a continuity of "edifice" providing, in Todorov's terms, a "primary rhythm" of the act, the secondary rhythm of the *rejet* of the act. [61]

Pure juxtaposition (*enchainement*) is found in chapters fifteen and sixteen of *Adam Bede.* In chapter fifteen, "The Two Bed-Chambers," Eliot strives for simultaneity in the presentation of Hetty Sorel and Dinah Morris. Her reference to mirrors suggests the diptych. The next chapter, appropriately titled "Links," is about Arthur and Adam, the men most involved in the fates of the two women. The literal diptych presented by these two chapters is suitably the end of the first book of the novel, because it mirrors "book" itself. Within each chapter we have clear antitheses of Hetty-Dinah and Arthur-Adam. The technique of alternating rhythm (*alternance*) functions in the structure of *War and Peace.* In the first part, one advances from the salon reception (chapters one through five) to Pierre visiting Prince Andrey to the Rostovs' home (chapters ten through fifteen). The movement is from the public to the private, from talk of war to a name-day celebration in peace, and so forth. The technique used by Dickens in *Bleak House,* of movement from an omniscient to a first person narrator, between the narrator and Esther Sommerson, pursues the functions of both parallelism (*enchainement*) and antithesis, (*alternance*) which Virginia Woolf later uses in *Mrs. Dalloway* and Faulkner in *As I Lay Dying* or, particularly, *The Wild Palms.*

The speed of the gradation of the development of character is also of architectural significance. In using the alternating method in *War and Peace,* or the shift between the stories of Anna and Levin in *Anna Karenina,* Tolstoy not only exploits parallelism and antithesis, but also manages to regulate the speed of revelation about the characters. Later in the novel's development, as in *Lord Jim* or *Victory, enchâssement,* in which one narrator's account is embedded in that of another, establishes a rhythm by which the *"differences progress uniformly."* It is especially through the narrative by *enchâssement* that Conrad can write about "how we know," how we learn information at all. Faulkner, in *The Sound and the Fury* or *Absalom, Absalom!,* is extremely careful to control the speed of the narration, which he does in *The Sound and the Fury* by *enchainement* and in *Absalom, Absalom!* by *encadrement.* [62]

A particularly important form of this speed involves sequence in the novel—how we enter, pass through, and exit—especially in connection with the problem of climax. In "The Construction of the Short Story and of the Novel," Victor Shklovsky examined the achieved and the illusory ending. In the former, he contended, we have both action and reaction; in the illusory, as in the tales of Maupassant, we have only the action with the other term missing (*forme négative* or *désinence zéro*). The extreme form of *désinence zéro*, he allows, is the conclusion of *The Sentimental Education*, where the final episode is an action never accomplished at all, and indeed where even the stage of action is not achieved. In "On the Theory of Prose," Eichenbaum distinguished the *nouvelle* from the *roman* by the fact that in the former the conclusion is the culmination of the narrative, while in the latter, which often contains an epilogue, the culmination is not the conclusion. Examples of such construction in the novel include the final book of *Anna Karenina* or *The Sentimental Education*, Charles's discovery of Emma's letters in *Madame Bovary*, and the sixth book of *The Return of the Native*. The problems of progression and climax, the province of sequence, are clearly evident. An author must control the reader's progress by the correct rhythm of revelation in order to make the conclusion seem inevitable, but at the same time he must never make the culmination the completion of the novel. From this perspective, one can see that the rapid conclusions of such novels as *Rob Roy* or *Emma* or *Jane Eyre* are not failures, but rather the results of the architectural norm of the *roman*. The individual chapters, as Shklovsky noted of *Little Dorrit*, both "retard the plot" and "undergo pressure from the plot," to achieve effects of slowing or acceleration, the control of sequence, the speed of "passage through." The speed of the three sections of *To the Lighthouse* is intriguing; the longest time is compressed into the short central section, "Time Passes." This passage of time, furthermore, is completely explained in terms of the architecture of the house during the ten years.[63]

The architectural nature of the chapter is illustrated with particular significance in Dickens's *Great Expectations*, a novel employing architectural illusion with a great sensitivity to rhythm and progression. Many writers have criticized the architecture of Dickens's novels: Flaubert complained of the "faulty construction" of *Pickwick Papers*; Poe, as Eichenbaum observes, felt that the serial publication of *Barnaby Rudge* prevented the author from having a detailed plan. George Orwell summed up the issue: "He is all fragments, all details—rotten architecture, but wonderful gargoyles." Shklovsky, however, initiated a revaluation of architecture in Dickens. Writing of *Little Dorrit*, he praised Dickens's use of the chapter to present "several simultaneous actions" and to create "plot impediment," both essential to the mystery novelist. Edgar Johnson declared that *Great Expectations* was "the most perfectly constructed . . . of all Dickens's works," while John Hagan contended it exhibited a "beauty of form, a shapeliness of design" that made it unique in the Dickens canon. Although published from 1 December 1860 to 3 August 1861 in weekly installments in *All the Year Round, Great Expectations* nevertheless reveals startling properties of architectural rhythm, scale, proportion, and sequence. It is, in consequence, a strong achievement of temporal art employing the spatial architectural illusion.[64]

In his essay on the structure of *Great Expectations*, John Hagan argues that the novel is divided into three parts: I, chapters 1–19, concern Pip's boyhood; II, chapters 20–39, concern his youth; III, chapters 40–59, concern his maturity. The overarching structure is clearly chiastic; part I shows a rise in hope and a fall in moral character, while II shows a fall in hope but a rise in moral character. Hagan further noted three methods of repetition which unify the work: first, of words and phrases; second, of characters, in the sense that they are variations on the theme of "great expectations"; and third, of incidents and locations, such as dinners, journeys, Satis House, the garden, mists, and visits to the "Castle." A recurrence of scenes and characters, however, has meaning only if it is structured in a certain way vis-à-vis all the other architecture of the novel. A close look at Hagan's schema indicates that the second part of the novel has no exact system of correspondence with the other two parts, and that the sections that do correspond are not composed of equal numbers of chapters.[65] A fine organization should not contain these anomalies. Is there a larger architecture, a more encompassing structure?

The table "Structure of *Great Expectations*" on pages 118–19 reveals what is in fact a systematic larger organization, one which indicates Dickens's close adherence to the qualities of architectural art. The basic clue is the opening unit of six chapters, extending from Christmas Eve to the end of Christmas Day. Within each division of six, there are subdivisions of three that reflect in miniature the relationship of parts I, II, and III to each other. In architecture, of course, the affinity of smaller to larger units is a problem of proportion, whose distinguishing element is scale; rhythm, the other large architectural element, is properly the function of sequence.

It is one of the achievements of *Great Expectations* that Dickens displays a remarkable sensitivity to scale and proportion. Dickens's concern for his audience is apparent, for it is the architectural impulse that is characterized by this regard for the individual entering, passing through, and exiting from the edifice. This book *is* indeed an object analogous to a building. Parts I, II, and III of the novel may be subdivided into three sections, which may be called A, B, and C. The reason for such a classification is obvious when their function is examined. The A section is

Structure of *Great Expectations*

Part I	1:	Christmas Eve; churchyard; Pip traces letters	
	2:	returns home	
	3:	Christmas morning; returns to churchyard	A
	4:	returns home; dinner	
	5:	marshes; convict arrested	
	6:	home; end of Christmas Day	
	7:	Biddy; writes on slate; mention of Miss Havisham	
	8:	Pumblechook; first interview at Satis House	
	9:	home; embarrassment	B
	10:	stranger with file; Magwitch's envoy	
	11:	Miss Havisham's birthday; fight with Herbert; sees Jaggers	
	12:	trust in Biddy	
	13:	with Joe to Satis House	
	14:	shame at home	
	15:	Orlick; Mrs. Joe injured	C
	16:	Biddy comes	
	17:	shame; Biddy vs. Estella	
	18:	Jaggers; "great expectations"	
	19:	visits Miss Havisham; to London	
Part II	20:	Jaggers and Wemmick	
	21:	Barnard's Inn	
	22:	Herbert tells of Miss Havisham	A
	23:	Drummle; Startop; the Pockets	
	24:	Wemmick and Pip	
	25:	the Aged	
	26:	dinner at Jaggers's; Molly	
	27:	sees Joe in London	
	28:	sees stranger again	B
	29:	to Satis House; sees Estella; "love her"	
	30:	tells Herbert of Estella	
	31:	the play	
	32:	Newgate	
	33:	Pip and Estella at Inn Yard	
	34:	Biddy and Joe vs. Estella	C
	35:	Mrs. Joe's funeral; mists	
	36:	Pip aged 21; money	
	37:	the Aged	
	38:	Estella and Miss Havisham: confrontation	
	39:	Pip 23; sees convict	
Part III	40:	Herbert and Magwitch	
	41:	Herbert, Magwitch, and Pip	
	42:	story of Magwitch and Compeyson	A

43:	Drummle; Pip thinks he sees Orlick on way to Miss Havisham's	
44:	Miss Havisham; "don't go home"	
45:	Wemmick; Magwitch lodged	
46:	begins boat training; Magwitch escaping	
47:	Compeyson seen	
48:	Molly Estella's mother; at Jaggers's	B
49:	Miss Havisham burns	
50:	Magwitch Estella's father	
51:	debate about Estella's parentage; Jaggers	
52:	escape plan; thinks of Joe; Wemmick's letter	
53:	confrontation with Orlick	
54:	fiasco of escape	C
55:	Magwitch in jail	
56:	Magwitch dies	
57:	reunion with Joe	
58:	Joe and Biddy married	
59:	ending one	
60:	ending two	

preparatory, the B, revelatory, and the C, climactic. This structure corresponds to the function of the three parts themselves: I is the entire novel's A; II is its B; III is its C. The division of each part into thirds is indicated by chapters 1, 7, and 13. Chapter 1 opens with a small boy tracing letters on a tombstone; chapter 7 specifically recalls this incident: "At the time when I stood in the churchyard, reading the family tombstones, I had just enough learning to be able to spell them out." Chapter 13, recounting the excursion of Joe and Pip to Satis House, opens with a statement involving an inscription: "Joe inscribed in chalk upon the door . . . the monosyllable HOUT." This division of 1-7-13 is pursued in part II with chapters 20-26-32, involving Jaggers, dinner at Jaggers's, and the tour of Newgate with Jaggers's clerk Wemmick. In part III, the structures of 40-46-52, all involving Pip, Herbert, and Magwitch, reflect this same ordering. The terminal points in each subdivision are similarly structured: 6-12-18 represents a pattern of intruders into the forge: Pip (as returning thief), Biddy, and Jaggers. In part II, the arrangement 25-31-37 indicates happier moments in Pip's London experiences, while in part III, 45-51-57 all comprise paternal figures for Pip: Magwitch, Jaggers, and Joe.

The relationships within the parts are as carefully structured. In I, chapters 1 and 6, 7 and 12, and 13 and 18 indicate parallel settings and mental attitudes. In II, however, the darkening London section, Dickens employs contrast rather than similarity: 20 and 25 move from Jaggers to the Aged, 26 and 31 from Jaggers to the play, 32 and 37 from Newgate to the Aged. Part III returns to parallels, with 40 and 45 involving Herbert and Magwitch with Pip, 46 and 51 joined by discussions of Clara's and Estella's fathers, and 52 and 57 made parallel by the fond recollection of Joe at the end of 52 and the reunion with him in 57. This structure in turn mirrors the exceptional nature of the B sections and of part II, the B of the entire novel. It is very evidently the classical figure of *variatio* ("variation"), a complex system of echoes and increments. The beginnings of all the triads are contrasting as well: in I, 1–4, 7–10, 13–16; in II, 20–23, 26–29, 32–35, all contrasting bleak locations; in III, 40–43, 46–49, 52–55, all in the movement from hope to despair. Thus as the openings of sextets are parallel, the openings of the triads are contrasting.

The same method of variation is maintained in the horizontal sequential rhythm of *Great Expectations*. The sequences leading from one subdivision to another, for example, involve contrasts: 6-7, 12-13, 25-26, 31-32, 45-46, and 51-52: Magwitch–Biddy; Biddy–Miss Havisham; the Aged–Jaggers; the play–Newgate; Magwitch lodged–Magwitch escaping; Jaggers–Joe. On the other hand, the chapters connecting triads indicate changes in attitude, but always in the direction of expansion or extension, never of contrast: 3-4, 9-10, 15-16, 22-23, 28-29, 34-35, 42-43, 48-49, 54-55. For example: 15-16, Mrs. Joe's injury brings Biddy; 34-35, Pip thinks favorably of Biddy and Joe, and then attends Mrs. Joe's funeral. This system of rhythm in the sequential chapters is reflected within each part as each part functions in the entire novel's rhythm. Architectural elements of proportion and scale, of rhythm and sequence, therefore, have received great attention from Dickens. This fact is not surprising, considering the great importance of the audience both to the architect in general and to a periodical novelist like Dickens in particular. Contrary to Poe's belief, periodical publication compelled Dickens to pay extreme attention to architecture. When Dickens completed *Great Expectations* on 11 June 1861, he was pleased, and the reader as architecture student may admiringly enter, pass, and exit.

The oblique axis, the relation of horizontal (sequential) rhythm to the vertical scale, is best indicated in one additional element of rhythm, which involves not merely sequence but the necessity of sequential differences to progress uniformly. This rhythm is seen in the larger structure, in the correspondence of the parts to one another: I, 18 + 1; II, 18 + 2; and III, 18 + 3. This concept, familiar from Dante's *Divine Comedy*, is sound architectural practice. The increment by one chapter in each part satisfies an important requirement of architecture, that the observer be guided through the edifice, and particularly that he be advised when one section has been left. The functions of chapters 19, 38, and 39, and 58, 59, and "60" are obviously of a summary nature, because they telescope the contrasting settings of the forge and Satis House with London. The two conclusions pursue the pattern established in parts I and II, and it is therefore completely acceptable to consider both of them as part of the architecture of the novel.[66] Considering both endings provides the final sextet which maintains the structure of the other sextets: 19 includes both the visit to Satis and the anticipation of London; 38 occurs at Satis and 39 at London; 58 returns to the forge, and 59 and 60, as ending one and ending two, preserve the contrast of the first and the fourth elements and the similarity of the first and the sixth elements demonstrated in the other sextets.

While Orwell considered that the parts of a Dickens novel did not constitute a satisfactory whole, it is possible to see in *Great Expectations* a controlling unity operating not only at the end of each part but also collectively for the novel. The method of *variatio* is perfectly suited to express the thoroughness of the oblique relations. Furthermore, the vertical relations, the beginnings of sextets and the endings of sextets, are parallels. The relation between the beginning and the ending of a sextet is parallel in parts I and III, but contrasting in II; the opening of each triad is contrasting. In the horizontal relations, the end of one sextet and the beginning of another are contrasting; between one triad and another there are expanding parallels. The meaning of *Great Expectations* was probably best expressed by Jung when he declared:

For the man who is dazzled by the light the darkness is a blessing and the boundless desert is a paradise to the escaped prisoner. It is nothing less than redemption for the medieval man of today not to have to be the embodiment of goodness and beauty and common sense. Looked at from the shadow-side, ideals are not beacons... but... gaolers foisted upon mankind by a clever ruse.[67]

Such is the meaning of the evening mists rising before Pip at the end of the novel. What Dickens achieved, however, by the architecture of *Great Expectations* was the erection of an edifice whose order provided the conviction that there can be a plan, itself the great expectation, to the entrance, the passage, and the exit.

The larger units of volumes, books, or parts are structured by the same techniques. The three volumes of Jane Austen's *Pride and Prejudice* or *Emma* were required by the demands of the circulating libraries, but frequently one may see the form of the syllogism in such tripartite arrangements. The novels present a major premise, minor premise, and conclusion. In *Pride and Prejudice*, for instance, we have: (1) the rejection of Darcy; (2) the understanding of Darcy; (3) the acceptance of Darcy by Elizabeth Bennet. In Tolstoy's *Resurrection*, the progressively shorter parts follow a similar structure: (1) Neklyudov becomes aware of Maslova

and her history; (2) Neklyudov seeks to act on the awareness; (3) Neklyudov is transformed by his action. The third short part by its very
brevity acts as a superb correlative to the sudden illumination experienced by the narrator. Stendhal, in *The Red and the Black,* prefers a dual
division; the two parts contain the act and the rejection of the act which is
thematically one of the central ideas of the novel, the elevation of reaction
over action. It is thus for a thematic reason that the longer part is devoted
to reaction. The two volumes of *The Charterhouse of Parma* reflect a
similar internal dichotomy of the psychological life, of act and contemplation of act. The tripartite division of *Madame Bovary* or of *Ulysses,* in
which the central section is larger than the other two, gives a hint of
epilogue to both works, as well as a disturbing "falling" difficult to interpret. Quadripartite novels echo the architectural edifice of four corners;
among such works are *The Princess of Clèves, Dangerous Liaisons,* and
Oblomov. Multiples of four appear in *The Golden Bowl* (twelve books)
and *Wilhelm Meister* (eight books).

The smaller units, of word, sentence, and paragraph, remain the minute blocks by which these houses of fiction are constructed. Gérard
Genette notes the importance not only of the word but the place of the
word in prose: "Each element is qualified by the place it occupies in a
total picture." In "The Meaning of the Word in Verse," Tynianov has
observed: "The word does not exist outside of a sentence. An isolated
word is not found in a nonphrasal environment." This is to say that in
prose, whatever the particular denotation (vertical relation) of a word, this
specific meaning is never found apart from a connotation (horizontal relation) by virtue of its placement in a phrase or sentence. In "Space and
Language," Genette indicates that the word as a signifier is a constant
"spatial term," while its signified meaning is a "variable object." To trans-
late Shklovsky's example, the word *earth* remains visually the same, but
of course is altered by what it signifies in context. The architectural element of the word is furthermore the product of placement. "I married
him, Reader," and "Reader, I married him," while conveying the same
information, vary in effect. The former sounds resigned; the strategic
repositioning of "Reader" achieves the conviction of the second sentence.
The rhetorical figures of juxtaposition, litotes, oxymoron, repetition, antithesis, or parallelism, of course, rely for their effect on their place in the
structure of the phrase or the sentence, as is also the case with *analepsis*
("retrospection") or *prolepsis* ("anticipation"), discussed by Genette in
Figures III. Genette declares that the place of the recollection or anticipation directly violates the linearity of the discourse.[68]

The style of sentence, furthermore, serves as an important function of
rhythm and of sequence, as well as of proportion. The lengths of sentences and the complexity of their structure (or, one might note, as of the

first paragraph of Dickens's *Bleak House,* the absence of sentences) influences the speed of reception by the reader. In *Jane Eyre,* for example, the opening, "There was no possibility of taking a walk that day," is abrupt, totally individual, an impression increased by the first line of the second paragraph: "I was glad of it." The elaboration that follows each of these utterances in their individual paragraphs, consisting in each case of a single longer sentence, provides a strong sense of rhythm (fast, slow), a feeling of sequence (entrance and passage), and an awareness of proportion in two senses. In each paragraph there is a great imbalance between the short first and long second sentence, but a feeling of balance between the two consecutive paragraphs. Such a movement reinforces the tension of surety and hazard throughout the novel. The contrast with, say, the first paragraph and sentence of *Middlemarch* is indicative: the first sentence there is complex, and is succeeded by a long paragraph explaining the statement, "Miss Brooke had that kind of beauty which seems to be thrown into relief by poor dress." Jane Austen always gives an indication of the speed of the narration to follow in her first paragraphs. The short single-sentence paragraphs of the openings of *Pride and Prejudice* and *Emma* contrast with the extended background analysis of the first paragraphs of *Mansfield Park.* If one considers the openings as vestibules, it is clear that the architecture establishes both the scale, or how the human figure stands in relation to the novel, and the sequence, or how one is to pass through the work. The paragraph is particularly important in scale. For example, one may speak of "monumental" scale in works involving long complex sentences and paragraphs (as in *Middlemarch* and *The Ambassadors*), and "shock" scale in the violent contrast of slowness and abruptness as in *Jane Eyre.* Furthermore, scale appears in the physical form of the book itself. The visual impression of *War and Peace* contrasted with *The Red Badge of Courage,* or of *A Portrait of the Artist as a Young Man* with *Ulysses,* for instance, establishes a clear feeling of scale, verifying the architectural significance of the book as object that Butor has recognized.[69]

One finds a particularly strong manifestation of the architecture of sentence, word, and paragraph in Flaubert's *Sentimental Education.* In the following two passages, for example, nearly all the possible architectural dimensions of these "materials" are exploited by careful position, interplay of proportions, balancing of complex and simple sentences, and progressive movement (sequence) to a climax:

On remarquait en entrant chez lui deux grands tableaux, où les premiers tons, posés çà et là, faisaient sur la toile blanche des taches de brun, de rouge et de bleu. Un réseau de lignes à la craie s'étendait par-dessus, comme les mailles vingt fois reprises d'un filet; il était même impossible d'y rien comprendre. Pellerin expliqua le sujet de ces deux compositions en indiquant avec le pouce les parties qui manquaient. L'une devait représenter *la Démence de Nabuchodonosor*, l'autre *l'Incendie de Rome par Neron*. Frédéric les admira.

Il admira des académies de femmes échevelées, des paysages où les troncs d'arbres tordus par la tempête foisonnaient, et surtout des caprices à la plume, souvenirs de Callot, de Rembrandt ou de Goya, dont il ne connaissait pas les modèles. Pellerin n'estimait plus ces travaux de sa jeunesse; maintenant il était pour le grand style; il dogmatisa sur Phidias et Winckelmann, éloquemment. Les choses autour de lui renforcaient la puissance de sa parole: on voyait une tête de mort sur un prie-Dieu, des yatagans, une robe de moine; Frédéric l'endossa.

(Going into his studio, one's eye was caught by two large pictures, in which the first tints, scattered here and there, formed patches of brown, red, and blue on the white canvas. Over them there stretched a tracery of chalk lines, like the meshes of a net which had been mended time and again; indeed it was absolutely impossible to make anything of it. Pellerin explained the subject of these two compositions by indicating the missing parts with his thumb. One was intended to represent *The Madness of Nebuchadnezzar*, the other *The Burning of Rome by Nero*. Frédéric admired them.

He admired some studies of nudes with dishevelled hair, some landscapes abounding in storm-twisted tree-trunks, and above all some pen-and-ink sketches, inspired by Callot, Rembrandt, or Goya, the originals of which were unknown to him. Pellerin thought very little of these early works of his; now he was for the grand manner; he pontificated eloquently on Phidias and Winckelmann. The objects around him gave added force to his argument; there was a skull on a prayer-stool, some scimitars, and a monk's frock, which Frédéric put on.)

There is here an extraordinary arrangement of primary and secondary rhythms: the paragraphs open with long sentences, and conclude with extremely abrupt rhythms: they are linked by "admira" as if by the binding of a diptych. Inside the second paragraph, the sentences themselves maintain the same rhythm as the part, as in "éloquemment": "Frédéric l'endossa." One need hardly note that the entire rhythm of the novel, the proportion of *ralentissement* to acceleration, occurs between the second and third parts of the novel, with the second noticeably longer, and the third summarizing the entire technique in the famous opening of part three, section six:

Il voyagea.

Il connut la mélancolie des paquebots, les froids réveils sous la tente, l'étourdissement des paysages et des ruines, l'amertume des sympathies interrompues.

Il revint.

Il fréquenta le monde, et il eut d'autres amours encore. Mais le souvenir continuel du premier les lui rendait insipides; et puis la véhémence du désir, la fleur même de la sensation était perdue. Ses ambitions d'esprit avaient également diminué. Des années passèrent; et il supportait le désoeuvrement de son intelligence et l'inertie de son coeur.

(He traveled.

He came to know the melancholy of the steamboat, the cold awakening in the tent, the tedium of landscapes and ruins, the bitterness of interrupted friendships.

He returned.

He went into society, and he had other loves. But the ever-present memory of the first made them insipid; and besides, the violence of desire, the very flower of feeling, had gone. His intellectual ambitions had also dwindled. Years went by; and he endured the idleness of his mind and the inertia of his heart.)

The architectural properties of rhythm and sequence, of proportion and scale, verify what Genette has called the province of architecture to make space speak of itself. In the novel, because "every language is composed of space," the elements of word, sentence, and paragraph, of chapter and book, comprise methods by which the novel may become its functional form, the building of an edifice, whether a house or a cathedral, by which the reader may enter, pass through, and exit. [70]

Such methods are brilliantly demonstrated in Hardy's final novel, *Jude the Obscure*. Here one experiences the consequences of volume in characterization along with the relation of modeled character to architectural enclosure. For the spatial study of Hardy, no criticism is more relevant than that by the Narrator in *The Captive* from Proust's *Remembrance of Things Past*. After telling the "captive" Albertine that "there are other typical phrases in Vinteuil like that stone-mason's geometry in the novels of Thomas Hardy," he continues: "Do you remember the stone-masons in *Jude the Obscure*, in *The Well-Beloved*, the blocks of stone which the father hews out of the island coming in boats to be piled up in the son's studio where they are turned into statues?" The spatial arts of both sculpture and architecture are essential to Hardy the novelist; the frequent appearance of characters who are sculptors suggests there is in fact an element of sculpture in characterization. It is hardly surprising that Hardy, mason and architect himself, should be a crucial exemplar of this practice. Proust's insights into Hardy's techniques—the attention to parallels in structure, not only in novels but between them, the reversal of the plot of one novel by that of another, the simultaneous verticality of all his works—point to the importance of spatial form in *Jude the Obscure*. If Hardy could refer to Raphael Brandon as a "literary architect," he is himself no less a sculptural and architectural novelist. [71]

The spatiality of Hardy's works derives particularly from a form of spatiality Genette discusses in *Figures II*: "the manifest spatiality of writing taken as the symbol of the profound spatiality of language." Proust's emphasis on the "simultaneous perception of the total unity of the work," Genette maintains, impelled him to compare his work to a cathedral. That is, the written text is a graphic product with clear visual and architectural properties. This architecture is a dimension of the spatial form of Hardy's works, which Proust emphasized. Ultimately, this geometry may be subsumed under the concept of secondary illusion, crucial to an author like Hardy, who worked in, wrote of (as in the *Dorset Chronicle*), and read widely about spatial art prior to and during his novelistic career. In the preface to *Jude the Obscure* he stated his objective in the novel: "to give shape and coherence to a series of seemings, or personal impressions." The words "shape" (spatial) and "series" (temporal) strongly indicate his personal experience of secondary illusion. [72]

"The letter killeth" is not only the epigraph but also the epitaph of this particular novel and of the novel as Hardy was to write it. As a mason Hardy was well aware that the earliest writing, for example the hieroglyph, was itself spatial art. In the hieroglyph the temporal letter and the spatial picture were one. Jude himself carves on stone as Hardy writes on paper. The greatest example of this writing on stone is, of course, the Ten Commandments, inscribed by the master carver, God. At the end of the novel Jude returns to the Book of Job, a defeated sculptor taking his text: "Let the day perish wherein I was born, and the night in which it was said, 'There is a man child conceived.'" Obviously, "The letter killeth" refers specifically to the sixth commandment and generally to all legislation governing personal morality. However, when a novelist says, "The letter killeth," one is compelled to ask how the novelist, he of the letter, kills.

Two declarations in Florence Hardy's *Early Life of Thomas Hardy*, about art and about the theme of Hardy's work, verify that form and theme are one:

> But in these Bible lives and adventures there is the spherical completeness of perfect art. . . . Is not the fact of their being so convincing an argument, not for their actuality, but for the actuality of a consummate artist who was no more content with what Nature offered than Sophocles and Phidias were content?

> It is the on-going—i.e., the 'becoming'—of the world that produces its sadness. If the world stood still at a felicitous moment there would be no sadness in it. The sun and the moon standing still on Ajalon was not a catastrophe for Israel, but a type of Paradise. [73]

Jude tells Sue she is far more classical than Christian, that he expects her "to have been watching Praxiteles chiselling away at his latest Venus." These references to Phidias, Praxiteles, and Ajalon invoke the architect's profound feeling toward building, toward sculpture, toward the timeless, toward stasis amid movement. Temporality was not a central objective for Hardy in *Jude the Obscure.* Jude's name itself, telescoping the Old Testament Judah and Judas Maccabaeus and the New Testament Judas and Saint Jude, amalgamates ideas of fervor, sterility, devotion, and rebellion in a timeless association. *Jude the Obscure,* for Hardy, was Ajalon.

But there was a further spatial route to the valley of Ajalon, the way of Praxiteles, of Phidias, of the sculptor of the *Laocoon.* Early in the novel Hardy describes Jude, almost destined to kill his sons, clenching his teeth like Laocoon in the statue; and Sue's statues of Venus and Apollo for a while become her patron saints, jarring against Calvary. Later, however, Jude savagely rebukes her when her fidelity to them reverts to a flagellant Christian penitence: "Can this be the girl who brought the Pagan deities into this most Christian city?... Where are dear Apollo, and dear Venus now!" Later Jude, after attempting to kill himself by seeing Sue and returning in the storm, fingers his own carving for the last time, out of recollection of her own once brave adherence to Venus and Apollo. Jude tells Arabella: "I have seen her for the last time, and I've finished myself—done." Coming from a stonemason, this "finishing" evokes the image of Praxiteles "finishing" Phryne as Venus. When at the end Jude has "marble features," the description, given all that prepares for it, is not a mere cliché. It is a recognition, rather, of the importance of sculptural secondary illusion to characterization in the novel, and of coextensive volume. All characterized figures in any novel, especially protagonists, strive for this volume, to connect not only with each other but also with the interpreting reader and his ideologies. Characters have, therefore, a plastic form, which in *Jude the Obscure* is reflected in the frequent associ-ation of the protagonists with sculptured objects. Hardy's association of sculpture and characterization anticipates Proust's recognition in *Swann's Way* of the virtual relation between the cathedral facade and young Théo-dore, or Faulkner's concept of the connection, in *The Sound and the Fury,* as *"moving sitting still,"* a novelist's definition of what Susanne Langer declares is the "virtual kinetic volume" of sculptural art.[74]

Langer asserts: "Almost as soon as buildings of hewn stone appear, sculpture becomes assimilated to architecture." This situation in the spa-tial arts poses an acute challenge to the temporal novelist dealing with sculptural and architectural secondary illusions. *Jude the Obscure* in par-ticular is so replete with architectural theory and debate that one can say that it not merely employs these secondary illusions but is primarily about them, and specifically about how sculptural coextensive volume in charac-terization is accommodated to the edifice of the book as an object. One recalls Genette's statement in *Figures II* of the preeminence of architec-tural space in the novel: "And the art of space par excellence, architec-ture, does not speak of space: it would be more true to say that it makes space speak, that it is space which speaks in it."[75]

The debate about architecture in *Jude the Obscure* decisively exposes how Hardy employed its secondary illusion. Of particular interest is the conflict between classical and Gothic. As a young apprentice Hardy destroyed much Gothic work in England, and throughout his life he read about this style—for example in Raphael Brandon's *Analysis of Gothic Architecture*.[76] Early in the novel we hear of an old temple site replaced by "modern Gothic":

In place of it a tall new building of modern Gothic design, unfamiliar to English eyes, had been erected on a new piece of ground by a certain obliterator of historic records who had run down from London and back in a day. The site whereon so long had stood the ancient temple to the Christian divinities was not even recorded on the green and level grass-plot.

This opposition between ancient and modern is soon transformed into characterization:

"Shall we go and sit in the Cathedral?" he asked, when their meal was finished.
"Cathedral? Yes. Though I think I'd rather sit in the railway station. . . . That's the centre of the town life now. The Cathedral has had its day!"
"How modern you are!"
"So would you be if you had lived so much in the Middle Ages as I have done these last few years! The Cathedral . . . is played out now. . . . I am not modern, either. I am more ancient than mediaevalism, if you only knew."
Jude looked distressed.

Later Jude proposes an excursion:

"Not ruins, Jude—I don't care for them."
"Well—Wardour Castle. And then we can do Fonthill if we like—all in the same afternoon."
"Wardour is Gothic ruins—and I hate Gothic!"
"No. Quite otherwise. It is a classic building—Corinthian, I think; with a lot of pictures."
"Ah—that will do. I like the sound of Corinthian."

Sue insists, "The mediaevalism of Christminster must go," further declaring, "You take so much tradition on trust that I don't know what to say." When Jude replies, "I take Christianity," she responds, "You might take something worse."

This architectural debate is, of course, central to Jude's (and Hardy's) ideology, with Jude's affinity for Gothic representing a lingering desire to cling to an outmoded faith. That this adherence is absolutely integral to the novel, however, is clear when one realizes that the architectural illusion used by Hardy is also Gothic. As a style, Gothic represented an inclination to "quicken spatial motion" by a strong verticality. Hardy's intention in his architectural practice in *Jude the Obscure* is clarified by

Erwin Panofsky's *Gothic Architecture and Scholasticism*. In a cathedral, Panofsky notes, the three locations, west, center, and east, were represented by nave, transept, and chevet. This "Trinitarian form," attributable to the triumph of scholasticism, made the architect of the Gothic cathedral "himself. . . a kind of Scholastic." Such is Jude and also Hardy. The division of *Jude the Obscure* into six books is a recreation of early Gothic style, exemplified in the cathedral at Noyon, where, as Pevsner observes, "the vaults are sexpartite, as they had been about 1115-20 in the Romanesque abbey churches of Caen."

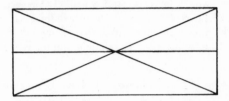

These six divisions correspond as well to a further subdivision of the parts of a Gothic structure into west facade, nave, aisles, transept, crossing, and chevet. Hardy's architectural illusion of Jude, Sue, and Arabella parallels Panofsky's tripartite scholastic system. Such a tripartite structure has an additional architectural parallel. At Noyon for the first time, as Fritz Baumgart asserts, "a genuine triforium appears, dissolving the remaining solid wall-surface between gallery and window area." As a result, Noyon exhibits a peculiar duality of lightness and of "Romanesque weight and stability." There lingers over it an unresolved opposition between the terrestrial and the transcendental.[77]

The Gothic structure of *Jude the Obscure* must be seen in the context of the great debate between classicists and the Gothic revivalists during the nineteenth century. As Kenneth Clark notes in *The Gothic Revival*, although Gothic was, in the eighteenth century, associated with enthusiasm, sensibility, or sublimity, in the early nineteenth century it became connected with the religious, producing an increased building of churches and an association of Gothic with popery. This connection became manifest when Augustus Pugin, a convert to Catholicism, was asked to design the medieval court for the Great Exhibition of 1851. Hardy, very familiar with Pugin's achievement, visited one of his chapels in 1862. As Pevsner observes, the result of Pugin's "equation of Christianity and Gothic" was that "Classicists began to brand the architect who favoured Gothic as an obscurantist." This is the logical explanation for Jude as "the Obscure." The epithet is applicable in a most technical way, derived from the Gothic architectural illusion of the text itself.[78]

The Gothic structure of *Jude the Obscure*, particularly its sexpartite division, is further clarified by Ruskin's description of "The Nature of Gothic" in *The Stones of Venice*:

I believe, then, that the characteristic or moral elements of Gothic are the following, placed in the order of their importance:

1. Savageness.	4. Grotesqueness.
2. Changefulness.	5. Rigidity.
3. Naturalism.	6. Redundance.

These characters are here expressed as belonging to the building; as belonging to the builder, they would be expressed thus:—1. Savageness or Rudeness. 2. Love of Change. 3. Love of Nature. 4. Disturbed Imagination. 5. Obstinacy. 6. Generosity. And I repeat, that the withdrawal of any one, or any two, will not at once destroy the Gothic character of a building, but the removal of a majority of them will.[79]

Hardy's own reading of Ruskin appears to have been crucial to the structure of *Jude the Obscure*. Ruskin's six characteristics apply effortlessly to the six books of the novel. Marygreen is savageness or rudeness, not particularly to be condemned, but simply there; Christminster, to say the least, is changefulness, as Jude begins to know Sue; Melchester is brutally natural, as the sexual conflicts between the two become unbearable and untenable; Shaston is grotesque, a place of "strange reports," "the city of a dream," where unconsummated sex becomes a violation of nature; Albrickham is characterized by the obstinacy of Sue and Arabella; and the final title, "At Christminster Again," reflects beyond question redundance.

The problem of sculptural coextensive volume, however, is reintroduced in Ruskin's last injunction for determining the value of architecture: *"Read* the sculpture." In addition to perceiving the formal Gothic arrangement, we must look at the sculpture, much as Sue and Jude do in the novel.

Read the sculpture. Preparatory to reading it, you will have to discover whether it is legible (and, if legible, it is nearly certain to be worth reading). On a good building, the sculpture is *always* so set, and on such a scale, that at the ordinary distance from which the edifice is seen, the sculpture shall be thoroughly intelligible and interesting. . . .

And having ascertained this, let him set himself to read them. Thenceforward the criticism of the building is to be conducted precisely on the same principles as that of a book.

The newly arrived Jude follows this advice when roaming the streets of Christminster.

The numberless architectural pages around him he read, naturally, less as an artist-critic of their forms than as an artizan and comrade of the dead handicraftsmen whose muscles had actually executed those forms. He examined the mouldings, stroked them as one who knew their beginning. . . .

What at night had been perfect and ideal was by day the more or less defective real. Cruelties, insults, had, he perceived, been inflicted on the aged erections. The condition of several moved him as he would have been moved by maimed sentient beings. They were wounded, broken, sloughing off their outer shape.

The sculptural secondary illusion associated with character likewise forces the reader to "*read* the sculpture," but the issue becomes extremely complicated in *Jude the Obscure*. We learn this fact only a bit later in the novel, when Sue seems to echo Jude's thought—"The mediaevalism of Christminster must go, be sloughed off"—but for the completely opposite intention. By his association of Sue and Jude with classical sculpture and sculptors, Hardy endows them with a classical coextension decidedly in conflict with his Gothic architectural form. [80]

Panofsky has observed that Gothic sculptured figures display a renewed interest in psychology, "the victory of Aristotelianism," which at first glance might appear to indicate a new individualism. This is in fact not so, for the Aristotelian urge in the sculpture conflicts with the transcendental intention of the edifice itself. In *Form in Gothic*, Wilhelm Worringer remarks: "This dualistic distraction . . . had lulled itself to quiescence in the great transcendental art of the Middle Ages." In fact, "Medieval culture . . . had known no differentiation of the individual—for the individual only dares to separate himself from the mass when dualistic fears have been overcome and a state of equilibrium and security in the relationship between the world and man has been attained." The precedent for Renaissance individualism was in fact classicism, as Alois Riegl pointed out long ago in *Spätrömische Kunstindustrie*: "The plastic art of the whole of antiquity sought as its ultimate goal to render external things in their clear material individuality, and in so doing to respect the sensible appearance of the outward things of nature and to avoid and suppress anything that might cloud and vitiate the directly convincing expression of material individuality." In fact, as Worringer argued in *Abstraction and Empathy*, the classical and the Gothic move in opposite directions.

In the urge to abstraction the intensity of the self-alienative impulse is incomparably greater and more consistent. Here it is not characterized, as in the need for empathy, by an urge to alienate oneself from individual being, but as an urge to seek deliverance from the fortuitousness of humanity as a whole, from the seeming arbitrariness of organic existence in general, in contemplation of something necessary and irrefragable.

Greek sculpture, therefore, from which Hardy in *Jude the Obscure* derives his sense of volume, is empathic and truly individual; Gothic architecture, on the other hand, is an attempt to achieve "deliverance from the fortuitousness of humanity."[81] This is the true explanation for Jude's, and Hardy's, attraction to Gothic architectural illusion.

In contrast to Gothic sculpture, which was frequently secondary to the edifice, the Greek statue was the motive for the temple; the volume of classical sculpture was as coextensive as possible, not only in the absoluteness of its own space but in its pivotal role as organizer of the surrounding space. Arabella, Sue, and Jude exhibit this same extreme extension, this strong independent volume, in the tenacity with which they maintain their individuality while absorbing others into it. They are repeatedly associated with classical (in Riegl's sense) sculpture for this reason. Nevertheless, this sculptural ideal conflicts with the Gothic architectural illusion of *Jude the Obscure*. Pevsner has observed that above all, the Gothic cathedral symbolized authority. In this novel, the Gothic form itself assumes the role of society. When Sue and Jude realize this fact, they cannot avoid the sculpturesque reference. Sue says: "I have been thinking . . . that the social moulds civilization fits us into have no more relation to our actual shapes than the conventional shapes of the constellations have to the real star-patterns." Much later the conflict of sculptural and architectural illusions proves fatal.

> "We must conform! . . . All the ancient wrath of the Power above us has been vented upon us, His poor creatures, and we must submit. There is no choice. We must. It is no use fighting against God!"
> "It is only against man and senseless circumstance," said Jude.
> ". . . But whoever or whatever our foe may be, I am cowed into submission. I have no more fighting strength left; no more enterprize. I am beaten, beaten! . . . 'We are made a spectacle unto the world, and to angels, and to men!' I am always saying that now."
> "I feel the same!"

The expression "I feel the same!" verifies the great sculptural coextension that is part of the operative illusion of Hardy's characterization in *Jude the Obscure:* without sculptural volume, no character may make such a statement.

Hardy, however, was too intellectually honest to give his classical characters a corresponding form. Instead, he deliberately ill-fitted them to the Gothic form of his novel, a form symbolic both of oppression and of failed faith. In Worringer's nomenclature, we have in *Jude the Obscure* an abstract transcendental Gothic architectural illusion subsuming an empathic classical volume in characterization.

In *Jude the Obscure* Hardy exploited sculptural and architectural secondary illusions, those of classical coextensive volume and Gothic form. He consciously made them ill-fitting, as God had done to man. Indeed, he says in the preface that the question of "consistency" or "discordance" was not primary. E. M. Cioran has observed in "The Fall out of Time" that "once we have penetrated someone, the best thing he can do is disappear."[82] "Penetrating someone" is the hallmark of coextensive volume, which both remains individual and absorbs. Like Jude, Hardy "finished" himself, killed himself to the novel forever. For the last time, like Jude, he "felt at the back of the stone for his own carving," demolished, like Jude, by authority. "The letter killeth."

The virtual spatiality which Proust recognized in the sculpture of Saint-André-des-Champs provides a novelist with some of his most decisive spatial functions. The correlation between the formalism of Tomashevsky's motifs and Wölfflin's categories verifies that the theory of the novel and the theory of painting converge, as in the encadred narratives of *Wuthering Heights, A Hero of Our Time,* and *Daphnis and Chloe.* Henry James's *Portrait of a Lady* employs spatial pictorial boundary to express the complex aesthetic morality suggested in its title. Through the method of sculptural relief, Balzac in *Cousin Bette* expresses his theory of environment as determinant as much as Hawthorne uses the atemporal quality of the sculpturesque to define romance as a spatial product in *The Marble Faun.* Novels like *The Red and the Black* and *Women in Love* develop the sculptural volume of character to present radical theories of the individual. In addition to the pictorial and the sculptural, the architectural concept of functional form underlies spatial strategies of the word, chapter, or part in such works as *The Sentimental Education* or *War and Peace,* of alternation in *Anna Karenina* or *Mrs. Dalloway,* and of spatial rhythm in a novel like *Great Expectations.* Hardy's *Jude the Obscure* is a consummate study of sculptural volume by development of a book's spatial architecture. Such methods of virtual spatiality have great consequences for literary interpretation, since these ideas of volume and of the book as object define the act of reading as well as the act of creation as reliant on spatial secondary illusion.

CHAPTER FOUR

The Genidentic

to try and grow a muff and canonise his dead feet down on the river airy by thinking himself into the fourth dimension

Joyce, *Finnegans Wake*

"maybe Father and I are both Shreve"

Faulkner, *Absalom, Absalom!*

One of the central concerns of architecture is the connection between exterior and interior space, the establishment of harmony between a building and its surroundings. Fritz Baumgart observes that in the twentieth-century building, with its final bridging of the gulf between engineering and architecture, one experiences "the unrestricted interpenetration of interior and exterior space." Frank Lloyd Wright's Robie House shows a "complete fusion of exterior and interior space." The so-called ethnic domain of architecture, as Susanne Langer has observed, is indicated by the fact that "it is the sphere of influence of a function," for it is the property of architectural space to be both self-contained and yet reflective of the world surrounding it. It is "the spatial *semblance* of a world, because it is made in actual space.... That is the image of an ethnic domain, the primary illusion in architecture." Furthermore, "architecture creates the semblance of that World which is the counterpart of a Self. It is a total environment made visible." "A virtual 'environment,' the created space of architecture, is a symbol of functional existence." Thus a Greek temple by "its outward appearance organizes the site of the town." Architecture is, in brief, "the human environment," "the complementary organic form," "an illusion of ethnic domain, or the environment created by Selfhood." These terms can also be used to describe the novel. It is certainly the "complementary organic form" of the reader's existence. While it relates to the space inside it, "it has its own center

134

and periphery"; it is "that World which is the counterpart of the Self."[1] The book is not only an object, but an architectural object; it is constructed, not written.

"In all matters... there are these two points: the thing signified, and that which gives it its significance," remarks Vitruvius in *On Architecture*. The contiguity of his terminology to modern critical thinking is provocative, for it suggests that the relation of signifier to signified has an architectural relation of "in" to "out." E. D. Hirsch has explored this relation in literary criticism in *Validity in Interpretation*. His central thesis may be summarized by saying that the object of interpretation is meaning, something determined; the object of criticism is significance, which is boundless. Interpretation is a "recognition of the author's meaning," a "verbal meaning" which is "determinate" and "reproducible." In addition to its "reproducibility," meaning also is characterized by "sharability," that is, verbal meaning is "a type experience that is common to author and reader." This "shared type of meaning" is an "intrinsic genre," and "all valid interpretation is thus intrinsic interpretation." Furthermore, "valid interpretation is always governed by a valid inference about genre." One may condense his argument thus: valid *in*terpretation is based on *in*ference about the *im*plication of an *in*trinsic genre. However, the method of this subtle interpretation, logical reasoning from hypotheses and premises, cannot be called complete, for it never confronts the problem of how one can participate with *in*. If, as Hirsch contends, the objective is the most correct *im*plication (etymologically, as he observes, "folded *in*") how does one "get in"? How is "sharability" not only an effect but a property? What does it mean when a genre is *in*trinsic (*intrinsecus*, "inwardly," "inside," "inwards")? How is an *in*ference, literally something "carried in," a part of interpretation (*inter-pretium*, "between" or "among price, value, worth")? An *interpres* was a mediator, a negotiator, and later an expounder (of law, not literature), a prophet. Interpretation, therefore, is concerned with two factors, one "in" and one "out," with a mediator between. How does one effect this mediation? Is there something about the "parties involved" that permits this conciliation to occur physically, or is it only the most adequate analogue for an elusive process?[2]

An initial step toward an explanation of interpretation is provided in Henri Bergson's *Time and Free Will*. In chapter three, discussing the question of real duration and prediction, Bergson stated: "Hence we have to distinguish two ways of assimilating the conscious states of other people: the one dynamic, which consists in experiencing them oneself; the other static, which consists in substituting for the consciousness of these states their image or rather their intellectual idea, their symbol." It is significant that Bergson in this same paragraph had selected the reading of a novel as an example of the process of assimilating "the conscious states of other people."

If Paul is to have an adequate idea of Peter's state at any moment of his history, there are only two courses open; either, like a novelist, who knows whither he is conducting his character, Paul must already know Peter's final act, and must thus be able to supplement his mental image of the successive states through which Peter is going to pass by some indication of their value in relation to the whole of Peter's history; or he must make up his mind to pass through these different states, not in imagination, but in reality. The former hypothesis must be put on one side since the very point at issue is whether, the antecedents *alone* being given, Paul will be able to foresee the final act. We find ourselves compelled, therefore, to alter radically the idea which we had formed of Paul: he is not, as we had thought at first, a spectator whose eyes pierce the future, but an actor who plays Peter's part in advance.

When Paul passes through the same successive stages as Peter, "Peter and Paul are one and the same person, whom you call Peter when he acts and Paul when you recapitulate his history." Bergson declares there are two ways of assimilating antecedents, "the one dynamic, the other static."

In the first case, we shall be led by imperceptible steps to identify ourselves with the person we are dealing with, to pass through the same series of states, and thus to get back to the very moment at which the act is performed; hence there can be no longer any question of foreseeing it. In the second case, we presuppose the final act by the mere fact of annexing to the qualitative description of the previous states the quantitative appreciation of their importance.

He contends that the identification of Paul with Peter permits them to occupy the same space, to experience simultaneous becoming, and he poses the central question: "Is time space?" Although Einstein provided the answer in 1905, Bergson suggested that the relation between two durations was a simultaneity which remained the same despite acceleration. The tendency of thought in *Time and Free Will* about the novel, about dynamism, and about simultaneity is crucial to a spatial analysis of literary texts.[3]

Some of Bergson's ideas are found in the literary criticism of Borges and Genette. In "The Reversible Universe" in *Figures I,* Genette cites this passage from Borges's *Other Inquisitions:*

Why does it make us uneasy to know that the map is within the map and the thousand and one nights are within the book of *A Thousand and One Nights?* Why does it disquiet us to know that Don Quixote is a reader of the *Quixote,* and Hamlet is a spectator of *Hamlet?* I believe I have found the answer: those inversions suggest that if the characters in a story can be readers or spectators, then we, their readers or spectators, can be fictitious.

In "Utopian Literature," Genette declared that literature is "a homogeneous and reversible space where individual particularities and chronological presences do not pass." Literature is in essence a single dynamic field, spatially reversible and atemporal. "Universal literature [is] a vast anonymous creation where each author is only the fortuitous incarnation of a Spirit atemporal and impersonal." He interprets Borges's statements as follows:

The world of books and the book of the world constitute only one, and if the hero of the second part of *Quixote* can be the reader of the first, and if Hamlet be the spectator of *Hamlet,* it follows that we, their readers or spectators, may be without knowing it fictive persons, and that at the moment we are reading *Hamlet* or *Don Quixote* someone may be occupied in reading us, writing us, or deleting us.

The world exists, Mallarmé said, to lead to a Book. The myth of Borges contracts the modern *everything is to write* and the classic *everything is written* into a formula even more ambitious, that is approximately: *everything is Writing.*

What is important in these observations is not only that the reader may be fictitious, but also that, by Genette's extension, the reader is himself a text. Jean Ricardou, in *Problems of the New Novel,* suggests yet another level of this dynamic situation. The reader is also an author.

The reader himself composes *another book,* of which certain pages, precisely, are divided, and inserted, according to his will, at other points of the narrative. The book we are considering could indeed be considered as a narrative which integrated to its own composition one of these alternative readings.

Criticism is in essence "a discourse on a discourse" or, as Genette notes, the text and its interpretation are "two languages of the same language." It is this dynamic quality, this identification in the same atemporal field, that was originally explained in Bergson's thought and that is verified by the theory of relativity.[4]

The principle of dynamism underlies a great part of Jurij Tynianov's literary analysis. "The unity of a work is not a closed symmetrical whole," he argues, "but an unfolding dynamic integrity; between its elements stands, not the static sign of equation and addition, but always the dynamic sign of correlation and integration." The literary work is therefore extensive beyond itself: "[Its] ... form must be perceived as a dynamic entity."

This dynamism is revealed, first of all, in the concept of the constructive principle. Not all aspects of a word are of equal value; dynamic form is not the result of uniting or merging such aspects ... but rather the result of their interaction which enhances one group of factors at the expense of another.... Second, the sensation of form in such a situation is always the sensation of flow ... of interrelation between the subordinating constructive factor and the subordinated factors. There is no need to introduce a *temporal* connotation into this concept of the progress of 'unfolding.' Flow dynamics may be taken in isolation, outside of time, as pure motion.

Tynianov's theory of form in art as dynamic is expanded by Victor Zuckerkandl's theories in *Sound and Symbol*. Discussing the temporal art of music, Zuckerkandl argues that music establishes a "dynamic field" for its experience and its interpretation. He refutes the idea that music is nonspatial by noting that it is impossible to talk of musical phenomena "except with words that, whether latently or patently, have a spatial meaning," particularly the words "within" and "without." Schopenhauer's contention, that music "is perceived solely in and through time, to the complete exclusion of space," is false: music is "flowing space." A central attribute of music is its coextensive volume; it is "not simply something that *is* in space but something that *occupies* space." Zuckerkandl continues: "Even where there is nothing to be seen, nothing to be touched, nothing to be measured, where bodies do not move from place to place, there is still space. And it is not empty space." Through examination of the triad, for example, one realizes that "the second tone is and remains audible *through the first*. The same is true of the third tone: the tones connected in the triad sound *through one another*. Or let us say that they interpenetrate one another." The concept of interpenetration arises because tones have "dynamic qualities." For this reason, "space . . . is not only that whence something encounters me; space is also that in which what encounters me is mutually related." The interpenetration establishes the presence of a "dynamic field," a reconciliation of "in" and "out." "The dynamic field that emanates from a body belongs to the body itself in the same sense as do its mass, its shape, its hardness, its color. . . . A body *is* where it *acts*." The limits of a work of art "do not coincide with the limits of its material form. With its dynamic field it extends into space," resulting in "superimposed, mutually interpenetrating dynamic states." Kurt Koffka relates this thought to spatial art itself: "Visual space is a dynamic event rather than a geometrical pattern." The experience of artistic space as force indicates interpenetration within its dynamic field. It is this intuition which permits Todorov in *The Poetics of Prose* to speak of the "lines of force of the narrative." Architecture, which is "the making of 'empty' space visible" to Zuckerkandl, operates as a force reconciling outside and inside.[5] The concept of an art work as a "dynamic field" resolves the opposition of "in" and "out." Through the dynamic field, *in*terpretation, *im*plication, and *in*trinsic genre, as described in Hirsch's *Validity in Interpretation,* scientifically and aesthetically realize the penetration suggested in their prefixes.

One of the properties of a novel, therefore, is that it is a dynamic field through which the reader may atemporally be the characters, be the author of his own text, and be an interpreter. The dynamic field of the novel, common to the work, to its author, and to its interpreter, is language, by its nature dynamic. This field permits the interpenetration of denotation and connotation, the two parts of metaphor or of metonymy. In "The Reverse of Signs" in *Figures I*, Genette explains this field:

All these facts of writing are the means of connotation, since in addition to their literal sense, sometimes fallible or negligible, they indicate an attitude, a choice, an intention. This result of sur-signification can be represented by a simple scheme, for which one can resort again to rhetoric in its classic example: in the synechdoche *sail* = *ship*, there is a signifying word [*mot signifiant*], *sail*, and an object (or concept) signified [*signifié*], the *ship*: hence the denotation; but as the word *sail* has been substituted for the proper word *ship*, the agreement (signification) which unites the signifiant to the signifié constitutes a figure; this figure indicates in its turn clearly, in the rhetorical code, a poetic state of discourse: it functions therefore as the signifiant of a new signifié, poetry, on a second semantic plane which is that of rhetorical *connotation*; the characteristic of connotation is as a result from being established above (or below) the first signification, but in a manner disconnected, in using the first sense as basis for designating a second concept.

Through the dynamic field, therefore, the "re-cognition" advocated by Hirsch may literally occur. "'Artistic' perception," Shklovsky observes, "is that perception in which we experience form—perhaps not form alone, but certainly form." Boris Eichenbaum adds about Shklovsky's statement: "The notion of 'form' here acquires new meaning; it is no longer an envelope, but a complete thing, something concrete, dynamic, self-contained, and without a correlative of any kind." Since this is so, "the perception of form results from special artistic techniques which force the reader to experience form." This direct experience of form is possible only through the dynamic field of a work of art. Eichenbaum even argues that Shklovsky's theory of defamiliarization has as its function not the "re-cognition" of the meaning of an object but "the creation of its 'vision.'" Because the act of reading is an act of creation, dynamic form explains why one response to a novel is another novel, why one *discours* compels another.[6]

This relation between two discourses, which reveals the inseparability of time from space, is strongly present in James Joyce's *Stephen Hero* and *A Portrait of the Artist as a Young Man*. Joyce, in "Proteus" in *Ulysses*, gave the suggestion that allowed Theseus to escape from the Daedalian labyrinth.

Ineluctable modality of the visible: at least that if no more, thought through my eyes. Signatures of all things I am here to read, seaspawn and seawrack, the nearing tide, that rusty boot. Snotgreen, bluesilver, rust: coloured signs. Limits of the diaphane. But he adds: in bodies. Then he was aware of them bodies before of them coloured. How? By knocking his sconce against them, sure. Go easy. Bald he was and a millionaire, *maestro di color che sanno*. Limit of the diaphane in. Why in? Diaphane, adiaphane. If you can put your five fingers through it, it is a gate, if not a door. Shut your eyes and see.

Stephen closed his eyes to hear his boots crush crackling wrack and shells. You are walking through it howsomever. I am, a stride at a time. A very short space of time through very short times of space. Five, six: the *nacheinander*. Exactly: and that is the ineluctable modality of the audible. Open your eyes. No. Jesus! If I fell over a cliff that beetles o'er his base, fell through the *nebeneinander* ineluctably. I am getting on nicely in the dark. My ash sword hangs at my side. Tap with it: they do. My two feet in his boots are at the end of his legs, *nebeneinander*. Sounds solid: made by the mallet of *Los Demiurgos*. Am I walking into eternity along Sandymount strand? Crush, crack, crick, crick. Wild sea money.

Although the novel is a temporal art form, the opening sentence is about the timeless world of the visible and the unavoidable presence of its modality. In other words, before all there is space, a pure Einsteinian relativity. All first knowledge is spatial. For example, one may read the colored signatures of space: "snotgreen, bluesilver, rust." Even the soul perceived by Aristotle in *De Anima* is spatial and relative in its diaphanous quality. In contrast to the first paragraph, which concerns the spatial, in the second Joyce evokes the world of the temporal: "Stephen closed his eyes to hear." Since by closing his eyes Stephen both sees and hears, it is evident one must pass through the spatial for the temporal to operate, and the temporal is not attained except by the spatial. For this reason, the spatial is "ineluctable," incorporating the temporal. "A very short space of time through very short times of space." Because of this space-time relativity, the temporal, the *nacheinander* or the successive, is less an object of fear than the inescapable spatial, the *nebeneinander*. This relativity is clear in the title, *A Portrait of the Artist as a Young Man*, where the spatial portrait is the structure of an essentially temporal subject, the maturing protagonist of a *Bildungsroman*. This relative nature is especially signified by "as," which unites the temporal and the spatial in a space-time bond. "Proteus" is thus about the nature of temporal texts like the novel vis-à-vis their spatiality. In particular, Joyce's work is concerned with the relationship of texts outside time, a nexus that can be grasped only spatially. The link between the *Odyssey* and *Ulysses*, between Ovid's *Metamorphoses* and *A Portrait of the Artist*, or between *Stephen Hero* and *A Portrait of the Artist*, reveals a dynamic interpenetrating field.

The nature of this interpenetrating field is apparent when one examines the epigraph from Ovid's *Metamorphoses* to *A Portrait of the Artist*, "et ignotas animum dimittit in artes" ("and he turns his mind to unknown arts"). [7] This epigraph is, first of all, a gloss on Aristotle's *De Anima* referred to in the first paragraph of "Proteus," for the meaning of *animum* in Ovid is expanded by Joyce's allusion to Aristotle's text. Thus the reader must work backwards, from *Ulysses* to *A Portrait* to Ovid to Aristotle. To Ovid, *animum* meant "mind," "spirit," or "inspiriting impulse," but from Aristotle via *Ulysses* one learns that *anima*, specifically "soul," is a visible spatial object. Thus the name "Dedalus," based on Ovid's Daedalus, who is Stephen's great progenitor, will be seen in a climactic epiphany as the young artist's soul. This spatiality is reinforced by consideration of the lines immediately preceding and following the epigraph. In his next line, Ovid records that Daedalus "changes nature." Joyce's method of changing nature, of achieving a metamorphosis, is spatial, for although the tyrant controls the sea and the land, "the sky is open." The dynamic penetration of the Joycean text by the Ovidian text constitutes the mythic method that metamorphosed twentieth-century literature. By exploring the spatial illusion, Joyce turned time into space-time. He "changes nature," as did his predecessor.

One is accustomed to startling transformations in *A Portrait of the Artist*. The young man is transformed into the artist; words and language transform the experience of the world; and most significantly, *Stephen Hero* is transformed into *A Portrait*. Joyce's transformation of the two works is in the nature of the palimpset; that is, a correct understanding of *A Portrait* results not from seeing it as a displacement of *Stephen Hero*, but as superimposed on it. (In the broadest sense, the same is true of *Ulysses*, which combines the "naturalistic" method of *Stephen Hero* and the symbolistic method of *A Portrait*.) If *A Portrait* is more "elliptical," that fact only emphasizes, rather than delimits, the significance of spatiality in the novel. Lessing's *Laocoon* is mentioned in the surviving pages of *Stephen Hero*, and it bears directly on *Portrait*. To Stephen in *Stephen Hero*, Lessing's speculations are "fanciful generalization"; they "irritate" him, but Lessing's legacy, the desire to codify the arts, is a major preoccupation of *Stephen Hero* and especially of *A Portrait*. [8] Concern with the nature of the arts provokes this rumination in *Stephen Hero:*

He proclaimed at the outset that art was the human disposition of intelligible or sensible matter for an esthetic end, and he announced further that all such human dispositions must fall into the division of three distinct natural kinds, lyrical, epical and dramatic. Lyrical art, he said, is the art whereby the artist sets forth his image in immediate relation to himself; epical art is the art whereby the artist sets forth his image in mediate relation to himself and to others; and dramatic art is the art whereby the artist sets forth his image in immediate relations to others. The various forms of art, such as music, sculpture, literature, do not offer this division with the same clearness and he concluded from this that those forms of art which offered the division most clearly were to be called the most excellent forms: and he was not greatly perturbed because he could not decide for himself whether a portrait was a work of epical art or not or whether it was possible for an architect to be a lyrical, epical or dramatic poet at will.

When Joyce handled the same material in *A Portrait*, he quoted the three types of art and their definitions nearly verbatim, but the speculation about the temporal and spatial arts is indeed mostly eliminated. Only Lessing's name and his *Laocoon* are mentioned; the insight that music, sculpture, and literature do not offer clear divisions and the striking thought about the architect as poet are omitted. The two opening paragraphs from "Proteus," however, indicate that the spatial and the temporal art forms, the *nebeneinander* and the *nacheinander*, are dynamically experienced by the Stephen of *Stephen Hero* and *A Portrait*.

The concept of two texts as a dynamic interpenetrating field has received clear definition by Tzvetan Todorov in "How to Read?" "To read, the text is never other; it is multiple," he declares. The relationship of *Stephen Hero* to *A Portrait* supports Todorov's idea:

An entire text can never be read in a satisfying and clear manner unless one places it in relation to other works, prior to it and contemporary with it. In a certain sense, all texts can be considered as parts of a single text which has been in the writing since the beginning of time.

When Stephen declares in "Proteus," "Signatures of all things I am here to read," he means reading in the dynamic sense indicated by Todorov. Todorov regards this dynamism as existing not only between texts by different authors, as in the relation of Ovid's *Metamorphoses* to *A Portrait*, but also between works by the same author. "The different texts of an author may appear as variations of one another, commenting on each other and mutually clarifying each other." The meaning of the epigraph to *A Portrait* is made clear by Todorov's recognition that "the text is always a transformation of another transformation."[9] When Joyce entitled his work *A Portrait* instead of *The Portrait*, he was recognizing it as a stage of transformation dynamically related to Aristotle and Ovid but also potentially the generator of succeeding texts. The existence of *Ulysses*, particularly given its concern with the spatial and the temporal arts derived from *A Portrait* and *Stephen Hero*, proves this is so.

This relationship between *A Portrait* and *Stephen Hero*, and Joyce's concern about the arts, has an important consequence in the development of his theory of the epiphany. The three qualities of the epiphany, *integritas*, *consonantia*, and *claritas* (including *quidditas*), the three constituent qualities of beauty, are emphatically spatial. In *A Portrait*, *integritas*, which can be "temporal or spatial," "is first luminously apprehended as selfbounded and selfcontained upon the immeasurable background of space or time which is not it." That is, the object is distinguished above all by its place in the surrounding space; the reason for the word "portrait" in the title becomes clear, for of the spatial arts, this one of painting alone is "selfbounded," since painting knows no volume. The second property, *consonantia*, is an awareness of the harmony of structure of the object "within its limits"; the emphasis is again on boundary. The perception of *quidditas*, which produces *claritas*, occurs when the imagination, "arrested" by the wholeness of the image and "fascinated" by its "harmony," experiences "the luminous *silent stasis* of esthetic pleasure." For such a feat to be accomplished of a word or of language, the spatiality of literature must be recognized. The "esthetic emotion," in the purest sense, is "static" not "kinetic," and in support of this idea Stephen mentions that Aquinas used the word *visa* to apply to the artistic experience, whether visual or aural; its importance is that "it means certainly a stasis and not a kinesis." Stephen's aesthetic ideas are thus a compound of Lessing's and Aquinas's. So true is this *visa* that Stephen speculates about the colors of words and wonders if color is their primary attraction. Harry Levin has recognized this static element when he states that, from *Stephen Hero* to *Portrait of the Artist as a Young Man*, "scenes were replaced by tableaux."[10]

The seen static epiphanic moment, however, is significantly spatial not only in itself but also in its location. Joyce wrote in *Stephen Hero:* "Your mind to apprehend that object divides the entire universe into two parts, the object, and the void which is not the object. To apprehend it you must lift it away from everything else." This idea is also expressed in *A Portrait:* "All these elements which he deemed common and insignificant fell out of the scene." Moreover, Stephen is "wondering always where [words] came from." The process of discovering a word in an epiphany is essentially, therefore, a discovery and recognition of its spatial place.

The element of the void assumes a strong ethical tone as well as aesthetic importance when considered in light of chapter three of *A Portrait*. This chapter locates God's position as in "space, even in the bottomless abyss." Hell itself is a true spatial location, where "time is gone: gone forever," where its peculiar pain is one of "extension," a veritable palimpsest of pain, with the forces not counteracting but superimposing. In addition to this "pain of extension and yet coexistent with it we have the pain of intensity." The two central properties of extension and of intensity are peculiarly spatial; torments are both "endless" and "infinite," properties far more spatial than temporal, for hell is a place "every instant of which is itself an eternity." Such a definition is the exact converse of that of an epiphany, where all eternity is an instant.

The verification of the spatial and religious nature of the epiphany is found in *Stephen Hero,* where the young Stephen, discovering Skeat's *Etymological Dictionary,* regards the phrases it suggests in a religious sense.

Phrases came to him asking to have themselves explained. He said to himself: I must wait for the Eucharist to come to me... he built a house of silence for himself wherein he might await his Eucharist, days and nights gathering the first fruits and every peace-offering and heaping them upon his altar whereon he prayed clamorously the burning token of satisfaction might descend.

At the end of chapter three of *A Portrait,* we recognize the significance when "the ciborium had come to him," bearing with it for the moment not his host of the word, but God's word of His host.

Stephen's desire in *Stephen Hero* that the "burning token of satisfaction might descend" occurs in *A Portrait,* of course, in the epiphany of his own name. "Now, at the name of the fabulous artificer, he seemed to hear the noise of dim waves and to see a winged form flying above the waves." This seen token, the graph of his name, is abstracted now from a space (himself). He is therefore not only his own God in space, but he has become in place his own epiphany, his own flesh made word, the priest offering his own Eucharist. The movement of *A Portrait* is essentially Stephen's acknowledgment that what was formerly a void is now a space, inhabited not by God but by him both as priest and receiver, object and worshiper, of himself.

Through the spatial penetration of *Stephen Hero* and *A Portrait,* Joyce powerfully conveys the spatial nature of the epiphany. The dynamism of the two texts, however, suggests the nature of Joycean transformation, that *A Portrait* itself is a potential text, the generator of other texts by Joyce, and particularly of *Ulysses.* The relativity of *A Portrait* is clear, with its recurring images as leitmotifs, its self-reflexive echoes of words, and its reiterated recognition of the ambiguity of words (for example, "suck," "belt," God/*Dieu,* or ivory/*ivoire/avorio/ebur*). The dynamic potential of the text is also reinforced by its elliptical nature, where the first, third, and fifth chapters are theses not intended to be resolved by the second and fourth chapters. This elliptical technique is the image of the movement from void to space that is the novel's function and theme. Joyce's definition of the artist in *A Portrait* supports the concept of a relative, potential text. "The artist, like the God of the creation, remains within or behind or beyond or above his handiwork, invisible, refined out of existence, indifferent, paring his fingernails." This is the ability to inhabit both place and space, to be both "remaining within" by the interpenetrating text and "refined out" by the elliptical, potential text. The Joycean text is genuinely Einsteinian.

The nature of spatial relativity in the temporal art of literature is clarified by the theory of *genidentity* developed by Kurt Lewin in 1922. According to Hans Reichenbach in *Space and Time*, genidentity "makes possible the concept of the individual that remains identical during the passage of time." This identity of time between the work of art and its interpreter rests on the eclipse of distance between their separate spaces produced by the dynamic field. Reichenbach's structure of particles reveals the nature of this field.

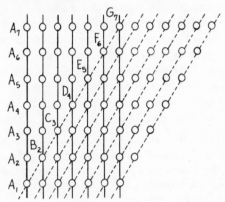

He explains: "Particle A_1 may thus be considered as genidentical with A_2 and A_3 . . . as well as with B_2, C_3, D_4. . . ." For purposes of literary theory and interpretation, one may assign various meanings to these particles. If one has two texts, A and B, the concept of genidentity reveals how they may remain both individual and multiple. The transformation of *Stephen Hero* into *A Portrait of the Artist as a Young Man* is dynamic in this sense. Similarly, if A is a text and B an interpreter of the text, their existence in a dynamic field uncomplicated by distance is manifest: the text and its interpreter occupy the same space, the dynamic field, in an atemporal relation. Likewise, words have genidentic extension. The structuralist word sign is constituted by a literal aspect and a signified aspect. From the perspective of genidentity, the literal aspect may be A, but the signified aspect B_2 or C_3 D_4. In changing the name of his protagonist from Daedalus to Dedalus, for instance, Joyce shows how his word *Dedalus* (A_1) is genidentic with Ovid's *Daedalus* (B_2), the concept of escape (C_3), the idea of inventor (D_4), the notion of artistic craft (E_5), and so on. Furthermore, Stephen can, through his experience of words and other texts, turn a void into a dynamic space. Whether A_1 is a text, an interpreter, or a word sign, it is significant that, as Reichenbach observes, "different states can be genidentical only if they are causally related." The causal connection, according to Reichenbach, constitutes a "signal, i.e., the transmission of a mark." Thus, one may speak of texts generating other texts, interpretations producing new interpretations, or words linking with other words. Michel Butor's conception of the book as an object demonstrates that its physicality is an architectural shaping of space, capable of exerting a volume through a dynamic field uniting text and interpreter, two texts, or the word in its literal and signified aspects. The acts of reading and of interpretation are thus spatial and atemporal.[11]

In *The Magic Mountain*, Thomas Mann analyzes the spatial nature of genidentity, especially its interpenetration, in an atemporal context. Of all the ideas that Hans Castorp must absorb during his residence on the mountain, the strangest but most compelling is stated earliest: "Space . . . possessed and wielded the powers we generally ascribe to time". This is to say that even before his arrival at the Berghof, Hans has already experienced its greatest power, the transmutation of time into space. In the preface to *The Magic Mountain*, Mann declares of his story:

It is far older than its years; its age may not be measured by length of days, nor the weight of time on its head reckoned by the rising or setting of suns. In a word, the degree of its antiquity has noways to do with the passage of *time*—in which statement the author intentionally touches upon the strange and questionable double nature of that riddling element.

The tale recounted, therefore, has nothing to do with chronological time; Mann even questions whether the double nature of time is valid. The other type of time, the psychological, which has nothing to do with the chronological, is unquestionably significant. In light of his statement about space at the beginning of the novel, however, Mann seems clearly to argue that the double nature of time is primarily illusory, imposed by man. In other words, absolute time does not exist. Time is only relative, and subsumed within space. Hermann Weigand observed of the novel:

Certainly, no other novel has ever aspired, in any way comparable to the *Zauberberg*, to be "all there" at any given moment.

The unique artistic aim of the *Zauberberg*, to be all there all the time, can, in the nature of things, be felt only more or less vaguely at the first reading.

Arnold Bauer can declare that one subject of the novel is "the mystical relativity of time, which has its scientific counterpart in Einstein's theories." As if to solidify the impression of this relativity, Mann constructs *The Magic Mountain* by "progressive foreshortening": chapter one, arrival; chapter two, past history; chapter three, first day; chapter four, first three weeks; chapter five, through the first seven months; chapter six, up to two years and four months after arrival; and chapter seven, four and one-half years. However one may regard the argument from the *Zeitgeist*, Thomas Mann and Einstein remain the literary and scientific cornerstones of the theory of relativity. Time is an element of space. If the subject of the novel is the consciousness of an era, that era has, with scientific precision, been "located" in space.[12]

Hans Castorp's introduction to the theory of relativity occurs on first meeting his cousin Joachim Ziemssen:

"It certainly is a change, anyhow, a break in the everlasting monotony."
"But time must go fast, living up here," was Hans Castorp's view.
"Fast and slow, as you take it," answered Joachim. "It doesn't go at all, I tell you. You can't call it time."

As his cousin notes, the diseased are "free" because "time is nothing to them." Hans is soon correcting Joachim:

"It might be possibly eight weeks ago—"
"Then you can hardly say lately," Hans Castorp pounced on him crisply.
"What? Well, not lately, then, since you're so precise. I was just trying to reckon. Well, then, some time ago, it was, I got a glimpse behind the scenes—purely by chance—and I remember it as if it were yesterday."

This initial education is reinforced by Settembrini's first words, "We are free with the time up here," and his subsequent analysis: "We up here are not acquainted with such an unit of time as the week.... Our smallest unit is the month. We reckon in the grand style—that is a privilege we shadows have." After this meeting, Hans and Joachim recall their earlier discussion. Hans declares: "Good Lord, is it still only the first day? It seems to me I've been up here a long time—ages." At the beginning of the fourth week, however, this relativity becomes more and more apparent:

It would be nearer the truth to call it a quarter after, but these odd quarter-hours outside the round figures do not count, they are swallowed up unregarded, in places where one reckons time in larger units—on long train journeys of many hours on end, or wherever one is in a state of vacant suspense, with all one's being concentrated on pulling the time behind one. A quarter past two will pass for half past, will even pass for three, on the theory that it is already well on the way toward it.

In this same chapter, the narrator himself confronts the problem of narrative time, what Ricardou in *Problems of the New Novel* calls the disparity between the "time of the narration" and the "time of the fiction."

And now we are confronted by a phenomenon upon which the author himself may well comment, lest the reader do so in his stead. Our account of the first three weeks of Hans Castorp's stay with "those up here" ... has consumed in the telling an amount of time and space only too well confirming the author's half-confessed expectations; while our narrative of his next three weeks will scarcely cost as many lines, or even words and minutes, as the earlier three did pages, quires, hours, and working-days. We apprehend that these next three weeks will be over and done with in the twinkling of an eye.

These same frustrations, of course, appeared much earlier in the novel's evolution in Sterne's *Tristram Shandy*.

After the experiences of the Walpurgis Night, it is the narrator himself who recalls the relativity of time, making it not only the subject but the method of *The Magic Mountain*.

Mountain and valley, then, had been lying in deep snow for six months; nay, seven, for as we talk, time strides on—not only present time, taken up with the tale we are telling, but also past time, the bygone time of Hans Castorp and the companions of his destiny.

We have elected to intermit the flow of our story along the stream of time, and let time flow on pure and free of any content whatever.

This onslaught of time, however, becomes overbearing, outside the control of the narrator: "We must bear in mind that while we tell the story, time streams silently and ceaselessly on." The problem becomes more and more acute:

Let us not forget the condition of life as of narration: that we can never see the whole picture at once.... The little hand on time's clock trips away as though measuring seconds; but God knows how much time it is covering when it whisks round heedless of the divisions it passes over!

Some day even the story itself will come to an end. Long has it lasted; or, rather, the pace of its contentual time has so increased that there is no more holding it, even its musical time is running out.

What Mann becomes aware of is that time, in relation either to the narration or to the fiction, is no longer an adequate method of conveying a subject itself subsumed within space.

One must find, to paraphrase Ricardou's terms, "the space of the fiction" and "the space of the narration." It is for this reason that Mann opens his sixth chapter with a statement of the problem.

What is time? A mystery, a figment—and all-powerful. It conditions the exterior world, it is motion married to and mingled with the existence of bodies in space, and with the motion of these. Would there then be no time if there were no motion? No motion if no time? We fondly ask. Is time a function of space? Or space of time? Or are they identical? Echo answers.... Furthermore, as our utmost effort cannot conceive a final limit either to time or in space, we have settled to think of them as eternal and infinite—apparently in the hope that if this is not very successful, at least it will be more so than the other. . . . Is it possible, in eternity, to conceive of a sequence of events, or in the infinite of a succession of space-occupying bodies? Conceptions of distance, movement, change, even of the existence of finite bodies in the universe—how do these fare? Are they consistent with the hypothesis of eternity and infinity we have been driven to adopt?

The first "answer" comes at the beginning of chapter seven.

Can one tell—that is to say, narrate—time, time itself, as such, for its own sake? . . . For time is the medium of narration, as it is the medium of life. Both are inextricably bound up with it, as inextricably as are bodies in space.

Time, while the medium of the narrative, can also become its subject. Therefore, if it is too much to say that one can tell a tale *of* time, it is none the less true that a desire to tell a tale *about* time is not such an absurd idea as it just now seemed.

One is particularly arrested in the German text by the appearance of scientific language like *Element* or *Masse*, or spatial artistic vocabulary like *perspektivisch*. These terms indicate that Mann has several solutions toward finding a "space" of fiction and of narration. The most apparent is to make the temporal medium the subject. The foreshortening technique of the chapters contributes to a spatial alteration of perspective; chronological time, once it has become a subject, ceases to be tyrannous, as Proust had recognized. The transmutation of the fundamentally temporal medium into a subject is the initial exploration of the spatial in *The Magic Mountain*.

Mann, however, associates the *Zeitroman* ("time novel") with the *Doppelsinn* ("ambiguity") peculiar to dreaming, to atemporal states of being. This ambiguity, this ability to exist in tension, becomes for Mann a crucial element for confronting the relativity of space and time in *The Magic Mountain*. The German *Zeitform* ("tense") contains, for example, a clear indication of this peculiarity. At several points in the novel Mann calls attention to the "spacious" nature of time at the Berghof. Hans loses contact with his uncle after contact with "the more spacious time conceptions" of the Zauberberg.

But to measure one's own private time, that time which for the individual in these parts was so closely bound up with space—that was held to be an occupation only fit for new arrivals and short-termers.

It is space-time that one experiences there; as Hans tells Joachim, "What we spend up here isn't time at all."

From this perspective, the device of antithesis in *The Magic Mountain* is fundamental to its space of narration and its space of fiction. The origin of the figure in *The Magic Mountain* is Germany itself, "the land of the middle." According to the ideas of Adam Müller and Nietzsche, the Germans are "the people of the middle." As Hermann Weigand puts it:

The German genius, according to Mann, does not subscribe to the formula "either-or," but rather to the formula "the one as well as the other." Not an out-and-out choice between opposites, but rather the inclusion of opposites, and the attempt to reconcile them as best one may, is characteristically German. [13]

At his first meeting with Hans Castorp, Settembrini tells him: "You represent now, in my eyes, the world of labour and practical genius." Germany, as he notes, is between Europe and Asian Russia:

"It is easy to see that the recklessness of these people where time is concerned may have to do with the space conceptions proper to a people of such endless territory. Great space, much time—they say, in fact, that they are the nation that has time and can wait. We Europeans, we cannot."

The international theme, the relation between countries, is an expression of Mann's formal problem in *The Magic Mountain*, which is how to express the relation of space to the temporal medium, the transformation of time into space. This thought is later expressed by Settembrini when he discusses Luther, a man who "flung a fatal preponderance into one of the two scales which in your country hang so dangerously even, into the scale of the East." Hans is the "man of the middle" confronted with "a choice between East and West." From the idea of the middle evolves the entire range of dualities observed by critics. Henry Hatfield has noticed the dual nature of the mountain itself (death and rebirth), and the dual aspect of Hans's isolation (educative freedom and disease), while Peeperkorn is both Dionysus and Christ and Behrens is ambivalent in his tyranny and toleration. Arnold Bauer considers Joachim Ziemssen an example of "noble" mediocrity because he does not learn about himself from his disease. Settembrini, the humanist from Bologna, and Naphta, the totalitarian Jewish Jesuit absolutist, alternate as Hans Castorp's two mentors. This ambiguity pervades even the location of the Zauberberg.

"You are bold indeed, thus to descend into these depths peopled by the vacant and idle dead—"

"Descend, Herr Settembrini? I protest. Here I have climbed up some five thousand feet to get here—"

R. P. Blackmur has noted that Mann's technique has been to present the equivocal and then make it familiar. "The relation between the simple and the equivocal . . . is the conceptual form of the book." Blackmur feels Mann's idea is that a human being may be the "lord of counterpositions," or as Arnold Bauer sees him, "the master of contradiction." The singularity of Mann's use of antitheses is that they result in a suspension in antithesis. [14]

The most basic formal manifestation of this relativity is the division of the book into two "volumes," the experiences before and those after the Walpurgis Night. One may summarize Weigand's commentary as follows: the first volume is concerned with disease, abandonment, adventure, and the body; the second involves health, restraint, responsibility, and the soul. A further formal extension of this relativity appears in the "fragmentary" manner in which Hans, and the reader, meet the characters. For example, through the successive meals one comes to grasp more and more the qualities of the inhabitants of the Berghof, but no absolute definition or description of the persons exists. The irony in *The Magic Mountain* also reflects the "suspension in antithesis," suggested by Schlegel's definition: "Irony is clear conviction of the everlasting movement of the infinite total Chaos." Hans defines the equivocal nature of this irony, which is relative by suspending its terms, in a passage exhibiting Mann's own authorial persona.

"Imagine," he said to himself, "he talks about irony just as he does about music, he'll soon be telling us that it is politically suspect—that is, from the moment it ceases to be a 'direct and classic device of oratory.' But irony that is 'not for a moment equivocal'—what kind of irony would that be, I should like to ask, if I may make so bold as to put in my oar? It would be a piece of dried-up pedantry!" Thus ungrateful is immature youth! It takes all that is offered, and bites the hand that feeds it.

Finally, the device of the leitmotif, by which ideas, phrases, debates, symbols, and images join in atemporal associations, suspended in their reflexiveness, was crucial to the making of the novel, as Mann declared in his essay, "The Making of *The Magic Mountain*." For Mann, antithesis, not antitheses, is the condition of mankind. Henry Hatfield is correct in stating that *The Magic Mountain* is Mann's "condemnation of thinking in antitheses." These would imply "either-or." Mann desired to give expression to atemporal suspension itself, and he achieved it by an intricate exploration of the space of the novel. The fact that the number of interconnections of the elements of this space are nearly infinite insures that one's impression of *The Magic Mountain* will remain "relative."[15]

Interpenetration, a further manifestation of spatial form in *The Magic Mountain*, relates it to other works by Mann, particularly to *Death in Venice* and *Tonio Kröger*. In his 1933 essay, "The Sufferings and Greatness of Richard Wagner," Mann spoke of the "three-dimensional rotundity" of Wagner, whose "genius lies in a *dramatic synthesis of the arts*." Wagner, he believed, was supreme in his ability to use music as a "method of characterization." Moreover, this "music" is peculiar: "His work, strictly speaking, has no chronology. It originates, of course, in time; but it is there all at once." The essay on Wagner is a more appropriate discourse on *The Magic Mountain* than Mann's essay devoted to it. The aim of the spatiality of the novel is for the entire work to be "there all at once," despite the fundamentally temporal medium of both opera and the novel. The "three-dimensional rotundity" Mann recognized in Wagner is of course sculptural; two words from *The Magic Mountain, Raum* and *Inhalts,* while more obviously "space" and "content," can both embrace the idea of "volume." Hermann Weigand has noted that in the novel one finds an "interpenetration of opposites," which is a particularly suitable definition of Mann's technique. This interpenetration by the leitmotif becomes a manifestation of characterization by sculptural volume.[16]

Mann had already employed such a method in *Death in Venice* (1911), making interpenetration in fact the theme of the novella. The Polish boy Tadzio mesmerizes and finally draws into himself the ruins of Aschenbach. Tadzio is himself "Greek sculpture": "What discipline, what precision of thought were expressed by the tense youthful perfection of this form?... Was not the same force at work in himself when he strove in cold fury *to liberate from the marble mass of language* the slender forms of his art?" Language itself is sculptural art, as is its object: "Thought that can merge wholly into feeling, feeling that can merge wholly into thought—these are the artist's highest joy." The essay on Wagner, *Death in Venice,* and *Tonio Kröger* provide a larger context for *The Magic Mountain* which is approved by Mann himself.

In a broader sense, the whole lifework of the author has its leading motifs, which serve to preserve its unity, to make that unity perceptible to the reader, and to keep the whole picture present in each single work. But just for that reason, it may be unfair to the single work to look at it by itself, disregarding its connection with the others, and not taking into account the frame of reference to which it belongs.

Mann implies that interpenetration among works is quite possible and intentional.[17]

The use of sculpture as a device of interpenetration in *The Magic Mountain* depends greatly on Joachim Ziemssen. The novel's image of interpenetration is the X ray, which is itself concerned with a form of penetration, disease. Staring at his cousin's body during an X ray in Behrens's office, Hans is drawn into it, experiencing its paradoxical nature of a diseased interior and an exterior "like a picture in a book, a regular Apollo Belvedere." The characterization of Joachim unites interpenetration to the antithesis that governs the book. During the experiences of "Snow," Hans Castorp sees an image reminiscent of Tadzio: "a lovely boy... that looked as though carven out of stone, inexpressive, unfathomable, a deathlike reserve." Surely this image is Joachim and Pribislav Hippe ("scythe," death) as well. In the succeeding chapter, when Joachim dies, it is Settembrini, whose words were called "plastic," who supports Hans. In the beginning of the final chapter, when Hans has his great epiphany of space and time, it is after recalling Joachim, whose silence is now seen as both prophetic and profound. Hans can speculate:

It would not be hard to imagine the existence of creatures, perhaps upon smaller planets than ours, practising a miniature time-economy, in whose brief span the brisk tripping gait of our second-hand would possess the tenacious spatial economy of our hand that marks the hours. And, contrariwise, one can conceive of a world so spacious that its time system too has a majestic stride, and the distinctions between "still," "in a little while," "yesterday," "to-morrow," are, in its economy, possessed of hugely extended significance. That, we say, would be not only conceivable, but, viewed in the spirit of a tolerant relativity, and in the light of an already-quoted proverb, might be considered legitimate, sound, even estimable.

Time is drowning in the measureless monotony of space, motion from point to point is no motion more, where uniformity rules; and where motion is no more motion, time is no longer time.

The figure of Hans Castorp, through his interpenetration by that of Joachim Ziemssen, becomes the embodiment of suspension in antithesis itself. His final appearance on the battlefields of Europe is neither the repudiation nor the victory of death, but rather the suspension by the man of the middle, who is every man. The "equivocal" power of sculpture to be both itself and to embrace what surrounds it is the paradigm of Mann's ideas in *The Magic Mountain*, the magic of the alchemy of time into space.

The concept of genidentity has, however, further importance. Reichenbach observes that "different states can be genidentical only if they are causally related." Consequently the existence of Ricardou's "another book" or of Genette's "two languages of the same language" is a result caused by the work of art itself. The language of a prose work, as Todorov argues in "Poétique" in *What is Structuralism?*, indicates its essential concern for the *lecteur virtuel* ("virtual reader"). The presence of the *lecteur virtuel* appears in what Mikhail Baxtin has called the "internal polemic" of prose.

In every style, properly speaking, there is an element of internal polemic, the difference being only in its degree and character. Any literary discourse more or less keenly senses its listener, reader, or critic, and reflects anticipated objections, evaluations, points of view. Moreover, literary discourse senses other literary discourse, other style alongside it. An element of the so-called reaction against a previous literary style which is present in every new style is just such an internal polemic.

This internal polemic is therefore an essential part of the dynamic field of the novel, as it creates the *lecteur virtuel*. Todorov observes that "literary points of view do not concern the actual perception by the reader, which remains always variable and dependent on factors external to the work, but concern a perception inherent to the work, attributed to the *destinataire virtuel* [virtual receiver] existing at the interior of this work." The ideal *lecteur virtuel*, one may contend, must be the *destinataire virtuel*, a conception made clear in "The Categories."

The image of the narrator is not a solitary image: when it appears on the first page, it is accompanied by what can be called "the image of the reader." Evidently, this image has as little rapport with a concrete reader as the image of the narrator has with the true author. The two are found in strict dependence on each other, and as the image of the narrator begins to stand out more clearly, the imaginary reader discovers himself drawn with more precision. The two images are proper to every work of fiction: the knowledge of reading a novel and not a document challenges us to play the role of this imaginary reader and at the same time the narrator appears, the one who recounts the narrative, since the narrative itself is imaginary. This dependence confirms the general semiological law according to which "I" and "you," the sender and the receiver of an utterance, always appear together.

The sender and the receiver of the enunciation may appear together through genidentic interpenetration. [18]

Todorov's *lecteur virtuel* is therefore an essential property of narrative discourse. Several recent studies have renewed attention to this reader, particularly Wolfgang Iser's *Implied Reader* and "The Writer's Audience Is Always a Fiction" by Walter Ong. Iser bases his contentions on an idea fundamental to Wayne Booth in *The Rhetoric of Fiction*. "The author creates . . . an image of himself and another image of his reader; he makes his reader, as he makes his second self, and the most successful reading is one in which the created selves, author and reader, can find complete agreement." The dynamic field through genidentity is the basis of this "complete agreement." For Iser, the meaning of a text cannot exist without "reader involvement." By a negation of customary norms in the novel, the reader is "forced to take an active part in the composition of the novel's meaning." The problem with Iser's statement, however, is that it requires one to regard this relationship as unnatural ("negation") and undesirable ("forced"). [19]

In *The Implied Reader* Iser investigates the creation and control of this reader from the eighteenth to the twentieth centuries. He analyzes the eighteenth-century narrative extensively, where the "novel reader was cast by the author in a specific role," particularly by such devices as the direct address of *Joseph Andrews.* Fielding leaves "deliberate gaps in the narrative . . . by which the reader is enabled to bring both scenes and character to life." The reader, Iser contends, is encouraged sometimes to collaborate with the author, sometimes to work independently on "vacant pages," occasionally to feel superior to the characters, and frequently to experience not only emulation but "discovery." All are parts of a process "whereby the reader formulates the unwritten text." In *Humphry Clinker,* the reader must "take the place of the recipients" of the letters. Scott in *Waverley* creates the "potential character" which the reader must fulfill.[20]

Iser's theory of reading, unfortunately, is extremely unrestricted. For example, he declares that not only the text but the "actions involved in responding to that text" constitute true meaning. One reads in the "virtual dimension" of the "unformulated part of the text." This theory becomes particularly tenuous for the twentieth century, when the author "disappears"—one of the two essential poles of Iser's experience fades and vanishes. Hirsch's ideas in *Validity in Interpretation* are at variance with Iser's contention that response may constitute meaning or that the "unwritten text" can be the author's text. Iser frequently uses the word "dynamic" to describe this relation without questioning how the relation may exist at all.[21]

Walter Ong decisively shifts the emphasis of Iser's argument. For him, the audience, the reader, is itself a part of the fictive process, not something external to it. Since Ong conceives of this relationship from the point of view of the author, there is not the adversary posture implicit in Iser's theory. The fact that the audience is a fiction has two results. First, "the writer must construct in his imagination, clearly or vaguely, an audience cast in some sort of role"; and second, "the audience must correspondingly fictionalize itself." The audience cannot maintain a separate identity. Chaucer, for example, through his group of listeners and tellers, has told "his readers how they are to fictionalize themselves." In contrast to Iser, Ong believes that Fielding, rather than having any established role for the reader, conceived it as "unsettled," which was "made acceptable by keeping the hero himself on the move." In the nineteenth century, he argues, this uncertainty is manifest in the "dear reader" convention. What Ong particularly recognizes, and what Todorov, Ricardou, and Genette have individually explored in depth, is illustrated by Paul de Man in *Blindness and Insight:* "The concept of intentionality is neither physical nor psychological in its nature, but structural." That the *lecteur virtuel* is an inherent part of the novel is demonstrated by the presence of authorial prefaces (*Roderick Random*), histories of the manuscript (*The Man of Feeling, Wuthering Heights, The Scarlet Letter*), publishers'

forewords and editors' prefaces (*Dangerous Liaisons*), and accounts of the
recounting (*Lord Jim, Absalom, Absalom!*). The genidentic experience
permits the "author/reader," a single individual, to create and to evaluate
the prose object. Such a process Jean Piaget in *Structuralism* called
"genetic homeostasis," a kinetic equilibration in the dynamic field. [22]

One work in which time is inseparable from space, and which therefore
requires the genidentic method, is Proust's *Remembrance of Things Past*,
especially *Time Regained*, where the creation of a work and its interpretation are both spatial. The conjunction of Albertine and Marcel in *The
Captive* produces several important colloquies, including that in which
their conversation shifts to *The Brothers Karamazov:* "But is it not a
sculpturesque and simple theme, worthy of the most classical art, a frieze
interrupted and resumed on which the tale of vengeance and expiation is
unfolded?" For Marcel the first episode of Dostoyevsky's novel is as "mys-
terious, grand, august as a Creation of Woman among the sculptures at
Orvieto." Proust's description of Hardy is masterly; he recognizes the
correspondence between the Hardy who was an architect and mason and
the Hardy who reproduced such men in art. In Marcel's discussion of the
relationship of *The Well-Beloved* to *A Pair of Blue Eyes*, Proust acknowledges the verticality of all the volumes of Hardy's work, their interrefer-
ence, and particularly the elements of line and of sculpture that are their
core, like Dostoyevsky's "frieze interrupted and resumed." This discussion of stonemasonry and sculpture is the clue to one element of Proust's
artistic resolution in his novel, the keystone to the two sides of his spatial
arch, the Méséglise way and Guermantes way. In *Figures III*, in his
"Discourse" about *Remembrance of Things Past*, Gérard Genette declares
that the *récit* of Proust's narrative is so free of time that it becomes
"temporally autonomous," as, for example, in the sequence from the first
appearance of Gilberte to the Duchess and the steeples of Martinville.

This succession has no agreement with the temporal order of events which
compose it, or only a rapport of partial coincidence. It depends essentially on the
placement of sites (Tansonville—plain of Méséglise—Montjouvain—return to
Combray—the Guermantes way), and therefore on a completely other temporality: the opposition between the walks to Méséglise and those to Guermantes, and
at the interior of each of these two series, an approximate order of "locations" of
the walk. One must naively merge the syntagmatic order of the narrative and the
temporal order of the story to imagine . . . that the meeting with the Duchess or
the episode of the steeples is after the scene at Montjouvain. The truth is that the
narrator had the most obvious reasons for grouping together, in spite of any
chronology, events in relation to a spatial proximity, by identity of climate (the
walks to Méséglise are always accompanied by bad weather, those toward Guermantes in good weather), or by thematic relation (the Méséglise way represents the
erotic-affective side, that of Guermantes is the aesthetic of the world of child-

hood), manifesting thus, more and better than anything before it, the capacity of *temporal autonomy* of narrative.

The question about Proust's art is really only how does *recherche* ("search") imply *retrouvé* ("regained")? Why is the one the other? Proust himself was clear about the meaning of the prefix *re-*, which meant both "back" and "again." In a letter to Paul Souday written 18 December 1919, he remarked: "The last chapter of the last volume was written immediately after the first chapter of the first volume. Everything in between was written subsequently." If Proust admired Balzac's *retour des personnages*, one is expected, in reading his novel, to become its own recreator by a *retour*, an understanding that forward can only be grasped by going back. [23]

There is no more suitable statement about Proustian time than this passage from *Swann:* "All these things made of the church for me something entirely different from the rest of the town; a building which occupied, so to speak, four dimensions of space—the name of the fourth being Time." The problem of time has been dealt with by several critics, notably by Robert Champigny, and their work has made it possible to study Proustian space. As Proust observed in *Against Sainte-Beuve:* "I found something else. . . . Time has assumed a dimension of space." Pursuing this insight, Georges Poulet demonstrated the importance of space in Proust, regarding it as the core of his artistic resolution of time. *Remembrance of Things Past*, Poulet contends, is a world where "thought marches in reverse," a "journey backwards," a work whose subject is "retrospective existence," "retrograde perspective," where the advance is "backwards." In *Proustian Space*, Poulet expanded the ideas of his *Studies in Human Time*. He distinguishes between Bergson's and Proust's concepts of space. "If the thought of Bergson denounces and rejects the metamorphosis of time into space, Proust not only accommodates himself to it, but installs himself in it . . . and makes of it finally one of the principles of his art." Bergson thinks space must be destroyed; for Proust, it is a salvation. "The work of Proust asserts itself as a search not only for lost time, but also for lost space." [24]

The consequence of this search for "lost space" as well as "lost time" is an extreme tension between the self and the world external to it. Germaine Brée has cited the "fusion of two worlds—the inner and the outer" as the central objective of Proust's work, while Poulet observes that for Proust the problem is how to "penetrate [the outside object] or draw it into ourselves," for Proust attempts "to reproduce it in himself." Poulet suggests two methods, "transcendence" and "equivalence," by which the Proustian man achieves such a fusion of inner and outer. For instance, in the passage about the hawthorns, the experience of what is outside is reproduced inside: "the operation by which, in miming within his own depths the exterior gesture of the sensible object, one imagines, one creates something which is still the object of sense, but this time no longer outside: rather, it is on the inside, no longer strange and impenetrable, but recognizable, identifiable: for this thing comes of us; it is us."[25] This internal miming of the external object, however, is only a partial solution to the eclipse of distance between the self and the external world.

The essential problem in the Proustian *recherche* is the method of the *retrouvé,* a method which must entail not only the recovery of *temps perdu* but of *espace perdu* as well, the entire tension of inner and outer. It is during the final pages of *Time Regained* that Proust suggests his concern for inner and outer.

I felt [happy impressions] as if they were occurring simultaneously in the present moment and in some distant past. . . . [They left] me uncertain in which period I was. In truth, the person within me who was at that moment enjoying this impression enjoyed it . . . independent of all considerations of time; and this person came into play only when . . . he could live and enjoy the essence of things, that is to say, entirely outside of time. . . . The person within me was a timeless person.

That these old impressions existed outside myself, at the corner of a certain square, could not be the means I was seeking. . . . [One had to] try to know them more completely at the spot where they were to be found, namely, within myself.

I was startled at the thought that it was, indeed, this bell which was still tinkling within me . . . to recapture it and hear it distinctly, I was forced to close my ears to the sound . . . around me. To endeavour to listen to it from nearby, I had to descend again into my own consciousness.

My head swam to see so many years below me, and yet within me . . . that past . . . which I was bearing so painfully within me.

Proust expresses the extraordinary necessity of the existence of the person within; separated from him, one is in exile. This being within is found not only by a confrontation with the outside but by its absorption—by drawing the hawthorns into ourselves. Georges Cattaui observes about Albertine that she is not only with him but in him by a metamorphosis whose essence is osmosis.[26] This centrifugal and centripetal action is the process by which " 'I' is another."

One need only look at a few of the "moments" to see the operation of this osmosis. It is at the heart of Marcel's experience of the trees at Hudimesnil in *In a Budding Grove:* "I sprang farther forward in the direction of the trees, or rather in that inverse direction at the end of which I could see them growing within myself." In *Sodom and Gomorrah* Marcel removes his boots: "The person who came to my rescue . . . was the same who, years before . . . in a moment when I was no longer in any way myself, had come in, and had restored me to myself, for that person was myself and more than myself." Or, when the twigs are ignited in *The Captive:* "There had been not merely a change in the weather outside, or, inside the room, the introduction of a fresh scent; there had been in myself a difference of age, the substitution of another person." This "substitution of person" is how "'I' is another." These three incidents demonstrate the importance of the internalization of the external world. The movement forward out is the growing within. The only life is the unobservable life, "the visible manifestations of which need to be translated and often *read backwards*" (italics added). The purpose of art is to help us "retrace," "recreate" this life: "One goes through an experience, but what one has felt is like these negatives which show nothing but black until they have been held up before a lamp and they, too, must be looked at from the reverse side." The truth is in something that is inverse, that can reverse, that can be backwards. "I had an imperative and vitally important engagement with myself." The process of reading as Proust explained it in *Time Regained* is similar to the method and goal of the novel. It does not merely juxtapose but interpenetrates the outside with the inside:

In reality, each reader reads only what is already within himself. The book is only a sort of optical instrument which the writer offers to the reader to enable the latter to discover in himself what he would not have found but for the aid of the book. It is this reading within himself what is also in the book which constitutes the proof of the accuracy of the latter and *vice versa.*

He continues: "They would not be my readers but readers of themselves . . . so that through my book I would give them the means of reading in their own selves."

The method of conducting the *recherche* and of gaining the *retrouvé* is sculpturesque and voluminous. "And my inner self of today is merely an abandoned quarry which believes that all the marble it contains is uniform and montonous, but out of which each remembrance, like a Greek sculptor, carves innumerable statues." Proust's sculptural imagery is almost entirely devoted to people, such as the frieze of young girls at Balbec. It is illuminating that in discussing Hardy, Dostoyevsky, or George Eliot, Proust finds the novelist's aim sculptural. Eliot's feeling for nature is one of "entering into it rather than describing it."[27] Sculptural volume is the core of his characterization of Mlle. de Saint-Loup in *Time Regained:*

Like most persons, moreover, did she not resemble the star-like crossroads in a forest where paths leading from the most different points converge, also for our life? Many were the paths of my life which met Mlle. de Saint-Loup and radiated outward from her. First of all, there came to an end in her the two principal "ways" where I had taken so many walks and dreamed so many dreams—through her father Robert de Saint-Loup, the Guermantes way; through Gilberte, her mother, the Méséglise way, which was Swann's way. One of them, through the young girl's mother and the Champs-Élysées, led me to Swann, to my evenings at Combray, to the Méséglise way; the other, through her father, to my afternoons at Balbec, where I saw him again beside the sunlit sea. And straight way crossroads between these two main roads defined themselves.

Mlle. de Saint-Loup may be the source of "radiation" by a sculpturesque notion of characterization, but she can as well enter into the narrator, himself a sculptured product. A few paragraphs later, the sculpturesque atemporal quality of characterization is overtly defined:

We could not recount our relations even with someone we have known only slightly without bringing in, one after the other, the most diverse settings of our life. Thus, every individual—and I was myself one of these individuals—measured the duration of time for me by the revolution he had accomplished, not only on his own axis, but about other individuals and notably by the successive positions he had occupied with relation to myself. And in truth, all these different planes on which Time, since I had come to grasp its meaning again at this reception, was arranging the different periods of my life, thereby bringing me to realise that in a book which aimed to recount a human life one would have to use, in contrast to the "plane" psychology ordinarily employed, a sort of three-dimensional, "solid" psychology, added a fresh beauty to the resurrections of the past which my memory had evoked as I sat musing alone in the library, because memory, by bringing the past into the present unmodified, just as it appeared when it was itself the present, eliminates precisely that great dimension of Time which governs the fullest realisation of our lives.

Of all definitions of the Proustian method, this is undoubtedly the greatest, for Proust expresses exactly how "that great dimension of Time" is eliminated: by "une psychologie dans l'espace." Time has become space, has become a sculptor: "Time, colourless and palpable, had, in order that I might, as it were, see and touch it, physically embodied itself in her and had moulded her like a work of art." A manuscript passage included at this point in the Pléiade edition reinforces the sculpturesque idea.

I was struck with the way in which her nose, modelled on her mother's and her grandmother's, ended sharply at a perfectly horizontal line below it, exquisite albeit not short enough. A single feature as distinctive, even had one seen nothing else, would have made it possible to identify one statue among thousands, and I marvelled how nature had come back in the nick of time for the granddaughter, as she had for the mother and grandmother, to give the mighty, deciding stroke of the chisel, like some great and unique sculptor.[28]

To write is to become spatial; there is no temporal art without its spatiality, as Marcel realizes.

Happy the man who could write such a book, I thought to myself; what a mighty task before him! To convey an idea of it, one would have to go to the noblest and most varied arts for comparisons; for this writer, who, moreover, would have to show the most contradictory sides of each of his characters in order to give his volume the effect of a solid, would need to prepare it with minute care, constantly regrouping his forces as if for an attack, endure it like an exhausting task, accept it like a rule of conduct, build it like a church.

Never in the history of literature has an author been so explicit about the sculpturesque notion of creation; Proust specifically cites the "volume" necessary for the reader to participate in his work, the volume that a writer like Lawrence sought in *Women in Love.* Sculptural volume is the only method in spatial art that inherently possesses the resolution of outer and inner; therefore Gilberte is Marcel. She is "fashioned of the very years I had lost; she seemed to me like my own youth."

The art of reading, like the art of writing, is a search, and not only for lost time. Gaston Bachelard's ideas in *The Poetics of Space* suggest that it is much more important from where, rather than when, one starts. Sculpture alone of the spatial arts overcomes the distance between outer and inner to generate a participatory experience of literature. The search for lost time requires that this time be lost forever. It is in this sense that Proust can believe that "the person I had been was a being outside time." This extratemporal being is found by extratemporal means. Proust describes his own achronic methods in the novel.

I was not mistaken, and I am going to relate at once the two incidents which afterwards proved it to me. (For the second of these incidents, I shall have to get far ahead of my story, as it happened after the death of M. de Charlus which did not occur until much later. . . .)

Proust's emphasis here on "retrospection," "anticipation," "seeing again," and "after" reveals how pervasive is the transformation of time into space in his novel. His conception of reading the work is completely genidentic.

It would be incorrect to say even that I was thinking of those who might read it as "my readers." For, as I have already shown, they would not be my readers but readers of themselves . . . so that *through my book* I would give them the means of *reading in their own selves.* Consequently, I would not ask them to praise or dispraise me but only to tell me if it is as I say, if the words they read in themselves are, indeed, the same as I have written [italics added].

The narrator, advising us not only how to create but to recreate, states: "One must return backwards." This is the novel that permits one to say: time regained is space.

In *Figures III,* Gérard Genette speaks of several achronic devices of prose narrative. Among them are *paralipse* (omission of information that ought to be given), *paralepse* (giving information that ought to be omitted), *analepse externe* (information supplied earlier than the beginning of the novel), *analepse interne* (information supplied later than the beginning), *prolepse externe* (anticipation of an event not occurring in the particular narrative), and *prolepse interne* (anticipation of what will follow in the next chapter). These strategies become logical in the timeless genidentic field, and are particularly explicable by the concept of "homeorhesis" Jean Piaget derives from C. H. Waddington in *Structuralism:* "a kinetic equilibration whereby deviations from certain necessary paths of development . . . are compensated for." The dynamic field of the novel, established in homeostasis, adjusted through homeorhesis, is the "hermeneutic circle" which Genette notes in *Figures I.* This circle is in fact a dynamic field, since the reader, confronting the figural nature of words, knows that interpretation "depends on a separation between these words and those that the reader, mentally, perceives beyond them, 'in a perpetual passing beyond the written thing.'" The code of rhetoric, Genette argues, establishes a "general consensus . . . a list, unceasingly reshaped but always tending to be exhaustive, of permissible figures"— that is, a genidentic dynamic field of language. For Genette, the classification of these figures is "subject to continuous modifications, but always organizing into a coherent functional system." He continues:

> The most apparent classification rests on these detailed forms: figures of words taken in their signification, or *tropes;* figures of words taken in their form, or figures of *diction;* figures resting on their order and the number of words in a phrase, or figures of *construction;* figures resting on "the choice and matching of words" (Fontanier), or figures of *elocution;* figures resting on the complete phrase, or figures of *style.*[29]

Genette's emphasis on the dynamism of the literary figure and of language itself reveals the particularly strong genidentity inherent in novels devoted to creations of dynamic fields involving an interaction of readers and characters as authors. Two novels in particular, William Faulkner's *Absalom, Absalom!* and Michel Butor's *Modification,* demonstrate the extreme extension of dynamism through language, that of creating a field totally absorbing the interpreter, who must become a recreator in a realm where time is completely inseparable from space, and where a "meaning" is found only through penetration in the dynamic field.

In the 1956 *Paris Review* interview, Faulkner declared:

> The aim of every artist is to arrest motion, which is life, by artificial means and hold it fixed so that a hundred years later, when a stranger looks at it, it moves again since it is life. Since man is mortal, the only immortality possible for him is to leave something behind him that is immortal since it will always move. This is the artist's way of scribbling "Kilroy was here" on the wall of the final and irrevocable oblivion through which he must someday pass.

Faulkner's belief that the artist's aim is to arrest motion had the following consequence in his work:

The fact that I have moved my characters around in time . . . . proves to me my own theory that time is a fluid condition which has no existence except in the momentary avatars of individual people. There is no such thing as *was*—only *is*. If *was* existed, there would be no grief or sorrow.

This perception of *is* is pervasive to Quentin Compson, as he notes on his last day in *The Sound and the Fury:* "The day like a pane of glass struck a light, sharp blow, and my insides would move, sitting still. *Moving sitting still.*" Richard Adams speaks of the "dynamic stasis" of Rosa's narrative in *Absalom, Absalom!*, and Sartre believes of *The Sound and the Fury:* "Nothing happens; the story does not unfold." "Faulkner has laid hold of a frozen speed at the very heart of things . . . fleeting and unimaginable immobility." "Faulkner is able to make man a sum total without a future." If for Proust the past is in some way salvation, for Faulkner it is hell. Michael Millgate, speaking of Quentin in *The Sound and the Fury*, notes that his is a "search for a means of arresting time," suggesting an important analogy between Faulkner's task and Quentin's. "What confronts [Quentin] is, among other things, a literary task, virtually a problem of authorship, involving questions of literary technique and of the author's attitude towards his material," a problem of which Quentin is himself conscious. Miss Rosa hopes he'll remember her kindly and be grateful for avoiding the actual experience of the events she is to narrate: "Maybe you will enter the literary profession . . . and write about it." Quentin thinks: *"Only she don't mean that,* he thought. *It's because she wants it told."* As several critics have noted, therefore, *Absalom, Absalom!* is preeminently a "narrative about narrative," with Quentin taking the "novel out of the hands of the novelist" by creating "fictions within fiction" in a "continuous pre-occupation with the novel as *form,*" to apply Aiken's words about Faulkner to Quentin himself. This narrative about narrative depends greatly on its spatial secondary illusion. As Hyatt Waggoner observes, the work is a "series of frames" with "picture containing a picture, and so on."[30]

The main element of Sutpen's plan was this spatial "design." He says: "You see, I had a design in my mind. Whether it was a good or bad design is beside the point; the question is, where did I make the mistake in it." There are at least two other designs in the novel, Quentin's and Faulkner's. This emphasis on design distinguishes *Absalom, Absalom!*, in which it is an obsessive interest. Faulkner provided a clue to the essence of design in *The Sound and the Fury:*

And Father said it's because you are a virgin: dont you see? Women are never virgins. Purity is a negative state and therefore contrary to nature. It's nature

that's hurting you not Caddy and I said That's just words and he said So is virginity
and I said you dont know. You cant know and he said Yes. On the instant when we
come to realise that tragedy is second-hand.

Much that is crucial to *Absalom, Absalom!* is contained here: the idea of
the "negative state," the problematic nature of words, and especially the
idea that tragedy is "second-hand." This is to say that the prevailing ethos
of *Absalom, Absalom!* is that of the future anterior ("there will have
been"), a strange state perfectly described by E. M. Cioran in "The Fall
out of Time." "When we are cast out, we *remember* the future, we no
longer run toward it." "When I see in the possible itself the past that is *to
come*, then everything turns into potential bygones, and there is no
longer any present, any future. . . . I generate dead time, wallowing in the
asphyxia of becoming. . . . Other people fall into time; I have fallen out of
it." Cioran is a lineal descendant of Quentin Compson. "If, on the surface,
I have a certain latitude of maneuver, in depth everything is *arrested*
forever." In other words, the idea of "second-hand tragedy" is peculiarly
bound with that abnormal, "static time" of the future anterior, a genuine
paradoxical, oxymoronic tense in language. The nature of Quentin's dilemma is revealed in an experience recounted by Cioran: "Hell is this
motionless present, this tension in monotony"; "the process of this fall
(out of time) and this adjustment is called History." Cioran's concept of
history is peculiarly the nature of "history" in *Absalom, Absalom!*. Its
advantage is that it is "paralysis on our own terms, and while certainly not
much comfort in words, still, life. Still-life. The methodical fall."[31] There
are then two essential spatial movements in this history—of simultaneity
and of the anterior.

Faulkner himself acknowledged the "simultaneous" element of *Absalom, Absalom!* when he noted that the similarities of the biblical allusions and the novel "were simultaneous. As soon as I thought of the idea
of the man who wanted sons and the sons destroyed him, then I thought
of the title." One may therefore read the accounts of David (Sutpen),
Absalom (Henry), Tamar (Judith), and Amnon (Bon) as a palimpsest for
Absalom, Absalom!. This principle of simultaneity, however, is pursued
not only by the palimpsest but also through the Balzacian principle of the
recurrence of characters. Michel Butor observes in his essay on Balzac
that by recurrence of characters Balzac "transposes this sequence into a
simultaneity." This technical recurrence, by which Quentin appears in "A
Justice," "That Evening Sun," and *The Sound and the Fury*, Sutpen is
alluded to in "An Odor of Verbena," and Wash Jones has his own account
in "Wash," operates, in Faulkner as in Balzac, as "a sort of novelistic
ellipsis," in that "a story which seemed linear . . . is later revealed as the

meeting point of a whole series of themes." The technique provides "a novelistic mobile... which we can approach in almost any order we please; each reader will follow a different trajectory." For both Balzac and Faulkner, "chronologic sequence... is... only a particular case of possible combinations." As Michael Millgate has observed, in *The Sound and the Fury* we have something very like a series of superimposed photographs which in *Absalom, Absalom!* become superimposed narratives superimposed on *The Sound and the Fury* itself. [32] Here is the simultaneous genidentic field of space-time theory.

The consequences of this simultaneity appear especially in Faulkner's method of repetition and suspension. If in the figures of Sutpen, Henry, Judith, and Bon we have the biblical David, Absalom, Tamar, and Amnon, Faulkner pursues the method of the palimpsest within the novel itself. Henry and Judith, for example, are a "single personality with two bodies both of which had been seduced almost simultaneously by a man whom at the time Judith had never even seen"; "She must have seen [Bon] in fact with exactly the same eyes that Henry saw him with." This results in a realization that "*I gave my life and Judith's both to him—.*"

Quentin thinks when Henry tells Judith he killed Bon: "the two of them, brother and sister, curiously alike as if the difference in sex had merely sharpened the common blood to a terrific, an almost unbearable, similarity." The result is that incest constituted part of the "truth."

So it must have been Henry who seduced Judith, not Bon: seduced her along with himself from that distance between Oxford and Sutpen's Hundred, between herself and the man whom she had not even seen yet, as though by means of that telepathy with which as children they seemed at times to anticipate one anothers' actions as two birds leave a limb at the same instant. [33]

This repetition, however, has one unusual element. It does not duplicate so much as it reduces to a unitary dimension. Quentin can think that Shreve "*sounds just like father,*" but there follows a later reduction to "*Maybe we are both Father,*" with the capital *F* seeming to indicate not a group of individuals but a generic kind. The motif of incest in the novel, important to Quentin and his attitude to Caddy in *The Sound and the Fury*, is essentially a subdivision of a much larger unitary simultaneous reduction in the novel. Bon thinks: "*All right. I want to go to bed with who might be my sister.*" Henry's torment, his attempts to dissuade Bon resulting in his final acquiescence to "*Write. Write. Write,*" reflects of course his own longing to be in the place of Bon. Or, rather, he wishes to have it both ways, to seduce his sister, and to be seduced by Bon.

The palimpsest of individual identities (Absalom/Henry/Quentin and Amnon/Bon/Shreve) becomes Faulkner's genidentitic dynamic field in

Absalom, Absalom! "So that now it was not two but four of them riding
the two horses through the dark over the frozen December ruts of that
Christmas Eve: four of them and then just two—Charles-Shreve and
Quentin-Henry." "The two the four the two facing one another in the
tomblike room." "Because now neither of them were there. They were
both in Carolina and the time was forty-six years ago, and it was not even
four now but compounded still further, since now both of them were
Henry Sutpen and both of them were Bon, compounded each of both yet
either neither." This genidentity of Henry and Judith, Henry and Bon
leads to that of Quentin and Shreve themselves: "It was Shreve speaking,
though . . . it might have been either of them and was in a sense both;
both thinking as one"; "it did not matter to either of them which one did
the talking." "*Yes, we are both Father. Or maybe Father and I are both
Shreve, maybe it took Father and me both to make all of us.*" Such
genidentity contributes to the simultaneous existence of one unit, that of
mankind itself, utterly timeless. This timeless essence is emphasized in
Sutpen, Bon, and Charles Etienne. Through this tenseless sense Faulkner declares: "There is no such thing as *was*—only *is.*" Sutpen himself
"fell into" the territory, with no one knowing where he came from;
Charles Bon is "impervious to time," "born of no woman." His son, when
brought by Judith and Clytie to Sutpen's Hundred, is a "child with a face
not old but without age." His son in turn, the idiot Jim Bond, is absolutely
timeless. One recognizes a clear manifestation in Faulkner's method of
characterization of a central spatial element, a "repetition" that is yet not a
recurrence, but rather a simultaneity. This is a method of characterization
close to the *polyptuton*, the variation of case endings for simultaneous
effects, of classical poets.

This simultaneity characterizes the minutest parts of Faulkner's construction and his style. There are similar chapter endings. At the close of
chapters three and four, Wash Jones's question, "Air you Rosie Cold-
field?," is repeated, followed by the information that "Henry has done
shot that durn French feller." Twice Rosa is stopped by Clytie, once when
Bon is shot and again when she tears through to find Henry in 1909. The
recurrence of the "boy-symbol" or of the winter motif verifies this design.
In his language, extensively studied by Warren Beck, Walter Slatoff, and
Florence Leaver, Faulkner carried this repetition that is yet not recurrence to an extreme level of thematic demonstration. Leaver notes that
four particular types of words recur: abstracts, "negative ultimates" (for
example, "inexorable" or "illimitable"), compounds, and repetitions. The
last three have strongly spatial overtones. The compounds ("torch-
disturbed") represent a superimposition of two ideas, the repetitions (in

Absalom, Absalom! particularly "outrage" and "wait") produce a further simultaneity, and the "negative ultimates" express a central element of Faulkner's ideology.[34] These practices are derived of course from the biblical story itself, with its reiterated exclamations and data: "Saul has slain thousands, David his tens of thousands."

Walter Slatoff has explored the "dynamic immobility" of other linguistic features. He points to Faulkner's use of the oxymoron (the "simultaneous suggestion of disparate or opposed elements"), of contradictory terms of equal rank ("at once corrupt and immaculate"), of an antizeugma maintaining a "tension of contradiction itself," and of synaesthetic images, which are inherently simultaneous. Slatoff and Leaver find that all of these practices contribute to what Conrad Aiken has stated to have been Faulkner's intention, the technique of "deliberately withheld meaning." "Faulkner is willing and even anxious to leave most of [the pieces of the story] in a high degree of suspension, or at least a suspension that cannot be resolved in logical or rational terms," "a juxtaposition of elements which do not seem to fit together and which to some degree resists synthesis or resolution." The result is the marathon sentences with "deliberate non-sequiturs," what Warren Beck called "kaleidoscopic disparaging suspension," with endings "designed to prevent . . . resolution." These sentences "leave unresolved the question of the meaningfulness of the human events and suffering we have witnessed," which reflects a "similar schizophrenia within ourselves." There is, however, a larger component of Faulkner's language operating here, in the exploitation of the spatial potential of the word, of the novel itself.[35] These "repetitions," whose effect is nevertheless "simultaneous," represent an exploration of the spatiality of novelistic language. If indeed *Absalom, Absalom!* is a novel about narrative and about novelistic method, then Faulkner's "suspensions" do not seem bizarre nor deliberately confusing, but rather the product of his intentional investigation of spatial genidentic language. This exploration of spatial illusion is what Quentin means by the "*ripple-space*" of events.

Faulkner's great achievement, however, exists in his discovery not only of "arrested motion" but of "negative motion." Characters in *Absalom, Absalom!* frequently "stop in motion." For example, Rosa says, "*I stopped in running's midstride again though my body . . . still advanced,*" and Sutpen and Henry "*kiss before Henry is aware that he has moved, was going to move, moved by what of close blood which in the reflex instant abrogates and reconciles.*" This is Quentin's state in *The Sound and the Fury* of "*moving sitting still.*" This frozen moment appears just before the fatal shot between Henry and Bon, when Faulkner alludes to the sculptural illusion underlying character:

> They faced one another on the two gaunt horses, two men, young, not yet in the world, not yet breathed over long enough, to be old but with old eyes, with unkempt hair and faces gaunt and weathered as if cast by some spartan and even niggard hand from bronze.

The spatial illusion is powerful: if this shot seems timeless it is primarily because the participants have assumed the spatial illusion of themselves.

However, this shot is peculiarly a "negative event." It is "a shot heard only by its echo," completing Bon's sequence: "He was absent, and he was, he returned, and he was not; three women put something into the earth and covered it, and he had never been." Here Faulkner begins to exploit a strange dimension of space that is solely his. This is negative space, whose corollary is the "negative ultimate" Florence Leaver finds in his language. And this shot which is only an echo is merely an echo of the Civil War itself, a "negative event":

> *I mean, there has never been any more of it, that there was that one fusillade four years ago which sounded once and then was arrested, mesmerized raised muzzle by raised muzzle, in the frozen attitude of its own aghast amazement and never repeated and it now only the loud aghast echo jarred by the dropped musket.*

Bon is "impervious to time," and his own death is even stranger: *"No, there had been no shot. That sound was merely the sharp and final clap-to of a door between us and all that was, all that might have been—a retroactive severance of the stream of event."* This shot which never occurred, only its echo, "destroyed" a man "impervious to time," "born of no woman," who at his "end" "had never been." Bon is the character above all whose realm is the future anterior by virtue of this "retroactive severance." Throughout the later part of *Absalom, Absalom!* Faulkner reiterates the concept of the retrograde. "And I reckon Grandfather was saying 'Wait, wait for God's sake wait' . . . until he finally did stop and back up"; *"with nothing remaining now but the ability to walk backward"*; *"what was left of them had been walking backward for almost a year."* Bon sees Sutpen during the retreat *"walking backward"* in Carolina.

If the retreat during the war is an historical event, it becomes the essential event of the race of mankind; it is during this walking backward that Henry gasps *"Write.Write.Write."* Bon's writing, which is his return, which is backward, which occurs during the retreat, becomes the paradigm of the writer confronting his material (Quentin/Henry/Bon/ Shreve), of recognition of the spatial illusion. Faulkner finds the strength of his own form of the novel in *Absalom, Absalom!*. That is, he finds in its spatial secondary illusion, its ability to be reversed by this illusion, the extraordinary complement of the nonevent, of the retreat, of the walk backwards. Conrad Aiken complained that in reading Faulkner's sentences it was "distracting to have to go back" to find the subject of the verb.[36] His statement reveals his failure to discover that Faulkner's techniques constitute a study in exploration of novelistic form by extreme probing of its spatial secondary illusion, and especially of its reversibility.

Through Jean Ricardou's observation that in the dialogue sections of a novel narrative and its narration become simultaneous in an "equilibrium," one finds a stronger definition of Faulkner's technique than the word "suspension" or "deliberately withheld meaning."[37] Since all of *Absalom, Absalom!* is dialogue, there is the most violent "arrest" of time in a novel about the novel, an enunciation of the novelist's exploration of spatial reversibility as the crucial illusion enabling this temporal art to extend to the depiction of man, the creature of the future anterior, forever observed in the conditional or subjunctive, uttering orders, in his solitude and his folly, in the imperative and subjunctive. All that returns is the echo, the echo that retreats from Quentin to Henry to Absalom. Man is a creature like Sutpen, who shouts "let there be" when there is no one to hear. This is the "true wisdom which can comprehend that there is a might-have-been which is more true than Truth." Or as Cioran observed: "When we are cast out, we *remember* the future."

The genidentity of *Absalom, Absalom!*, resulting from its simultaneity of character and its dynamism of language, is extended even more radically in the finest spatial novel of the present day, *The Modification*, by Michel Butor. The term *nouveau roman* has by now been so broadly applied as to be almost meaningless, and time itself has made what once was new seem familiar. Our understanding of the relation of cinema to fiction and of the introduction (or reintroduction) of the concept of surfaces and things to the novel has accustomed us to such "experimental" novels and techniques. However, one may cite Butor as an exception even to the experimental tradition. He has shed the affiliation with the traditional novel easily, in a manner more radical than that of Robbe-Grillet. For example, to contrast the titles of Robbe-Grillet's fiction with Butor's indicates the nature of their revolts: works like *Jealousy, The Voyeur, La Maison de Rendez-vous* and *The Erasers* indicate Robbe-Grillet's interest in subjects that are traditional concerns of the novel— passion, observation, location, suspense. Butor's titles, with the possible exception of *Passage from Milan*, reflect technical assaults: *Passing Time, Degrees, Mobile*. Their predominant emphasis is on the conscious exploration of the technique of writing. Two of Butor's best-known essays contain the word *recherche*, indicating their affiliation not only with Proust but with "research"; he is the greatest spatial novelist of the present day. If Robbe-Grillet developed his theories of things, of surfaces, in part from cinema, he nevertheless did so by connecting two temporal art forms. Butor, on the other hand, whose interest in painting extends to writing on Mondrian, Pollock, and Rothko, dedicated his *Mobile* to Pollock, which indicates the direction of his inquiries. Other essays, such as "The Space of the Novel" and "The Book as Object," indicate the explorations of secondary illusion that have characterized his work. *The Modification* is in reality about spatiality per se in the novel.

Butor's interest in the spatial is enduring in both his creative and his critical works. In "Research on the Technique of the Novel," he argues that the chronological arrangement of events has little to do with the effect of a novel; when two central characters are separated, the interest, for example, immediately becomes simultaneity. What are they doing at commensurate moments? Time to Butor is rarely experienced as continuous; the novel's preoccupation with this type of time is its greatest falsity to actual experience. Even the use of words and sentence patterns, which make the novel in essence temporal, are not principal to experience. Time in the novel is a superimposition of at least three temporal structures, those of adventure, of writing, and of reading. In "The Book as Object," Butor presents theories of secondary illusion; he believes that the novel cannot function without the plastic element. In his "Time of the Narration; Time of the Fiction," Jean Ricardou, with more implication than he perhaps suspects, discusses both Lessing's *Laocoon* and Butor's work in the same pages. In modern fiction, states Ricardou, the drama of fiction is the struggle between the writing and the architecture, between the narration and that which contains it: "the *act of writing* is no longer disguised by the unwinding of the story, but it has been challenged in its very reiteration, by the *architecture* of the book."[38]

Such is the nature of *The Modification*, whose subject is relativity itself. On a thematic level, the story recounts the excursion by train of Léon Delmont from Paris to Rome to secure his mistress Cécile by telling her he has found a position for her. In the course of the journey, however, his original plans change as recollections and projections of Rome, Paris, Cécile, and his wife Henriette modify his ideas. When he alights in Rome he has decided to abandon his original idea, return to his wife, and write of his experiences in a novel. As Michel Leiris observes, the theme is "abandonment of a project and the decision instead to write of the abandonment in *The Modification*." The subject has complex implications. Léon Roudiez argues that the book is about *la mauvaise foi* ("bad faith").

Until this time Léon has never made an authentic decision; his decision not to change his circumstances is the first. Michael Spencer, however, contends that Roudiez's interpretation is untenable because of the strong determinism pervading the book. While either of these positions may be questioned, Delmont's decision to write of his experiences is indisputable: "You take [the book] in your hand, saying to yourself, I ought to write a book; that would be the way to fill this hollow emptiness within me, now that I've lost all other freedom." His statement is nearly verbatim Butor's own: "a void, an absence is at the origin of each novel"; "only the writing of the novel will permit one to elucidate the void." Thus, the void is the origin of the novel, according to Butor, and the essence of the novel according to Ricardou, who earlier declared that Butor's *Passing Time* was "a narrative of the hiatus." *The Modification* is a confrontation with spatiality itself, represented first by the void and then by the object which fills the void to create a dynamic field. It is in this sense that Butor titles his essay "The Book as Object." Delmont finds his objective: "Then in that hotel room, alone, you'll begin writing a book, to fill the emptiness of those days in Rome deprived of Cécile."[39]

The Modification reflects, moreover, two elements central to Butor's thought about fiction—"mobility" and "openness." Delmont notes he has no other freedom except to write; this is the only truly determined thing about his decision. But it reflects Butor's sense of the importance of mobility, of freedom, as much in structural as in metaphysical terms. The concept of openness, derived by Butor from Umberto Eco, states in effect that every good book is constantly potential (as opposed to "closed" books which have no potentiality). Butor furthers this idea by stating that in the final structure of a book should be reflected the ideal history of that structure. Mobility and openness expand the idea of genidentic spatiality to mean the dynamic field may include not only that work and its reader but all literature. At the end of the novel, Delmont moves "toward this book, this future necessary book of which you're holding in your hand the outward form." It is, as Roland Barthes observes, both compensatory and redemptive to write the book. Furthermore, as Ricardou claims, it is the only thing that can be written: "The novel ceases to be the writing of a story to become the story of a writing."[40]

The title is crucial to understanding the work. Butor himself cites it as a "micro-grammaire" of the novel. Embracing the concept of change or qualification of an original essence, the title is itself dynamic and potential. Barthes insists:

If Robbe-Grillet describes objects quasi-geometrically, it is to release them from their human significance, to *purge* them of metaphor and anthropomorphism.

This detailed regard... is purely negative, it establishes nothing, or rather it establishes anything, or rather it establishes precisely the *nothing human* of the object.

By contrast, in *The Modification*, "the object is rendered in its sorrowful intimacy with man, it becomes part of man, it 'dialogues' with him." Out of this phenomenological connection between man and the exterior world arises the physical and spiritual modification that is the work's concern. As Françoise Rossum-Guyon observes in her *Critique of the Novel*: "The modification of route and that of the soul are not only parallels of one another but correlatives of one another. The indications of the stations and of the time-table, the transformation in the compartment, reveal indirectly the internal modification, the growth of internal disorientation." In *The Modification*, "the traveler no longer has the power to separate the exterior from the interior, the causes from the effects, the reality from the dream."[41] He has become an extraordinary dynamic field.

Handling the spiritual and the physical modifications in conjunction is one of Butor's most notable secondary spatial practices; it constitutes the creation of the work as a dynamic field. In fact he used superimposed sheets of paper as the graph for *Degrees* (1960). This concept of superimposition is one of his most important functional elements, as in his essay on *The Princess of Clèves* (1959). Butor demonstrates the unity of that work by superimposing the deaths of Henry II and M. de Clèves. The "limitless space of our consciousness" is, as Georges Markow-Totovy observes, the subject of *The Modification*, a space found in the interpenetration of the physical and spiritual modifications. The complex system of temporal arrangement in this novel follows and pursues that of the earlier *Passing Time*. There are at least two structures in *The Modification*. Jean Roudaut has found the following levels: (1) the present, 1955: Delmont's visit to Rome; (2) the previous week: visit to Rome; (3) the previous year, 1954: Cécile to Paris; (4) two years previous, 1953: Delmont meets Cécile on the train to Rome; (5) three years previous, 1952: to Rome with Henriette; (6) 1938: honeymoon in Rome with Henriette; (7) the future. Rossum-Guyon has distinguished ten excursions by further subdividing departing and returning journeys, but the seven levels distinguished by Roudaut are enough to prove, in effect, Butor's own dictum: "Every displacement in space will imply a reorganization of the temporal structure." Employing Richardou's concept of two axes makes evident that there is a schematization of the changes of levels within each chapter.[42]

Rossum-Guyon has indicated five sequences of time which are varied in "strophes" throughout each chapter: A, the present; B, the future; C, the near past; D, the past with Cécile; E, the past with Henriette. They appear in the following order, constituting a true literary genidentic field.

Chap. 1	A C A
2	A B C B A
3	A B C D C B A
4	A B C B A C D C A D E D A
5	A B C D C B A C D E D C A
6	A B C D C A C D E D A
7	A B C D A C D E A
8	A B C A C D A D E A
9	A B A C A D A E A

Whether or not one can credit Butor with such complexity (and there is much evidence to suggest one can), what is indisputable is the method of creation of a genidentic dynamic field in *The Modification*. This novel resembles in many ways the projected scheme for *Degrees,* although Butor contends he used a letter system as the graph of *The Modification*. This spatiality provides the two qualities of openness (ending and beginning with A) and mobility (engaging not only the protagonist but also the reader) valued by the author. Roudaut finds chapters 1–3 symmetrical in their arrangement of the time strophes, 4-6 partially symmetrical, and 7-9 dissymmetric (in order to implement even more the concept of potentiality). The work, as Butor wished, bears the imprint of its own ideal structure. His aim in *The Modification* was absolutely fulfilled, according to Barthes in his "Literature and Discontinuity," whereas *Mobile,* by its discontinuity and possibility, represented the extreme form of potentiality. Barthes has well observed that the physical and the spiritual journeys both align Butor with the great tradition of narrative (e.g., epic) and modify the tradition: "The spatial itinerary, the temporal itinerary and the spiritual itinerary . . . exchange their literalness, and it is exchange which is signification." Butor has admitted that the mobile place of the train compartment was a method of "projecting time into space."[43]

The technique of modification in the structure of the novel itself is constantly interesting, but one may cite in particular the modification of myth and the modification of point of view as reflecting specific results of this technique. The mythic base of the novel is Rome, as both a pagan and a Christian city; the pagan element is associated with Cécile and the Christian with Henriette. As Michel Leiris notes, in either instance Rome is the eternal feminine, the Blessed Virgin, the reconciliation point of contraries, the location to which all paths lead.[44] Delmont has certain affinities with Aeneas, who must read the future by the light of the past: "Is there not a Golden Bough to guide me and open the gates for me?" For example, there are the long dream episodes of the Great Huntsman of the Forest of Fontainebleu, who poses the central questions of the novel: "Do you hear me?," "What are you waiting for?," "Where are you?," "Are you mad?," "Who are you?" The final summation of these questions is a variation on the insistent Mercury who taunts Aeneas in the fourth book of the *Aeneid* prior to his departure from Dido. This interrogator probes Delmont in much the same fashion before his decision to abandon Cécile. This modification of the myths of Rome, of the golden bough, and of Mercury (the guiding spirit of travelers) represents one of the variations Butor effects, both to locate *The Modification* traditionally and to open it potentially.

A further method, and one provoking extraordinary critical controversy, is the use of the second person *vous* as the point of view in the novel. This *vous* of *The Modification* is the key to its genidentic dynamism; it is the point of view, if one can even use the expression, of a dynamic field. Butor himself has said that in *The Modification* the *vous* is both singular and plural, a statement verifying what Leiris has called the "universalization" of the novel. For Butor this *vous* represents the self and the other, the dialogue between author and reader, the activity between the acting and the perceiving dimensions of a single person, "between him who speaks and him who borrows the speech." Tracing the use of *vous* back to *Absalom, Absalom!, For Whom the Bell Tolls,* or *A Farewell to Arms,* Bruce Morrissette believes the *vous* is less author or protagonist than a persona, a center of consciousness in the novel belonging to neither author nor protagonist, but mediating between them. For W. M. Frohock, the *vous* bridges the aesthetic distance between reader and character as well as permitting the character to observe himself. He declares that Butor's characters are engaged "in identifying themselves to themselves."[45]

In his own "Research on the Technique of the Novel," Butor has claimed that point of view changes constantly in any novel. In an epistolary work, for example, a character is "I," "you," and "he" during the course of the narrative. In an interview with Paul Guth in *Figaro littéraire,* Butor declared:

It is absolutely necessary that the narrative be made from the point of view of a character. If he is disturbed by a grasp of consciousness, it is necessary only for him to say *I*. I needed an interior monologue beneath the level of language of the person himself, in a form intermediary between the first and the third person. This *you* allows me to describe the situation of the character and the manner in which language is born in him.

In "The Use of Personal Pronouns in the Novel," Butor has defined the great advantage of the second person: "It is here that the use of the second person intervenes, so that one can characterise in the novel someone to whom is recounted his own proper story." This strategy, he claims, re-

sults "always, in a 'didactic' narrative." The modification of this unusual
point of view, which Barthes conceives as involving the dialectic of creator
and created, is pursued further when the viewpoint at times alternates to
il ('he") in the story, particularly in dreams and frequently in episodes
involving the Great Huntsman and Roman myths, especially the she-wolf
and Charon. In such situations the shift to *he* involves the confrontation of
the other self, but under what specific guise it is difficult to say. Is it the
archetypal mythic self, the potential self (that is, the Aeneas who will
leave Dido), the idealized self of lofty aspiration, or the superego (the
future writer of the book)? It is significant that the Roman god Janus
appears in this frenzied dream as a customs official. Here is one of the
finest "modifications" in the novel, when through this two-faced god
Butor finds the perfect mythic prototype for his modification of *vous* to
il.[46]

What is being said of the genidentic dynamic field in *The Modification*
directs one to its finest modification, which is of the novel itself. Of no
other book is Ricardou's comment in "Time of the Narration" more true:
"The novel ceases to be the writing of a story and becomes the story of a
writing." In "The Story in the Story," Ricardou states the nature of this
modification: "It is represented as the grip of consciousness of narrative
by itself. It becomes a narrative, which, in its making, is forced to define
the making which is its narrative." If Delmont has reached a modification,
a redefinition, how much more true is this of the structure of narrative
itself. Michel Leiris has recognized the presence of "the book" in *The
Modification*—Delmont is a representative of a typewriter firm. Guide
books, law books, breviaries, papers, the sibylline books, and the *Aeneid*
make their appearance in its pages. To illustrate his belief that the book is
an object and a construct, Butor uses paragraphs that begin in mid-
sentence, with small letters, italics, and "epic" listing. Thus Ricardou
declares that there is "a narration within a narration" in Butor's work, the
account of the making of the novel in itself. Although itself part of a
narrative tradition dating back to *Henry von Ofterdingen* or *Wilhelm
Meister*, and of course Proust, Butor's particular place in this tradition is
the very clarification of his particular element of this idea, the *mise en
abyme*: "The *mise en abyme* is before everything else the structural revolt
of a fragment of narrative against the totality which contains it." This *mise
en abyme* was given exposure in *Passing Time*. In *The Modification*, this
exposure has been further pursued with complex time strophes arranged
from symmetric to dissymmetric patterns, and with levels superimposed
in arrangements recalling the palimpsest sheets Butor used to create
Passing Time, itself the palimpsest of *The Modification*. Each datum is
altered by new placement, modified by itself in the dynamic field. Every

Notes

CHAPTER ONE

1. Max Jammer, *Concepts of Space*, p. 10; this chapter is generally indebted to Jammer's study.
2. Rex Warner, *The Greek Philosophers* (New York: New American Library, 1962), p. 33.
3. Plato, *Timaeus*, trans. H. D. P. Lee (Baltimore: Penguin, 1965), p. 70; Jammer, p. 15; *Timaeus*, pp. 75–77.
4. Jammer, p. 18; Aristotle, *Physics* in *Selections*, Oxford translation, ed. W. D. Ross (New York: Scribner's, 1927), pp. 123–24; Jammer, p. 24.
5. René Descartes, *Principles of Philosophy*, in *Problems of Space and Time*, ed. J. J. C. Smart, p. 76; Gottfried Leibniz, *Third Paper*, ibid., p. 89; *Fifth Paper*, ibid., p. 94.
6. Isaac Newton, *Mathematical Principles of Natural Philosophy*, ibid., pp. 81, 87; John Locke, *An Essay Concerning Human Understanding*, ibid., p. 99; Immanuel Kant, *Critique of Pure Reason*, ibid., pp. 105, 107, 112; Ernst Mach, ibid., p. 130; Henri Bergson, *Introduction to Metaphysics*, ibid., p. 139.
7. Hermann Minkowski, "Space and Time," ibid., pp. 297–98.
8. C. D. Broad, *Examination of McTaggart's Philosophy*, ibid., pp. 325–26, 334–36; J. N. Findlay, "Time: A Treatment of Some Puzzles," ibid., pp. 343–47; Nelson Goodman, *The Structure of Appearance*, ibid., pp. 359–60, 367–68.
9. Émile Borel, *Space and Time*, pp. 163–64; Hans Reichenbach, *Space and Time*, trans. Maria Reichenbach and John Freund, pp. 274, 286.
10. Richard Taylor, "Spatial and Temporal Analogies and the Concept of Identity," in Smart, pp. 381–82; 392–93; Roland Barthes, *Writing Degree Zero*, pp. 5, 10; Adolf Grünbaum, "Time, Irreversible Processes, and the Physical Status of Becoming," in Smart, p. 402.
11. Augustine, *Confessions*, trans. R. S. Pine-Coffin (Baltimore: Penguin, 1961), pp. 264, 276; Hans Meyerhoff, *Time in Literature*, p. 9.
12. Meyerhoff, pp. 80, 85, 54, 67; important critical studies include Jean Pouillon, *Temps et roman;* Georges Poulet, *Studies in Human Time, The Interior Distance*, and particularly *Proustian Space*; Leon Edel, *The Modern Psychological Novel*; Robert Humphrey, *Stream of Consciousness in the Modern Novel.*
13. Henry James, in *The Art of the Novel*, ed. R. P. Blackmur, p. 14 (all citations of James's prefaces are to this edition); E. M. Forster, *Aspects of the Novel*, p. 29.
14. Gotthold Lessing, *Laocoon*, p. 20; A. A. Mendilow, *Time and the Novel*, pp. 23, 26–28.
15. Mendilow, pp. 25–28.
16. Joseph Frank, "Spatial Form in Modern Literature," in *The Widening Gyre*, pp. 8–9, 13, 15, 19, 24; this essay, originally published in 1945, was an early and provocative

influence on my book. See also Murray Krieger, *"Ekphrasis* and the Still Movement of Poetry: or, *Laokoön* Revisited," in James L. Calderwood and Harold E. Toliver, eds., *Perspectives on Poetry,* p. 323.

17. Susanne Langer, *Feeling and Form,* pp. 86–103.

18. Barthes, *Writing Degree Zero,* pp. 10–11; Wayne Booth, *The Rhetoric of Fiction,* pp. 243–66 et passim.

19. Forster, p. 67; Bertrand Russell, "The Problem of Infinity Considered Historically," in Smart, pp. 145–50; Borel, pp. 163–64.

20. Paul de Man, *Blindness and Insight,* p. 31; Virginia Woolf, *A Writer's Diary* (New York: New American Library, 1953), p. 101; Joseph Conrad, preface to *The Nigger of the Narcissus,* included in *Typhoon and Other Tales,* intro. Albert Guerard (New York: New American Library, 1962), p. 21; William Faulkner in Jean Stein, "William Faulkner: An Interview," *Paris Review* (1956), Frederick J. Hoffman and Olga W. Vickery, eds., *William Faulkner: Three Decades of Criticism* (New York: Harcourt, Brace & World, 1960), p. 80; on genidentity, see Reichenbach, pp. 270–72; Wolfgang Iser, *The Implied Reader,* passim.

21. Mary Gaither, "Literature and the Arts," in Newton P. Stallknecht and Horst Frenz, eds., *Comparative Literature: Method and Perspective,* p. 183; an excellent appraisal is contained in Ulrich Weisstein, "The Mutual Illumination of the Arts," *Comparative Literature and Literary Theory,* pp. 150–66; Krieger, p. 346, n. 1; Heinrich Wölfflin, *Principles of Art History,* p. 14.

22. Rensselaer Lee, *Ut Pictura Poesis,* p. 3, n. 3; Aristotle, *Poetics,* in T. S. Dorsch, trans., *Classical Literary Criticism* (Baltimore: Penguin, 1965), p. 40; Horace, *Ars Poetica,* ibid., p. 91; Lee, p. 4.

23. Lee, pp. 57, 11.

24. John Dryden, "A Parallel of Poetry and Painting," in *Essays of John Dryden,* ed. W. P. Ker (Clarendon Press, 1900; rprt. ed. New York: Russell and Russell, 1961), 2: 124–25, 130–31, 137–38, 143, 145, 147, 149, 151; Joseph Addison, *Spectator* 416, in Lee, p. 58.

25. Lee, pp. 60–61, 68–69.

26. See René Wellek, "The Parallelism between Literature and the Arts," *English Institute Annual* (New York: Columbia University Press, 1942), pp. 33–40, for a summary of treatises based on Wölfflin.

27. Laurence Binyon, "English Poetry in Its Relation to Painting and the Other Arts," *Proceedings of the British Academy* (London: Oxford University Press, 1918), pp. 381, 398–400; Edmund Blunden, "Romantic Poetry and the Fine Arts," *Proceedings of the British Academy* (London: Oxford University Press, 1943); Herbert Read, "Parallels in Painting and Poetry," in *In Defence of Shelley and Other Essays* (London: Heinemann, 1936), pp. 228, 230, 240, 247. In 1927, Roger Fry spoke of a caesura in Cézanne (*Cézanne* [New York: Farrar, Strauss and Giroux, 1958], p. 53).

28. Wellek, "Parallelism," pp. 50, 51–53, 56.

29. Helmut Hatzfeld, "Literary Criticism through Art and Art Criticism through Literature," *Journal of Aesthetics and Art Criticism* 6 (September 1947): 1–21; Giovanni Giovannini, "Method in the Study of Literature in Its Relation to the Other Fine Arts," *Journal of Aesthetics and Art Criticism* 8 (March 1950): 191, 193; Wallace Stevens, "The Relations between Poetry and Painting," in *The Necessary Angel* (New York: Knopf, 1951), pp. 171, 175; one should also note Mario Praz, *Mnemosyne,* particularly chapter seven. An annual bibliography is produced from the National Modern Language Association session, "Literature and the Other Arts."

30. Sypher, *Four Stages,* pp. 19–34; *Rococo to Cubism,* pp. 307, 297–311.

31. John Henry Raleigh, "The English Novel and the Three Kinds of Time," in Robert

Murray Davis, ed. *The Novel*, p. 244; James, *Art of the Novel*, p. 14; Humphrey, pp. 64, 86; Gérard Genette, "Discours du récit," in *Figures III*, passim; Genette's *Figures III*, a distinguished achievement, has exerted particular influence on my thinking.

32. Henry James, "The Art of Fiction," in *The Future of the Novel*, pp. 5, 6, 9, 23, 27; review of *Our Mutual Friend*, ibid., p. 78.

33. James, review of *Middlemarch*, ibid., pp. 81, 88; James, "The Lesson of Balzac," ibid., pp. 110, 115, 121; James, "Gustave Flaubert," ibid., p. 140.

34. James, ibid., p. 155; James, *Art of the Novel*, as follows: *donnée*, pp. 5, 15, 42, 48, 119, 178, 182, 235, 299, 307, 334; *centre*, pp. 37, 294, 317; *organic theory*, pp. 84–85, 219; *foreshortening*, pp. 14, 278; *scene*, pp. 157, 251, 300, 311, 323; *Turgenev*, pp. 42, 139, 332; *Daisy Miller*, p. 268; *environment and character*, pp. 64–65; Langer, pp. 88–92; James, *Art of the Novel*, pp. 46, 109, 301, 308, 312. I have retained James's British spelling of *centre* for this concept.

35. Percy Lubbock, *The Craft of Fiction*, pp. 80, 45, 84, 233, 103, 62, 68, 93, 110, 119, 250, 268, 244, 49, 257; Forster, pp. 8, 30, 39, 74, 132, 150, 153, 168, 67.

36. Edwin Muir, *The Structure of the Novel* (New York: Harcourt, Brace, 1929), pp. 57, 63–65, 88; Robert Scholes and Robert Kellogg, *The Nature of Narrative* (New York: Oxford University Press, 1966); Alan Friedman, *The Turn of the Novel* (New York: Oxford University Press, 1966); Philip Stevick, "The Theory of Fictional Chapters," in Stevick, ed., *The Theory of the Novel*, pp. 171–84; E. K. Brown, *Rhythm in the Novel* (Toronto: University of Toronto Press, 1950); Frank Kermode, *The Sense of an Ending* (New York: Oxford University Press, 1967); R. S. Crane, "The Concept of Plot and the Plot of *Tom Jones*," in Calderwood and Toliver, eds., *Perspectives on Fiction*, p. 306; Gaston Bachelard, *The Poetics of Space*, trans. Maria Jolas.

37. In my text I have translated the titles of a few books and articles that are not available in published English translations; all such items are cited by their original titles in the notes and bibliography. Michel Butor, *Essais sur le roman*, p. 49; Gérard Genette, *Figures I*, pp. 101, 108; Tzvetan Todorov, *Qu'est-ce que le structuralisme?*, pp. 100–103, 107. All translations from Butor, Genette, and Todorov, unless otherwise indicated, are mine.

38. Gérard Genette, *Figures II*, p. 45; Butor, *Inventory*, trans. here Patricia Dreyfus, pp. 44–46, 55–56; Genette, *Figures I*, pp. 39–67, 69–90, 223–43; *Figures II*, pp. 57, 58, 60 (this study first appeared in the essential *Communications* 8 [1966] devoted to "L'Analyse structurale du récit"); *Figures III*, p. 280.

39. Butor, *Essais*, pp. 112–13, 116, 118; Butor, "Balzac and Reality," in *Inventory*, trans. here Remy Hall, pp. 102–5; Butor, *Essais*, p. 53.

40. Victor Shklovsky, "La construction de la nouvelle et du roman," in Tzvetan Todorov, ed. and trans., *Théorie de la littérature*, pp. 184, 189, 191; Jurij Tynianov and Roman Jakobson, "Problems in the Study of Literature and Language," in Ladislav Matejka and Krystyna Pomorska, eds., *Readings in Russian Poetics*, p. 80 (hereafter *MP*); Shklovsky, "The Mystery Novel: Dickens's *Little Dorrit*," ibid., pp. 220–26. This selection in *MP* is included in Shklovsky's *Sur la théorie de la prose*, pp. 169–208; of particular importance is the chapter "Comment est fait *Don Quichotte*," pp. 107–45.

41. Tzvetan Todorov, "Les catégories du récit littéraire," *Communications* 8 (1966), pp. 126, 128, 140; Todorov, *Poétique de la prose*, pp. 16–18; like Wellek, Todorov alludes to the hazards of the *Geistesgeschichte* theories based on Wölfflin, p. 19; Todorov, "Comment lire?," ibid., pp. 245, 248–52. Todorov's text has been translated as *The Poetics of Prose* by Richard Howard (Ithaca: Cornell University Press, 1977), but all translations from it in this book are my own. Jean Ricardou, *Problèmes du nouveau roman*, pp. 161–65, 181–82. Translations from Ricardou are mine.

One must mention Barthes's important *Essais critiques*, particularly "Littérature objective" on Robbe-Grillet, "Littérature et discontinu," "L'activité structuraliste," and "Littérature et signification." His introductory essay in *Communications* 8, "Introduction à l'analyse structurale des récits," surveys, for example, the work of Todorov, pp. 5–6, of Propp, pp. 12–13, 16, and the concept of codes, pp. 25–27. All translations from Barthes are mine.

Several additional collections of Russian criticism influential in later parts of this study are Lee T. Lemon and Marion J. Reis, eds. and trans., *Russian Formalist Criticism*, including essays by Shklovsky, Tomashevsky, and Eichenbaum (subsequently cited as *LR*), and two specialized compilations, Robert A. Maguire, ed., *Gogol from the Twentieth Century*, with its important studies by Eichenbaum and Chizhevsky; and Victor Erlich, ed., *Twentieth-Century Russian Literary Criticism*, including studies by Shklovsky, Eichenbaum, and Tynianov.

42. De Man, pp. 160, 163. The importance of space as an architectonic construct for novelists is particularly emphasized in Sharon Spencer, *Space, Time, and Structure in the Modern Novel*.

CHAPTER TWO

1. Fanny Burney, *Evelina* (New York: Norton, 1965); Samuel Richardson, *Pamela*, intro. William M. Sale, Jr. (New York: Norton, 1958).
2. Johann Wolfgang von Goethe, *Wilhelm Meister's Apprenticeship*, trans. Thomas Carlyle (New York: Collier, 1962); Friedrich Hölderlin, *Hyperion*, trans. Willard R. Trask (New York: New American Library, 1965); Novalis, *Henry von Ofterdingen*, trans. Palmer Hilty (New York: Ungar, 1964).
3. Jean-Paul Sartre, *Nausea*, trans. Lloyd Alexander (New York: New Directions, 1964); Alain Robbe-Grillet, *Jealousy*, trans. Richard Howard (New York: Grove, 1965).
4. James, *Art of the Novel*, pp. 15, 37–38, 84, 21, 322–23.
5. George Eliot, *Adam Bede*, intro. Gordon S. Haight (New York: Holt, Rinehart and Winston, 1964). All subsequent references to *Adam Bede* are to this edition.
6. Darrell Mansell, "George Eliot's Conception of 'Form,'" in George R. Creeger, ed., *George Eliot* (Englewood Cliffs: Prentice-Hall, 1970), p. 68; on George Eliot's relation to Comte and Feuerbach, see Bernard Paris, "George Eliot's Religion of Humanity," ibid., pp. 11–36.
7. George Eliot, "Notes on Form in Art," in *Essays of George Eliot*, ed. Thomas Pinney (New York: Columbia University Press, 1963), pp. 433, 434.
8. Marcel Proust, *Swann's Way*, trans. C. K. Scott-Moncrieff (New York: Modern Library, 1928); Nathaniel Hawthorne, *The Scarlet Letter*, intro. Austin Warren (New York: Holt, Rinehart and Winston, 1963); Virginia Woolf, *To the Lighthouse* (New York: Harcourt, Brace, 1955); *The Waves* (London: Penguin, 1964).
9. André Gide, *The Counterfeiters*, trans. Dorothy Bussy and Justin O'Brien (New York: Modern Library, 1955); Robert Louis Stevenson, *The Weir of Hermiston* (New York: Dutton, 1965); E. M. Forster, *Howards End* (New York: Random House, Vintage, 1921); Joseph Conrad, *Victory* (New York: Modern Library, 1921).
10. Eugène Delacroix, in Rudolf Arnheim, *Art and Visual Perception*, p. 175; James, *Art of the Novel*, pp. 322–23.
11. Shklovsky, "La construction," p. 193 (translation here and subsequently mine); Todorov, *Poétique de la prose*, p. 161.
12. Shklovsky, "La construction," p. 187.
13. Tolstoy citations are to R. F. Christian, *Tolstoy's "War and Peace"* (Oxford: Clarendon Press, 1962), pp. 21–22; *War and Peace*, ed. George Gibian (New York: Norton, 1966),

pp. 1363, 1365; Christian, pp. 104, 178–79; Käte Hamburger, "Tolstoy's Art," in Ralph E. Matlaw, ed., *Tolstoy* (Englewood Cliffs, N. J.: Prentice-Hall, 1967), pp. 69, 61; the English translation is by Louise and Aylmer Maude, 2 vols. (New York: Heritage, 1938) (all subsequent references are to this edition).

14. James Curtis, "The Function of Imagery in *War and Peace*," *Slavic Review* 29 (September 1970): 480; Christian, pp. 124, 130, 173; Boris Eichenbaum, *The Young Tolstoy*, ed. Gary Kern (Ann Arbor, Mich.: Ardis, 1972), p. 49.

15. Tolstoy, as cited in Curtis, p. 460; Shklovsky, "La construction," p. 187; see also Shklovsky, "Parallels in Tolstoy," in Erlich, *Twentieth-Century Russian Literary Criticism*, pp. 81–85, especially his analysis of the spatial plane method "staircase-construction," p. 85; Christian, p. 172; Shklovsky, selection from his *Tolstoy's "War and Peace*," in Gibian, p. 1440.

16. Shklovsky, in Gibian, p. 1437; Christian, p. 126.

17. Boris Eichenbaum, "Tolstoy's Essays as an Element of Structure," in Gibian, p. 1444; Christian, p. 156; Stasov, in Christian, pp. 143–44.

18. Herman Melville, *Moby Dick*, ed. Charles Feidelson (New York: Bobbs-Merrill, 1964).

19. Genette, *Figures I*, pp. 39–49; Todorov, *Poétique de la prose*, pp. 245, 248, 250; Boris Eichenbaum speaks of "layers" of sound and of narrative superimposed and interwoven in *The Overcoat* in Maguire, *Gogol*, pp. 275, 284, 288.

20. Dorothy Van Ghent, *The English Novel*, p. 9; Gerald Brennan, *The Literature of the Spanish People* (New York: Meridian, 1957), p. 30; Erich Auerbach, "The Enchanted Dulcinea," from *Mimesis*, quoted in Lowry Nelson, Jr., ed., *Cervantes* (Englewood Cliffs: Prentice-Hall, 1969), p. 107; Harry Levin, "The Example of Cervantes," ibid., p. 34; E. C. Riley, "Literature and Life in *Don Quixote*," ibid., p. 124; Leo Spitzer, "On the Significance of *Don Quijote*," ibid., p. 93.

21. Spitzer, in Nelson, *Cervantes*, pp. 88–91; Nelson, Introduction, ibid., p. 4; A. Castro, cited by Riley, ibid., p. 123; Auerbach, p. 111; Van Ghent, pp. 11–13.

22. Thomas Mann, "Voyage with Don Quixote," in *Essays*, trans. Helen T. Lowe-Porter (New York: Knopf, 1957), pp. 326, 342; Nelson, p. 8.

23. Jorge Luis Borges, "Kafka and His Precursors," in *Labyrinths* (New York: New Directions, 1964), p. 201; Levin, p. 39; Miguel de Cervantes, *Don Quixote*, trans. Samuel Putnam (New York: Modern Library, 1949) (all subsequent references are to this edition); Leo Spitzer, *Linguistics and Literary History*, pp. 43–48; Ortega y Gasset, *Meditations on Quixote*, trans. Evelyn Rugg (New York: Norton, 1963), p. 132; Borges, "Partial Magic in the Quixote," in *Labyrinths*, p. 194.

24. Borges, *Labyrinths*, p. 242.

25. Genette, *Figures III*, pp. 82–114; Julian Marias, ed., *Meditations*, pp. 176–77.

26. Ortega y Gasset, in Marias, p. 69; Borges, *Labyrinths*, pp. 39, 42.

27. Riley, p. 136.

28. Shklovsky, *Sur la théorie*, pp. 118, 119; Spitzer, "Perspectivism," p. 62; Ortega y Gasset, in Marias, p. 161.

29. Gustave Flaubert, *L'Éducation sentimentale*, preface by Marcel Proust and Albert Thibaudet (Paris: Gallimard, 1965), p. 5; all French quotations from this edition; *Letters*, trans. J. M. Cohen (New York: Philosophical Library, 1951), pp. 225, 228–29, 191, 117; *Selected Letters*, trans. Francis Steegmuller (New York: Vintage, 1957), p. 142.

30. Henri Céard, as quoted in Benjamin F. Bart, *Flaubert* (Syracuse: Syracuse University Press, 1964), p. 540; Flaubert, *Flaubert in Egypt*, trans. Francis Steegmuller (Boston: Little, Brown, 1972), pp. 56, 52, 128–29.

31. Flaubert, *The Sentimental Education*, trans. Robert Baldick (Baltimore: Penguin, 1964); all subsequent translations are from this edition; Jean Prévost, in Martin Turnell,

The Novel in France (New York: Random House, Vintage, 1951), p. 299; Genette, *Figures I*, pp. 237, 242, 243; Poulet, *Studies*, pp. 253, 254, 255, 258.

32. Victor Brombert, *The Novels of Flaubert* (Princeton: Princeton University Press, 1966), pp. 9-10; E. W. Fisher, ed., "Un inédit de Gustave Flaubert: *La Spirale*," *La Table ronde* 124 (April 1958): 101; translation mine.

33. Fisher, ed., *The Spiral*, pp. 97, 98; translation mine.

34. Genette, *Figures I*, p. 226.

35. Bachelard, pp. 25, 57, 106, 114, 109, 214, 222; Brombert, pp. 147, 32; Jean-Pierre Richard, "The Creation of Form in Flaubert," in Raymond Giraud, ed., *Flaubert* (Englewood Cliffs, N.J.: Prentice-Hall, 1964), pp. 38, 46-56.

36. Robert Adams, *Nil* (New York: Oxford, 1966), pp. 68, 89, 92, 127; Turnell, p. 290; Flaubert, *Selected Letters*, pp. 128, 126; Brombert, pp. 125, 133, 178, 181.

37. I. Rice Pereira, *The Nature of Space*, pp. 31, 25, 31-32.

38. James, *Future of the Novel*, p. 147; Arnheim, pp. 248, 266-67, 287; Ricardou, p. 165.

39. I have here modified the Penguin translation.

40. Jean-Paul Sartre, "Flaubert," in Giraud, p. 14.

CHAPTER THREE

1. Langer, p. 86.

2. Boris Tomashevsky, "Thematics," *LR*, pp. 67, 57, 67-68, 70; Victor Shklovsky, "Sterne's Tristram Shandy: Stylistic Commentary," *LR*, p. 57.

3. Tomashevsky, "Thematics," p. 70; Lubomír Doležel, "Toward a Structural Theory of Content in Prose Fiction," in Seymour Chatman, ed., *Literary Style*, p. 99.

4. Wölfflin, pp. 14-16; Gérard Genette, *Figures II*, p. 59.

5. Thomas Hardy, *The Mayor of Casterbridge*, intro. Harvey Webster (New York: Holt, Rinehart and Winston, 1964); Leo Tolstoy, *Anna Karenina*, trans. David Magarshack (New York: New American Library, 1961); George Eliot, *Felix Holt the Radical* (New York: Dutton, 1966); Petronius, *The Satyricon*, trans. John Sullivan (Baltimore: Penguin, 1965).

6. Shklovsky, "Dickens's *Little Dorrit*," *MP*, pp. 221-22.

7. Butor, *Essais*, p. 53; Todorov, "Les catégories," p. 140; Shklovsky, "La construction," pp. 194, 190.

8. Charles Maturin, *Melmoth the Wanderer*, intro. William Axton (Lincoln: University of Nebraska Press, 1961); Mary Shelley, *Frankenstein*, in *Three Gothic Novels*, ed. Peter Fairclough, intro. Mario Praz (Baltimore: Penguin, 1968); Emily Brontë, *Wuthering Heights*, ed. Mark Schorer (New York: Holt, Rinehart and Winston, 1963).

9. Krieger, p. 325; Longus, *Daphnis and Chloe*, trans. Paul Turner (Baltimore: Penguin, 1968); all subsequent references are to this edition; the Greek text is from Otto Schönberger, ed., *Hirtengeschichten von Daphnis und Chloe* (Berlin, 1960).

10. Krieger, p. 338.

11. De Man, p. 163; Bachelard, pp. 81, 78.

12. James, *Art of the Novel*, pp. 49, 40, 42-43, 46, 48.

13. Van Ghent, pp. 213, 216, 219; Marion Montgomery, "The Flaw in the Portrait," in *Interpretations of "The Portrait of a Lady,"* ed. Peter Buitenhuis (Englewood Cliffs: Prentice-Hall, 1968), pp. 64, 65; Henry James, *The Portrait of a Lady*, intro. Fred R. Millett (New York: Modern Library, 1951) (all subsequent references are to this edition).

14. C. M. Bowra, *The Greek Experience* (New York: Praeger, 1957), p. 159; Homer, *The Iliad*, trans. Richmond Lattimore (Chicago: University of Chicago Press, 1961); Hagstrum, pp. 23, 29, 31-33.

15. Thomas, *Tristran*, trans. A. T. Hatto (Baltimore: Penguin, 1960).
16. Honoré de Balzac, *Cousin Bette*, trans. Marion Crawford (Baltimore: Penguin, 1965); William Thackeray, *Vanity Fair*, ed. Geoffrey and Kathleen Tillotson (Boston: Houghton Mifflin, 1963).
17. Charles Augustin Sainte-Beuve, *Selected Essays*, trans. Francis Steegmuller and Norbert Guterman (Garden City: Doubleday, 1964), p. 288; Harry Levin, *James Joyce* (New York: New Directions, 1960), p. 210; Hagstrum, p. 34; Émile Zola, *Nana*, trans. anon., intro. Henri Peyre (New York: Collier, 1962).
18. D. H. Lawrence, *The Rainbow* (New York: Viking, 1961); prologue to *Women in Love*, in Mark Schorer, *D. H. Lawrence* (New York: Dell, 1968), p. 206; William Faulkner, *The Hamlet* (New York: Random House, Vintage, 1964).
19. Henry James, *Hawthorne* (New York: Collier, 1966), pp. 138, 141, 142, 144, 145.
20. See John Barron, *Greek Sculpture* (London: Dutton, 1965), p. 120.
21. Anthony Bertram, *Florentine Sculpture* (London: Dutton, 1969), p. 81.
22. Richard Chase, *The American Novel and Its Tradition* (Garden City: Doubleday, 1957), p. 13; James, *Art of the Novel*, p. 34; Nathaniel Hawthorne, *The Marble Faun*, afterword by Murray Krieger (New York: New American Library, 1961) (all subsequent references are to this edition).
23. Krieger, p. 342.
24. Bachelard, pp. 5, 14, xxxiii, 34, 65, 49, 51.
25. Langer, pp. 71–72, 88–90; Elizabeth Bowen, "Jane Austen," in *The English Novelists*, ed. Derek Verschoyle (New York: Harcourt, Brace, 1936), p. 108.
26. W. J. Harvey, *Character and the Novel*, pp. 52, 54, 55; Forster, pp. 67, 74–75.
27. D. H. Lawrence, "Art and Morality," in *Phoenix*, ed. Edward McDonald (New York: Viking, Compass, 1972), pp. 521, 526; Nikolai Gogol, *Dead Souls*, trans. David Magarshack (Baltimore: Penguin, 1961); William Faulkner, *Light in August*, intro. Cleanth Brooks (New York: Modern Library, 1968).
28. Gustave Flaubert, Appendix to *Salammbô*, trans. J. C. Chartres, intro. F. C. Green (New York: Dutton, 1931), p. 318; Joseph Conrad, *Lord Jim*, ed. Thomas C. Moser (New York: Norton, 1968).
29. Gogol, *Dead Souls*; Melville, *Moby Dick*; Kate Chopin, *The Awakening and Other Stories*, ed. Lewis Leary (New York: Holt, Rinehart and Winston, 1970). George Eliot, *Middlemarch*, ed. Gordon S. Haight (Boston: Houghton Mifflin, 1956); George Eliot, *The Mill on the Floss*, ed. Gordon S. Haight (Boston: Houghton Mifflin, 1961).
30. Gide, *The Counterfeiters*, trans. Dorothy Bussy and Justin O'Brien.
31. Lawrence, "Introduction to His Paintings," in *"A Propos of Lady Chatterley's Lover" and Other Essays* (London: Penguin, 1961), pp. 22, 36, 38, 51.
32. Lawrence, "Morality and the Novel," in McDonald, pp. 526, 527, 528, 529; "Why the Novel Matters," ibid., p. 538; *Lady Chatterley's Lover*, preface by Lawrence Durrell (New York: Bantam, 1968).
33. Letters quoted from D. H. Lawrence, *Selected Literary Criticism*, ed. Anthony Beal (New York: Viking, Compass, 1966), pp. 15, 17, 18.
34. Marinetti, *Futurist Manifesto*, in Eugen Weber, ed., *Paths to the Present* (New York: Dodd, Mead, 1971), p. 244; for Lawrence's ideas about Futurism applied to Melville, see *Studies in Classic American Literature* (New York: Viking, Compass, 1964), p. 146; for further information on the subject, see the essay by Jack Lindsay in Mervyn Levy, ed., *The Paintings of D. H. Lawrence* (London: Cory, Adams, and Mackay, 1964), pp. 43–44.
35. These statements are quoted in Sypher, *Rococo*, p. 322.
36. D. H. Lawrence, *The Rainbow* (New York: Viking, Compass, 1961) (all subsequent

references are to this edition); one should note that Lawrence mentioned the painter Frank Brangwyn in his essay "Making Pictures," in Levy.

37. F. R. Leavis, *D. H. Lawrence: Novelist* (New York: Simon and Schuster, 1955), p. 170; the separatist assumption underlies such criticism as Angelo Bertocci, "Symbolism in *Women in Love*," in Harry T. Moore, ed., *A D. H. Lawrence Miscellany* (Carbondale: Southern Illinois University Press, 1959), pp. 92–98; and Edward Engelberg, "Escape from the Circles of Experience: D. H. Lawrence's *The Rainbow* as a Modern *Bildungsroman*," *PMLA* 78 (March 1963): 103–13.

38. D. H. Lawrence, *Women in Love* (New York: Viking, Compass, 1960); subsequent references are to this edition.

39. Lawrence, prologue to *Women in Love*, in Schorer, p. 206.

40. "Making Pictures," in Levy, unnumbered end pages; the paintings cited are from this edition; in the same volume, see Harry T. Moore's appraisal, "D.H. Lawrence and His Paintings;" introduction, p. 51.

41. De Man, pp. 152, 42.

42. Langer, pp. 101–2; Schorer, "*Women in Love* and Death," in Harry T. Moore et al., eds., *The Achievement of D. H. Lawrence* (Norman, Okla.: University of Oklahoma Press, 1953), p. 175.

43. Harvey, pp. 120, 16, 152–54, 52.

44. Sartre, *Nausea*, trans. Alexander; Gide, *The Counterfeiters*, trans. Bussy and O'Brien.

45. Kenneth Clark, *The Nude* (Garden City: Doubleday, 1956), p. 74; on Verrocchio, see Bertram, *Florentine Sculpture*, p. 98; Howard Hibbard, *Bernini* (Baltimore: Penguin, 1965), p. 57.

46. Thomas Hardy, *The Return of the Native*, intro. Albert J. Guerard (New York: Holt, Rinehart and Winston, 1950).

47. Honoré de Balzac, *Père Goriot*, trans. Marion Crawford (Baltimore: Penguin, 1951).

48. Stendhal [Marie-Henri Beyle], *The Charterhouse of Parma*, trans. C. K. Scott-Moncrieff, afterword by Jacques Barzun (New York: New American Library, 1962); *Scarlet and Black* [*The Red and the Black*], trans. Margaret R. B. Shaw (Baltimore: Penguin, 1953); Henry James, *The Ambassadors*, ed. F. W. Dupee (New York: Holt, Rinehart and Winston, 1960); James Joyce, *Ulysses* (New York: Modern Library, 1961) (all subsequent references are to this edition); Mark Twain, *Adventures of Huckleberry Finn*, ed. Leo Marx (New York: Bobbs-Merrill, 1967); Melville, *Moby Dick*.

49. Norman Friedman, "Point of View in Fiction: The Development of a Critical Concept," in *The Theory of the Novel*, ed. Philip Stevick (New York: Free Press, 1967), p. 127; Stendhal, *Scarlet and Black*, trans. Shaw.

50. Jane Austen, *Pride and Prejudice*, ed. Mark Schorer (Boston: Houghton Mifflin, 1956).

51. Jurij Tynianov, "On Literary Evolution," in *MP*, pp. 71, 72, 77; Langer, pp. 94–98.

52. Richard Macksey, "Architecture of Time: Dialectics and Structure," in René Girard, ed., *Proust* (Englewood Cliffs, New Jersey: Prentice-Hall, 1962); Proust's letter to Jean Gaigneron, p. 105; Cremieux, p. 104; Macksey, pp. 105–6; Genette, *Figures II*, p. 44; Michel Butor, "Balzac and Reality," in *Inventory*, p. 25.

53. Butor, "The Book as Object," *Inventory*, pp. 40, 41, 42, 44, 50, 52, 55; *Essais*, p. 127.

54. Shklovsky, "La Construction," pp. 179–80, 189–90; *Sur la théorie*, pp. 99–101; Todorov, "Les catégories," pp. 128, 140.

55. Eugene Raskin, *Architecturally Speaking* (New York: Bloch, 1966), pp. 42, 45–51, 61, 64; Henry Hope Reed, *The Golden City* (New York: Norton, 1970), p. 114.

56. Reed, p. 114; Raskin, p. 95; Boris Eichenbaum, "The Theory of the 'Formal Method,'" *LR*, p. 116.

57. Genette, *Figures II*, pp. 44–45.

58. Ibid., pp. 45–47; Todorov, "Les catégories," pp. 125–26.
59. James, *Art of the Novel*, p. 5; Stevick, pp. 175–77; Reed, p. 114.
60. Henry Fielding, *Joseph Andrews*, ed. Martin Battestin (Boston: Houghton Mifflin, 1961).
61. Jane Austen, *Emma*, ed. Lionel Trilling (Boston: Houghton Mifflin, 1957); Stevick, p. 176; Todorov, "Les catégories," pp. 131–32.
62. On the "speed of the narration," see Ricardou, p. 162.
63. Shklovsky, "La construction," p. 177; Eichenbaum, "Sur la théorie de la prose," in Todorov, ed., *Théorie de la littérature*, pp. 202–3, 207–8; Shklovsky, "Dickens's *Little Dorrit*," *MP*, p. 226.
64. Gustave Flaubert, *Letters*, trans. J. M. Cohen (New York: Philosophical Library, 1951), p. 182; George Orwell, *Essays* (Garden City: Doubleday, 1954), p. 103; Eichenbaum, "Sur la théorie," p. 210; Shklovsky, *MP*, pp. 221, 222; Edgar Johnson, *Charles Dickens*, 2 vols. (Boston: Little Brown, 1952), 2:993; John Hagan, "Structural Patterns in Dickens' *Great Expectations*," *ELH* 21 (March 1954): 66.
65. Hagan, pp. 55–65; Charles Dickens, *Great Expectations*, ed. Earle Davis (New York: Holt, Rinehart and Winston, 1949); all subsequent references are to this edition.
66. Both conclusions intend a physical parting, but with a spiritual unity, between Pip and Estella. Commentators ignore the fact that in the revised conclusion, presumably including all data Pip wished one to know, the final phrase is "'friends apart.'" Had Dickens's intention been otherwise, that expression would not have been the final statement from Estella, who never lied. There will be no "shadow of another parting" for the reason that there will not be another meeting.
67. C. G. Jung, *The Spirit in Man, Art, and Literature*, trans. R. F. C. Hull (Princeton: Princeton University Press, 1966), p. 122.
68. Genette, *Figures II*, p. 45; Tynianov, *MP*, p. 136; Genette, *Figures I*, p. 103; Charlotte Brontë, *Jane Eyre*, ed. Mark Schorer (Boston: Houghton Mifflin, 1959); Genette, *Figures III*, pp. 82–114.
69. *Jane Eyre*, ed. Schorer; *Middlemarch*, ed. Haight.
70. Genette, *Figures I*, p. 107.
71. Marcel Proust, *The Captive*, from *Remembrance of Things Past*, trans. C. K. Scott-Moncrieff and Frederick Blossom, 2 vols. (New York: Random House, 1932). Throughout this book, this translation has been used with small changes, among them the translation of *Le Temps retrouvé* as *Time Regained;* Florence Emily Hardy, *The Early Life of Thomas Hardy* (London: Macmillan, 1928), p. 101.
72. Genette, *Figures II*, pp. 45–46; Hardy, *Early Life*, p. 43; Thomas Hardy, *Jude the Obscure*, ed. Irving Howe (Boston: Houghton Mifflin, 1965) (all subsequent references are to this edition).
73. Hardy, *Early Life*, pp. 223, 265.
74. William Faulkner, *The Sound and the Fury* (New York: Random House, Vintage, 1956); all subsequent references are to this edition.
75. Langer, p. 101; Genette, *Figures II*, p. 44.
76. Hardy, *Early Life*, p. 101.
77. Erwin Panofsky, *Gothic Architecture and Scholasticism*, pp. 45, 36, 26; Nikolaus Pevsner, *An Outline of European Architecture*, pp. 90, 98; Fritz Baumgart, *A History of Architectural Styles*, p. 92.
78. Kenneth Clark, *The Gothic Revival*, pp. 78, 81, 90, 112; Hardy, *Early Life*, p. 50; Pevsner, p. 381.
79. John Ruskin, *The Stones of Venice*, in Charles Harrold and William D. Templeman, eds., *English Prose of the Victorian Era* (New York: Oxford University Press, 1962), p. 900.

80. Ibid., p. 923.

81. Panofsky, p. 6; Wilhelm Worringer, *Form in Gothic*, p. 114; Worringer, *Abstraction and Empathy*, p. 24; Riegl, ibid., p. 21.

82. E. M. Cioran, "The Fall out of Time," in *The Fall into Time*, trans. Richard Howard (New York: Quadrangle, 1970), p. 177.

CHAPTER FOUR

1. Baumgart, pp. 277, 282; Langer, pp. 95, 97–99, 101.

2. Vitruvius, *On Architecture*, trans. M. H. Morgan (New York: Dover, 1960). The Latin text is as follows: "Cum in omnibus enim rebus, tum maxime etiam in architectura haec duo insunt, quod significatur et quod significat" (Loeb text, ed. Frank Granger [New York: Putnam, 1931]). E. D. Hirsch, *Validity in Interpretation*, pp. 143, 26–27, 31, 66, 92, 113, 63.

3. Henri Bergson, *Time and Free Will* [*Essai sur les données immédiates de la conscience*], trans. F. L. Pogson, pp. 186–90, 193. It is important that both Bergson and James use the concept *donnée*, since the method of reading and its object have a similar genesis.

4. Genette, *Figures I*, pp. 17, 125, 126; Jorge Luis Borges, *Other Inquisitions*, trans. Ruth Simms (New York: Washington Square, 1966), p. 48; Ricardou, p. 190; Genette, *Figures I*, p. 221.

5. Jurij Tynianov, "Rhythm as the Constructive Factor of Verse," *MP*, p. 128; Victor Zuckerkandl, *Sound and Symbol*, pp. 267, 268, 270, 278, 275, 292, 299, 302, 304, 305; Todorov, *Poétique de la prose*, p. 161.

6. Genette, *Figures I*, p. 192; Shklovsky, cited by Eichenbaum, *LR*, p. 112; Eichenbaum, *LR*, pp. 114, 113; Shklovsky, "Art as Technique," *LR*, pp. 12–13; quoted by Eichenbaum, p. 114.

7. James Joyce, *A Portrait of the Artist as a Young Man* (New York: Viking, Compass, 1964); all subsequent references are to this edition.

8. James Joyce, *Stephen Hero* (New York: New Directions, 1963); all subsequent references are to this edition.

9. Todorov, *Poétique de la prose*, pp. 245, 250, 251.

10. Harry Levin, *James Joyce* (New York: New Directions, 1960), p. 48.

11. Reichenbach, pp. 270–71. On the relation of language to generalized physics, see Kenneth L. Pike, "Language as Particle, Wave, and Field," *Texas Quarterly* 2 (Summer 1959): 37–54; William Holtz, "Field Theory and Literature," *Centennial Review* 2 (Fall 1967): 532–48. Holtz notes: "Any given 'thing' participates in many larger systems (fields) which *always include the observer himself*" (p. 534).

12. Thomas Mann, *The Magic Mountain*, trans. H. T. Lowe-Porter (New York: Modern Library, 1952) (all subsequent references are to this edition); Hermann J. Weigand, *Thomas Mann's Novel "Der Zauberberg"* (New York: AMS, 1971), pp. 91, 95; Arnold Bauer, *Thomas Mann*, trans. Alexander and Elizabeth Henderson (New York: Ungar, 1971), p. 44; Weigand, p. 15.

13. Weigand, p. 106.

14. Henry Hatfield, *Thomas Mann* (New York: New Directions, 1962), pp. 69, 70; Bauer, p. 46; R. P. Blackmur, "The Lord of Small Counterpositions: Mann's *The Magic Mountain*," in *Eleven Essays in the European Novel*, pp. 82, 90, 95; Bauer, p. 48.

15. Weigand, pp. 49, 63; Thomas Mann, "The Making of *The Magic Mountain*" (from the English edition); Hatfield, p. 80.

16. Thomas Mann, "The Sufferings and Greatness of Richard Wagner," in *Essays*, trans. H. T. Lowe-Porter (New York: Random House, Vintage, 1957), pp. 200, 210, 215, 218; italics added.

17. Thomas Mann, *Death in Venice* and *Tonio Kröger,* trans. H. T. Lowe-Porter (New York: Random House, Vintage, 1964); italics added.

18. Reichenbach, p. 271; Todorov, "Poétique," from *Qu'est-ce que le structuralisme?*, p. 116; Mikhail Baxtin, "Discourse Typology in Prose," *MP*, p. 189; Todorov, "Poétique," p. 117; "Les catégories," p. 147.

19. Booth, p. 138; Iser, pp. ix, xii.

20. Iser, pp. 40, 45, 44, 99.

21. Ibid., pp. 274, 287, 48, 275, 280.

22. Walter J. Ong, "The Writer's Audience is Always a Fiction," *PMLA* 90 (January 1975): 12, 16, 17; Jean Piaget, *Structuralism,* trans. Chaninah Maschler, p. 49; De Man, p. 25.

23. Genette, *Figures III,* pp. 120–21; Marcel Proust, *Letters of Marcel Proust,* trans. Mina Curtiss (New York: Random House, 1949), pp. 337–38.

24. Robert Champigny, "Proust, Bergson and Other Philosophers," in René Girard, ed., *Proust,* (Englewood Cliffs, N. J.: Prentice-Hall, 1962), pp. 122–31; Marcel Proust, *Marcel Proust on Art and Literature,* trans. Sylvia Warner (New York: Meridian, 1958), p. 249; Poulet, *Studies in Human Time,* pp. 297, 320–21; Poulet, *Proustian Space,* pp. 3–4, 12.

25. Germaine Brée, *The World of Marcel Proust* (Boston: Houghton Mifflin, 1966), p. 179; Poulet, *Studies in Human Time,* pp. 307, 309, 308.

26. Georges Cattaui, "Images as Instruments," in Girard, pp. 88–89.

27. Proust on George Eliot in *Marcel Proust on Art and Literature,* p. 376.

28. The French text used is *A la recherche du temps perdu,* ed. Pierre Clarac and André Ferré, 3 vols. (Paris: Gallimard, 1954).

29. Piaget, p. 49; Genette, *Figures I,* pp. 216, 125.

30. Hoffman and Vickery, pp. 80, 82; Richard P. Adams, *Faulkner: Myth and Motion* (Princeton: Princeton University Press, 1968), p. 201; Jean-Paul Sartre, "On *The Sound and the Fury:* Time in the Works of Faulkner," in Robert Penn Warren, ed., *Faulkner* (Englewood Cliffs: Prentice-Hall, 1966), pp. 87, 89, 90; Michael Millgate, *The Achievement of William Faulkner* (New York: Random House, Vintage, 1966), pp. 88, 154; William Faulkner, *Absalom, Absalom!* (New York: Modern Library, 1964) (all subsequent references are to this edition); Joseph W. Reed, Jr., *Faulkner's Narrative* (New Haven: Yale University Press, 1973), pp. 147, 152; Laurence Thompson, *William Faulkner: An Introduction and Interpretation* (New York: Holt, Rinehart and Winston, 1967), p. 56; Conrad Aiken, "William Faulkner: The Novel as Form," in Warren, ed., *Faulkner,* p. 49; Hyatt Waggoner, "Past as Present: *Absalom, Absalom!,*" ibid., p. 175.

31. Cioran, *The Fall into Time,* pp. 179, 174, 178, 180.

32. Frederick L. Gwynn and Joseph L. Blotner, eds., *Faulkner in the University* (New York: Random House, Vintage, 1959), p. 76; Butor, "Balzac," in *Inventory,* pp. 103, 104, 105; Millgate, p. 98.

33. For Faulkner, "truth" is an atemporal, spatial, composite: "I think that no one individual can look at truth. It blinds you. You look at it and you see one phase of it. Someone else looks at it and sees a slightly awry phase of it. But taken all together, the truth is in what they saw though nobody saw the truth intact.... But the truth ... comes out, that when the reader has read all these thirteen different ways of looking at the blackbird, the reader has his own fourteenth image of that blackbird which I would like to think is the truth" (Gwynn and Blotner, eds., *Faulkner in the University,* pp. 273–74).

34. Florence Leaver, "Faulkner: The Word as Principle and Power," in *Three Decades,* p. 200.

35. Walter J. Slatoff, "The Edge of Order: The Pattern of Faulkner's Rhetoric," ibid.,

pp. 177, 178, 174, 181, 186, 196; Aiken, p. 48; Warren Beck, "William Faulkner's Style," in Warren, ed., *Faulkner*, p. 63.

36. Aiken, p. 48.
37. Ricardou, p. 164.
38. Butor's *Essais* and *Inventory* cited passim; Ricardou, pp. 166, 170.
39. Michel Leiris, "Le réalisme mythologique de Michel Butor," included in the text of *La Modification* (Paris: Éditions de Minuit, 1957), p. 292; Léon Roudiez, *Michel Butor* (New York: Columbia University Press, 1965), pp. 20–21; Michael Spencer, *Michel Butor* (New York: Twayne, 1974), pp. 66, 69; Georges Markow-Totevy, "Michel Butor," *Bucknell Review* 10 (May 1962): 284; Ricardou, p. 185; the English version of *La Modification* used here is *A Change of Heart*, trans. Jean Stewart (New York: Simon and Schuster, 1969), but I have retained the more literal title, *The Modification*.
40. Georges Charbonnier, *Entretiens avec Michel Butor* (Paris: Gallimard, 1957), pp. 59, 129; Roland Barthes, "Il n'y a pas d'école Robbe-Grillet," *Essais critiques*, p. 104 (translation mine); Ricardou, p. 166.
41. Charbonnier, *Entretiens*, p. 12; Barthes, *Essais*, pp. 102–3; Françoise van Rossum-Guyon, *Critique du roman* (Paris: Gallimard, 1970), p. 194; translations mine.
42. Markow-Totevy, p. 285; Butor, *Répertoire I*, pp. 74–78; Markow-Totevy, p. 279; Jean Roudaut, "Répétition et modification dans deux romans de Michel Butor," in Spencer, p. 76.
43. Rossum-Guyon, p. 249; Roudaut, in Spencer, p. 76; Barthes, "Littérature et discontinu," *Essais*, p. 187; Barthes, "Il n'y a pas," pp. 102–3; Markow-Totevy, p. 287.
44. Leiris, p. 306.
45. Ibid., p. 299; Markow-Totevy, pp. 282, 288; Bruce Morrissette, "Narrative 'You' in Contemporary Literature," *Comparative Literature Studies* 2 (1965): 15; W. M. Frohock, "Introduction to Butor," *Yale French Studies*, no. 24 (Summer 1959), pp. 59, 60.
46. Butor, *Essais*, pp. 121–22; *Figaro littéraire*, 7 December 1957; Butor, "L'usage des pronoms personnels dans le roman," *Essais*, p. 80.
47. Ricardou, cited passim; Butor, *Inventory*, pp. 286, 290; Leiris, p. 303; Butor, *Inventory*, p. 19; Bernard Dort, "Are These Novels 'Innocent?'," *Yale French Studies*, no. 24 (Summer 1959), pp. 23–29.
48. Leiris, p. 299; Jean Roudaut, *Michel Butor ou le livre futur* (Paris: Gallimard, 1964); Markow-Totevy, p. 285.

Bibliography

ARNHEIM, RUDOLF. *Art and Visual Perception: A Psychology of the Creative Eye.* Berkeley: University of California Press, 1969.

AUERBACH, ERICH. *Mimesis: The Representation of Reality in Western Literature.* Translated by Willard Trask. Garden City, N. Y.: Doubleday, Anchor Books, 1957.

BACHELARD, GASTON. *The Poetics of Space.* Translated by Maria Jolas. Boston: Beacon, 1969.

BARRON, JOHN. *Greek Sculpture.* London: Dutton, 1965.

BARTHES, ROLAND. *Critique et vérité.* Paris: Seuil, 1966.

———. *Essais critiques.* Paris: Seuil, 1964.

———. "Introduction à l'analyse structurale des récits." *Communications* 8 (1966): 1–27.

———. *On Racine.* Translated by Richard Howard. New York: Hill and Wang, 1964.

———. *Writing Degree Zero.* Translated by Annette Lavers and Colin Smith. Boston: Beacon, 1967.

BAUMGART, FRITZ. *A History of Architectural Styles.* London: Praeger, 1970.

BAXTIN, MIKHAIL. "Discourse Typology in Prose." Translated by Richard Balthazar and I. R. Titunik. In *Readings in Russian Poetics,* edited by Ladislav Matejka and Krystyna Pomorska. Cambridge, Mass.: MIT Press, 1971.

———. *La Poétique de Dostoïevski.* Paris: Seuil, 1970.

BERGSON, HENRI. *Time and Free Will.* Translated by F. L. Pogson. New York: Harper Torchbooks, 1960.

BERNSTEIN, JEREMY. *Einstein.* New York: Viking, 1973.

BERTRAM, ANTHONY. *Florentine Sculpture.* London: Dutton, 1969.

BLACKMUR, R. P. *Eleven Essays in the European Novel.* New York: Harcourt, Brace, 1964.

BLANCHOT, MAURICE. *L'Espace littéraire.* Paris: Gallimard, 1955.

BOLLNOW, OTTO F. *Mensch und Raum.* Stuttgart: Kohlhammer, 1963.

BOOTH, WAYNE. "Distance and Point of View." In *The Theory of the Novel,* edited by Philip Stevick. New York: Free Press, 1967.

———. *The Rhetoric of Fiction.* Chicago: University of Chicago Press, 1961.

BOREL, ÉMILE. *Space and Time.* New York: Dover, 1960 (reprt. of 1st English ed., 1926).

BOULTON, MARJORIE. *The Anatomy of Prose.* London: Routledge and Kegan Paul, 1954.

BOURNEUF, ROLAND. "L'organisation de l'espace dans le roman." *Études littéraires* 3 (1970): 77–94.

BREMOND, CLAUDE. *Logique du récit.* Paris: Seuil, 1973.

BROWN, CALVIN. *Music and Literature: A Comparison of the Arts.* Athens, Ga.: University of Georgia Press, 1948.

BUTOR, MICHEL. *Essais sur le roman.* Paris: Gallimard, 1964.

———. *Inventory.* Edited by Richard Howard. New York: Simon and Schuster, 1968.

CALDERWOOD, JAMES L. and TOLIVER, HAROLD E., eds. *Perspectives on Fiction.* New York: Oxford University Press, 1968.

CAPEK, MILIC. *Bergson and Modern Physics.* Dordrecht: Reidl, 1971.

———. *The Philosophical Impact of Contemporary Physics.* Princeton, N.J.: Van Nostrand, 1961.

CARROLL, DAVID. "Diachrony and Synchrony in *Histoire.*" *Modern Language Notes* 92 (May 1977): 797–824.

CHATMAN, SEYMOUR, ed. *Literary Style: A Symposium.* New York: Oxford University Press, 1971.

CHIZHEVSKY, DMITRY. "About Gogol's 'Overcoat.'" In *Gogol from the Twentieth Century,* edited by Robert A. Maguire. Princeton, N.J.: Princeton University Press, 1974.

CLARK, KENNETH. *The Gothic Revival.* Baltimore, Md.: Penguin, 1962.

———. *The Nude: A Study in Ideal Form.* Garden City, N.J.: Doubleday, 1956.

COHEN, JONATHAN. "Tense Usage and Propositions." *Analysis* 11 (March 1951): 80–87.

CULLER, JONATHAN. *Structuralist Poetics.* Ithaca, N.Y.: Cornell University Press, 1975.

DAVIS, ROBERT, ed. *The Novel: Modern Essays in Criticism.* Englewood Cliffs, N.J.: Prentice-Hall, 1969.

DE GEORGE, RICHARD, and DE GEORGE, FERNANDE, eds. *The Structuralists from Marx to Lévi-Strauss.* Garden City, N.Y.: Doubleday, Anchor Books, 1972.

DE MAN, PAUL. *Blindness and Insight.* New York: Oxford University Press, 1971.

DE SAUSSURE, FERDINAND. *Course in General Linguistics.* Translated by Wade Baskin. New York: McGraw-Hill, 1966.

EDEL, LEON. *The Modern Psychological Novel.* New York: Grosset and Dunlap, 1964.

EHRMANN, JACQUES, ed. *Structuralism.* Garden City, N.J.: Doubleday, 1970.

EICHENBAUM, BORIS. "How Gogol's 'Overcoat' Is Made." In *Gogol from the Twentieth Century,* edited by Robert A. Maguire. Princeton, N.J.: Princeton University Press, 1974.

———. "O. Henry and the Theory of the Short Story." Translated by I. R. Titunik. In *Readings in Russian Poetics,* edited by Ladislav Matejka and Krystyna Pomorska. Cambridge, Mass.: MIT Press, 1971.

———. "On Tolstoy's Crises." Translated by Carol A. Palmer. In *Twentieth-Century Russian Literary Criticism,* edited by Victor Erlich. New Haven, Conn.: Yale University Press, 1975.

———. "Sur la théorie de la prose." In *Théorie de la littérature,* edited by Tzvetan Todorov. Paris: Seuil, 1965.

———. "The Theory of the Formal Method." Translated by I. R. Titunik. In *Readings in Russian Poetics,* edited by Ladislav Matejka and Krystyna Pomorska. Cambridge, Mass.: MIT Press, 1971.

EINSTEIN, ALBERT. *Relativity, the Special and General Theory.* London: Methuen, 1960.

ERLICH, VICTOR, ed. *Twentieth-Century Russian Literary Criticism.* New Haven, Conn.: Yale University Press, 1975.

FORSTER, E. M. *Aspects of the Novel.* New York: Harcourt, Brace and World, Harvest Books, 1954.

FRANK, JOSEPH. "Spatial Form: An Answer to Critics." *Critical Inquiry* 4 (Winter 1977): 231–52.

———. *The Widening Gyre: Crisis and Mastery in Modern Literature.* Bloomington, Ind.: Indiana University Press, Midland Books, 1968.

FRIEDLAENDER, WALTER. *David to Delacroix*. Translated by Robert Goldwater. New York: Schocken, 1968.

FRIEDMAN, NORMAN. "Point of View in Fiction: The Development of a Critical Concept." In *The Theory of the Novel*, edited by Philip Stevick. New York: Free Press, 1967.

GALE, RICHARD M. "Tensed Statements." *Philosophical Quarterly* 12 (January 1962): 53–59.

GENETTE, GÉRARD. *Figures I*. Paris: Seuil, 1966.

———. *Figures II*. Paris: Seuil, 1969.

———. *Figures III*. Paris: Seuil, 1972.

———. *Mimologiques*. Paris: Seuil, 1976.

GOMBRICH, E. H. *Art and Illusion*. Princeton, N.J.: Princeton University Press, 1961.

GOODMAN, NELSON. *The Structure of Appearance*. Cambridge, Mass.: Harvard University Press, 1951.

GRÜNBAUM, ADOLF. *Philosophical Problems of Space and Time*. New York: Knopf, 1963.

HAGSTRUM, JEAN. *The Sister Arts: The Tradition of Literary Pictorialism and English Poetry from Dryden to Gray*. Chicago: University of Chicago Press, 1958.

HARDY, BARBARA. *The Appropriate Form: An Essay on the Novel*. London: Athlone, 1964.

HARVEY, W. J. *Character and the Novel*. Ithaca, N.Y.: Cornell University Press, 1965.

HARTMAN, GEOFFREY. *Beyond Formalism: Literary Essays 1958–1970*. New Haven, Conn.: Yale University Press, 1970.

HATZFELD, HELMUT A. *Literature through Art: A New Approach to French Literature*. Chapel Hill, N.C.: University of North Carolina Press, 1969.

HIBBARD, HOWARD. *Bernini*. Baltimore, Md.: Penguin, 1965.

HIRSCH, E. D. *Validity in Interpretation*. New Haven, Conn.: Yale University Press, 1967.

HOLTZ, WILLIAM. "Field Theory and Literature." *Centennial Review* 2 (Fall 1967): 532–48.

———. "Spatial Form in Modern Literature: A Reconsideration." *Critical Inquiry* 4 (Winter 1977): 271–83.

HUMPHREY, ROBERT. *Stream of Consciousness in the Modern Novel*. Berkeley: University of California Press, 1968.

ISER, WOLFGANG. *The Implied Reader*. Baltimore, Md.: Johns Hopkins University Press, 1974.

JAKOBSON, ROMAN. "The Dominant." Translated by Herbert Eagle. In *Readings in Russian Poetics*, edited by Ladislav Matejka and Krystyna Pomorska. Cambridge, Mass.: MIT Press, 1971.

———. "On Realism in Art." Translated by Karol Magassy. In *Readings in Russian Poetics*, edited by Ladislav Matejka and Krystyna Pomorska. Cambridge, Mass.: MIT Press, 1971.

———. *Questions de poétique*. Paris: Seuil, 1973.

———, and TYNIANOV, JURIJ. "Problems in the Study of Literature and Language." Translated by Herbert Eagle. In *Readings in Russian Poetics*, edited by Ladislav Matejka and Krystyna Pomorska. Cambridge, Mass.: MIT Press, 1971.

JAMES, HENRY. *The Art of the Novel: Critical Prefaces*. Edited by R. P. Blackmur. New York: Scribner's, 1934.

———. *The Future of the Novel: Essays on the Art of Fiction*. Edited by Leon Edel. New York: Random House, Vintage, 1956.

JAMMER, MAX. *Concepts of Space: The History of Theories of Space in Physics*. Cambridge, Mass.: Harvard University Press, 1969.

JUNG, C. G. *Mandala Symbolism*. Translated by R. F. C. Hull. Princeton, N.J.: Princeton University Press, Bollingen Series, 1972.

KESTNER, JOSEPH. *Jane Austen: Spatial Structure of Thematic Variations*. Salzburg: University of Salzburg Press, 1974.

————. "Keats: The Solace of Space." *Illinois Quarterly* 35 (November 1972): 59–64.

————. "Pindar and Saint-Exupéry: The Heroic Form of Space." *Modern Fiction Studies* 19 (Winter 1973–74): 507–16.

————. "*Sanditon* or *The Brothers:* Nature into Art." *Papers on Language and Literature* 12 (Spring 1976): 161–66.

————. "The Spatiality of Pasternak's *Aerial Ways.*" *Studies in Short Fiction* 10 (Summer 1973): 243–51.

KRIEGER, MURRAY. "*Ekphrasis* and the Still Movement of Poetry: or, *Laokoön* Revisited." In *Perspectives on Poetry*, edited by James L. Calderwood and Harold E. Toliver. New York: Oxford University Press, 1968.

LANE, MICHAEL, ed. *Introduction to Structuralism.* New York: Harper, Torchbooks, 1972.

LANGER, SUSANNE. *Feeling and Form: A Theory of Art.* New York: Scribner's, 1953.

LEE, RENSSELAER. *Ut Pictura Poesis: The Humanistic Theory of Painting.* New York: Norton, 1967.

LEMON, LEE T., and REIS, MARION J., eds. and trans. *Russian Formalist Criticism: Four Essays.* Lincoln, Nebr.: University of Nebraska Press, 1965.

LESSER, SIMON. *Fiction and the Unconscious.* New York: Random House, Vintage, 1962.

LESSING, GOTTHOLD. *Laocoon.* Translated by Ellen Frothingham. New York: Noonday, 1969.

LOCKSPEISER, EDWARD. *Music and Painting: A Study in Comparative Ideas from Turner to Schoenberg.* New York: Harper and Row, 1973.

LODGE, DAVID. *Language of Fiction: Essays in Criticism and Verbal Analysis of the English Novel.* New York: Columbia University Press, 1966.

LORENTZ, HENDRIK. *The Principle of Relativity.* London: Methuen, 1923.

LUBBOCK, PERCY. *The Craft of Fiction.* New York: Viking, Compass Books, 1957.

LUCID, DANIEL P., ed. *Soviet Semiotics: An Anthology.* Baltimore, Md.: Johns Hopkins University Press, 1977.

LUKÁCS, GEORG. *Studies in European Realism.* Translator anonymous. New York: Grosset and Dunlap, Universal Library, 1964.

————. *The Theory of the Novel.* Translated by Anna Bostock. Cambridge, Mass.: MIT Press, 1971.

MACKSEY, RICHARD, and DONATO, EUGENIO, eds. *The Languages of Criticism and the Sciences of Man.* Baltimore, Md.: Johns Hopkins University Press, 1970.

MAGUIRE, ROBERT A., ed. *Gogol from the Twentieth Century.* Princeton, N.J.: Princeton University Press, 1974.

MATEJKA, LADISLAV, and POMORSKA, KRYSTYNA, eds. *Readings in Russian Poetics: Formalist and Structuralist Views.* Cambridge, Mass.: MIT Press, 1971.

MENDILOW, A. A. *Time and the Novel.* New York: Humanities Press, 1972.

MEYERHOFF, HANS. *Time in Literature.* Berkeley: University of California Press, 1968.

ONG, WALTER J. "The Writer's Audience is Always a Fiction." *PMLA* 90 (January 1975): 9–21.

ORTEGA y GASSET, JOSÉ. "On Point of View in the Arts." Translated by Paul Snodgrass and Joseph Frank. In *The Dehumanization of Art and Other Essays on Art, Culture, and Literature.* Princeton, N.J.: Princeton University Press, 1968.

PANOFSKY, ERWIN. *Aufsätze zu Grundfrager der Kunstwissenschaft.* Berlin: Haude and Spenersche, 1974.

————. *Gothic Architecture and Scholasticism.* New York: World, 1957.

————. *Meaning in the Visual Arts.* Garden City, N.Y.: Doubleday, Anchor Books, 1955.

————. *Studies in Iconology.* New York: Harper Torchbooks, 1967.

PEREIRA, I. RICE. *The Nature of Space: A Metaphysical and Aesthetic Inquiry.* Washington, D.C.: Corcoran Gallery, 1968.

PEVSNER, NIKOLAUS. *An Outline of European Architecture*. Baltimore, Md.: Penguin, 1968.

PHILIPSON, MORRIS, ed. *Aesthetics Today*. New York: World, 1961.

PIAGET, JEAN. *Structuralism*. Translated by Chaninah Maschler. New York: Harper Torchbooks, 1970.

PIKE, KENNETH L. "Language as Particle, Wave, and Field." *Texas Quarterly* 2 (Summer, 1959): 37–54.

POUILLON, JEAN. *Temps et roman*. Paris: Gallimard, 1946.

POULET, GEORGES. *The Interior Distance*. Translated by Elliott Coleman. Ann Arbor, Mich.: University of Michigan Press, 1964.

———. *Proustian Space*. Translated by Elliott Coleman. Baltimore, Md.: Johns Hopkins University Press, 1956.

———. *Studies in Human Time*. Translated by Elliott Coleman. Baltimore, Md.: Johns Hopkins University Press, 1956.

PRAZ, MARIO. *Mnemosyne: The Parallel between Literature and the Visual Arts*. Princeton, N.J.: Princeton University Press, Bollingen Series, 1974.

PROPP, VLADIMIR. *Morphologie du conte*. Paris: Seuil, 1970.

RABKIN, ERIC S. "Spatial Form and Plot." *Critical Inquiry* 4 (Winter 1977): 253–70.

RASKIN, EUGENE. *Architecturally Speaking*. New York: Bloch, 1966.

RASMUSSEN, STEEN EILER. *Experiencing Architecture*. Cambridge, Mass.: MIT Press, 1962.

REED, HENRY HOPE. *The Golden City*. New York: Norton, 1970.

REICHENBACH, HANS. *The Direction of Time*. Edited by Maria Reichenbach. Berkeley: University of California Press, 1956.

———. *The Philosophy of Space and Time*. Translated by Maria Reichenbach and John Freund. New York: Dover, 1958.

RICARDOU, JEAN. *Problèmes du nouveau roman*. Paris: Seuil, 1967.

ROBBE-GRILLET, ALAIN. *For a New Novel, Essays on Fiction*. Translated by Richard Howard. New York: Grove, 1965.

ROBEY, DAVID, ed. *Structuralism: An Introduction*. Oxford: The Clarendon Press, 1973.

ROSSUM-GUYON, FRANÇOISE VAN. *Critique du roman*. Paris: Gallimard, 1970.

RUSSELL, BERTRAND. "On the Experience of Time." *Monist* 25 (January 1915): 212–33.

———. "The Philosophy of Bergson." *Monist* 22 (July 1912): 321–47.

SARTRE, JEAN-PAUL. *What is Literature?* Translated by Bernard Frechtman. New York: Harper, Colophon Books, 1965.

SCHOLES, ROBERT. *Structuralism in Literature: An Introduction*. New Haven, Conn.: Yale University Press, 1974.

———, ed. *Approaches to the Novel*. San Francisco: Chandler, 1966.

——— and KELLOGG, ROBERT. *The Nature of Narrative*. New York: Oxford University Press, 1966.

SCHORER, MARK. "Fiction and the 'Matrix of Analogy.'" *Kenyon Review* 11 (Autumn 1949): 539–60.

———. "Technique as Discovery." In *The Theory of the Novel*, edited by Philip Stevick. New York: Free Press, 1967.

SCOTT, GEOFFREY. *The Architecture of Humanism*. New York: Norton, 1974.

SHKLOVSKY, VICTOR. "Art as Technique." In *Russian Formalist Criticism*, translated and edited by Lee T. Lemon and Marion Reis. Lincoln, Nebr.: University of Nebraska Press, 1965.

———. "La construction de la nouvelle et du roman." In *Théorie de la littérature*, edited by Tzvetan Todorov. Paris: Seuil, 1965.

————. "The Mystery Novel: Dickens's *Little Dorrit.*" Translated by Guy Carter. In *Readings in Russian Poetics*, edited by Ladislav Matejka and Krystyna Pomorska. Cambridge, Mass.: MIT Press, 1971.

————. "Parallels in Tolstoy." Translated by Victor Erlich. In *Twentieth-Century Russian Literary Criticism*, edited by Victor Erlich. New Haven, Conn.: Yale University Press, 1975.

————. *Sur la théorie de la prose*. Translated by Guy Verret. Lausanne: L'Age d'Homme, 1973.

SMART, J. J. C., ed. *Problems of Space and Time*. New York: Macmillan, 1964.

————. "Spatialising Time." *Mind* 64 (April 1955): 239–41.

SOUVAGE, JACQUES. *An Introduction to the Study of the Novel*. Ghent: Story, 1965.

SPENCER, SHARON. *Space, Time, and Structure in the Modern Novel*. Chicago: Swallow, 1971.

SPITZER, LEO. *Linguistics and Literary History*. Princeton, N.J.: Princeton University Press, 1967.

STALLKNECHT, NEWTON P., and FRENZ, HORST, eds. *Comparative Literature: Method and Perspective*. Carbondale, Ill.: Southern Illinois University Press, 1971.

STEVICK, PHILIP, ed. *The Theory of the Novel*. New York: Free Press, 1967.

SUTTON, WALTER. "The Literary Image and the Reader: A Reconsideration of the Theory of Spatial Form." *Journal of Aesthetics and Art Criticism* 16 (1957): 112–23.

SYPHER, WYLIE. *Four Stages of Renaissance Style*. Garden City, N.Y.: Doubleday, Anchor Books, 1955.

————. *Rococo to Cubism in Art and Literature*. New York: Random House, Vintage, 1960.

TODOROV, TZVETAN. "Les catégories du récit littéraire." *Communications* 8 (1966): 125–51.

————. *Littérature et signification*. Paris: Larousse, 1967.

————. "Poétique." In *Qu'est-ce que le structuralisme?*, edited by François Wahl. Paris: Seuil, 1968.

————. *Poétique de la prose*. Paris: Seuil, 1971.

————, ed. *Théorie de la littérature*. Paris: Seuil, 1965.

TOMASHEVSKY, BORIS. "Thematics." In *Russian Formalist Criticism*, translated and edited by Lee T. Lemon and Marion Reis. Lincoln, Nebr.: University of Nebraska Press, 1965.

TYNIANOV, JURIJ. "The Meaning of the Word in Verse." Translated by M. E. Suino. In *Readings in Russian Poetics*, edited by Ladislav Matejka and Krystyna Pomorska. Cambridge, Mass.: MIT Press, 1971.

————. "Rhythm as the Constructive Factor of Verse." Translated by M. E. Suino. In *Readings in Russian Poetics*, edited by Ladislav Matejka and Krystyna Pomorska. Cambridge, Mass.: MIT Press, 1971.

————, and JAKOBSON, ROMAN. "Problems in the Study of Literature and Language." Translated by Herbert Eagle. In *Readings in Russian Poetics*, edited by Ladislav Matejka and Krystyna Pomorska. Cambridge, Mass.: MIT Press, 1971.

VAN GHENT, DOROTHY. *The English Novel: Form and Function*. New York: Harper, 1953.

VINOGRADOV, V. V. "Des tâches de la stylistique." In *Théorie de la littérature*, edited by Tzvetan Todorov. Paris: Seuil, 1965.

VOLOSINOV, V. N. "Reported Speech." Translated by Ladislav Matejka and I. R. Titunik. In *Readings in Russian Poetics*, edited by Ladislav Matejka and Krystyna Pomorska. Cambridge, Mass.: MIT Press, 1971.

WAHL, FRANÇOIS, ed. *Qu'est-ce que le structuralisme?* Paris: Seuil, 1968.

WEISSTEIN, ULRICH. *Comparative Literature and Literary Theory*. Bloomington, Ind.: Indiana University Press, 1973.

WELLEK, RENÉ. *Concepts of Criticism*. New Haven, Conn.: Yale University Press, 1963.

———. *Discriminations: Further Concepts of Criticism*. New Haven, Conn.: Yale University Press, 1970.

———. "The Parallelism between Literature and the Arts." In *English Institute Annual*. New York: Columbia University Press, 1942.

——— and WARREN, AUSTIN. *Theory of Literature*. New York: Harcourt, Brace and World, 1956.

WÖLFFLIN, HEINRICH. *Principles of Art History: The Problem of the Development of Style in Later Art*. Translated by M. D. Hottinger. New York: Dover, 1950.

WORRINGER, WILHELM. *Abstraction and Empathy*. Translated by Michael Bullock. New York: International Universities Press, 1967.

———. *Form in Gothic*. Authorized translation. New York: Schocken, 1964.

ZEVI, BRUNO. *Architecture as Space*. Translated by Milton Gendel. New York: Horizon, 1974.

ZUCKERKANDL, VICTOR. *Sound and Symbol: Music and the External World*. Translated by Willard Trask. Princeton, N. J.: Princeton University Press, Bollingen Series, 1969.

Index

197

Joseph A. Kestner graduated magna cum laude from The University of New York at Albany in 1965, and received his M.A. (1966) and Ph.D. (1969) from Columbia University, where he was also a President's Fellow and a Woodrow Wilson Fellow. He has taught at Princeton University and at The City University of New York. He is currently an associate professor in the Graduate Faculty of Modern Letters, The University of Tulsa.

The manuscript was edited by Sherwyn Carr. The book was designed by Edgar Frank. The typeface for the text is Caledonia, designed by W. A. Dwiggins about 1938. The display face is Caslon Old Style No. 337, with swash initials.

The text is printed on International Bookmark text paper. The book is bound in Holliston Mills Kingston Vellum cloth over binder's boards. Manufactured in the United States of America.